Interior Lighting
for Designers

Interior Lighting for Designers

FOURTH EDITION

Gary Gordon FIES, FIALD, LC

Illustrations by Gregory F. Day

John Wiley & Sons, Inc.

Published by John Wiley & Sons, Inc., Hoboken, New Jersey
Published simultaneously in Canada

No part of this publication may be reproduced, stored in a retrieval system, or transmitted in any form or by any means, electronic, mechanical, photocopying, recording, scanning, or otherwise, except as permitted under Section 107 or 108 of the 1976 United States Copyright Act, without either the prior written permission of the Publisher, or authorization through payment of the appropriate per-copy fee to the Copyright Clearance Center, Inc., 222 Rosewood Drive, Danvers, MA 01923, (978) 750-8400, fax (978) 750-4470, or on the web at www.copyright.com. Requests to the Publisher for permission should be addressed to the Permissions Department, John Wiley & Sons, Inc., 111 River Street, Hoboken, NJ 07030, (201) 748-6011, fax (201) 748-6008, e-mail: permcoordinator@wiley.com.

Limit of Liability/Disclaimer of Warranty: While the publisher and author have used their best efforts in preparing this book, they make no representations or warranties with respect to the accuracy or completeness of the contents of this book and specifically disclaim any implied warranties of merchantability or fitness for a particular purpose. No warranty may be created or extended by sales representatives or written sales materials. The advice and strategies contained herein may not be suitable for your situation. You should consult with a professional where appropriate. Neither the publisher nor author shall be liable for any loss of profit or any other commercial damages, including but not limited to special, incidental, consequential, or other damages.

For general information on our other products and services or for technical support, please contact our Customer Care Department within the United States at (800) 762-2974, outside the United States at (317) 572-3993 or fax (317) 572-4002.

Wiley also publishes its books in a variety of electronic formats. Some content that appears in print may not be available in electronic books.

Library of Congress Cataloging-in-Publication Data

Gordon, Gary, 1957-
  Interior lighting for designers / Gary Gordon ; illustrations by
Gregory F. Day.— 4th ed.
       p.   cm.
Includes bibliographical references and index.
  ISBN 0-471-44118-X (Cloth)
  1. Electric lighting. 2. Lighting, Architectural and decorative. I. Title.
  TK4175 .G67 2003
  729'.28—dc21
                                        2002152368

Printed in the United States of America
10 9 8 7 6 5

For
my grandfather,
Louis Becker,
who first inspired me to look at buildings

Contents

Preface to the Fourth Edition

This Fourth Edition expands upon the foundation established in the previous edition, with the added benefit of greater clarity throughout. While it retains the mark of the thorough copy and technical edit provided for the Third Edition by the late luminaire-design genius Edison Price, chapters 9, 10, and 11 have been reorganized to correspond more closely with professional practice. New to this edition is material on the latest advances in lighting technology and practice; state-of-the-art light sources, equipment, and systems; and a comprehensive glossary. For the first time, an Instructor's Manual is available on-line from the publisher to accompany the text.

As with the Third Edition, this book is intended to serve as both a textbook for architecture and interior design students and a manual for practicing professionals. It provides a simple framework for understanding the lighting design process. More than 250 line drawings, photographs, and color plates, many of them new to this edition, illustrate the text. The design of light for interiors is emphasized; tools and techniques are presented as a means by which to achieve the design. This is an architectural approach to lighting design, based on my apprenticeship with the talented architect and lighting designer Carroll Cline, as well as twenty years of professional practice.

The lighting design process outlined in this book parallels the methodology used by lighting professionals to provide solutions for architectural interiors around the world. I developed this system for describing the lighting design process while teaching graduate and undergraduate students at the Parsons School of Design Lighting Institute in New York City. The success of this method is demonstrated by the great number of my former students who professionally practice lighting design today.

ACKNOWLEDGMENTS
This work owes an enormous debt to Caryl Gordon and Mary Hebert for their help with copy-editing and proofreading; to Dr. Kevin Houser for his exceptionally thorough techni-

cal edit; and to David Marini for his assistance with the layout and design.

Valuable research assistance was provided by the able crew of the Gary Gordon LLC office in New York: Kevin Frary, Justin Horvath, Michael Haslam, Christine Kong, Ryan Stromquist, Rob Thomas, and Ryan Wither. Rob Thomas skillfully coordinated all of the drawings, color plates, and photographs.

I am also grateful for the support of Aneeahseah Lefler and Jennifer Downey. At John Wiley & Sons, Amanda Miller provided editorial guidance, and Jennifer Ackerman made working on this book a joy.

Gary Gordon FIES, FIALD, LC
New York, New York
September 2002

Introduction

Lighting design is a process. It is the process of integrating light into the fabric of architecture. Regardless of the space to be lighted—a bank, a church, an office, a gallery, a restaurant, a store, a classroom—and regardless of the light sources available for use, the process is always the same.

Because lighting design is a process, it can be learned. This book traces the steps in the lighting design process much as a professional performs them in practice. Design, of course, is not always a linear process. At times some of these steps are used simultaneously. But, on the whole, the order of the material corresponds to professional practice.

This book does not describe *the* lighting design process; it describes *a* lighting design process. It is one that has been used successfully by Gary Gordon LLC to provide solutions for more than one thousand architectural projects around the world. It is a process built on the conviction that the lighting condition of a space has enormous emotional impact on people.

A common mistake when providing light for buildings is to select the lighting equipment first. Selecting luminaires is the last step in the process. What is important is not what makes the light, but which objects and surfaces receive it. The key to successful lighting design is to decide *what* you want to light first, and then work backward to determine the solution.

In chapter 1, we learn by understanding the human visual system that perception of the world around us is based not on the quantity of light entering the eye but on the quantity of contrast. In chapter 2, we learn from psychology that because the sense of sight is contrast-sensitive, the brightness contrast of a space determines its emotional impact. In chapter 3, we learn how the direction and distribution of light determine the brightness contrasts that yield the desired emotional setting.

Once the emotional setting and brightness contrast have been established, we begin our selection of light sources by determining the color of light in chapter 4. The next three chapters provide a thorough knowledge of light sources, from daylight (chapter 5) through incandescent and tungsten-halogen (chapter 6) to discharge sources: fluorescent, mercury, metal halide, and high-pressure sodium (chapter 7). Chapter 8 describes the auxiliary equipment required to operate discharge and low-voltage incandescent lamps.

Chapter 9 explains the external devices employed to modify light sources so that they provide the desired direction and distribution of light and control glare. With the light source modified, Chapter 10 illustrates how we use photometry to predict the quantity of light in completed space. Chapter 11 provides an understanding of the electrical requirements of light sources and methods of lighting system control.

Once the source, with its external devices, methods of modifying distribution and controlling glare, and electrical requirements, is established, we are at last ready to select the luminaire in chapter 12. It is only at this point in the lighting design process that a suitable luminaire can be chosen: after the designer has identified the activity in a space and degree of contrast required, and has determined the color of light, light sources, modifications to control source distribution and glare, and locations of light sources.

Our final chapter looks at the elements that produce visual clarity; design techniques for lighting architectural surfaces, tasks, and art; the balance of brightness; energy-effective design; and integrating light and architecture.

The architectural lighting design process described in this book produces a space where the casual observer is unaware of the mechanics of light production; he perceives only a comfortable environment that supports his activities and enhances his wellbeing. With practice, the designer learns to apply this process in ways that go even further, producing environments that stimulate the mind and inspire the spirit.

Perception

1

Perception of the world around us is based not on the quantity of light entering the eye, but on the quantity of contrast.

VISIBLE LIGHT

What we perceive as light is a narrow band of electromagnetic energy, ranging from approximately 380 nanometers (nm) to 760 nm. Only wavelengths in this range stimulate receptors in the eye that permit vision (figure 1.1 and color plate 1). These wavelengths are called *visible energy* even though we cannot directly see them.

In a perfect vacuum, light travels at approximately 186,000 miles per second. When light travels through glass or water or another transparent substance, it is slowed down to a velocity that depends on the density of the medium through which it is transmitted (figure 1.2). This slowing down of light is what causes prisms to bend light and lenses to form images.

When light is bent by a prism, each wavelength is refracted at a different angle so the emergent beam emanates from the

Figure 1.1 Visible light is a narrow region of the total electromagnetic spectrum, which includes radio waves, infrared, ultraviolet, and x-rays. The physical difference is purely the wavelength of the radiation, but the effects are very different. Within the narrow band to which the eye is sensitive, different wavelengths give different colors. See also color plate 1.

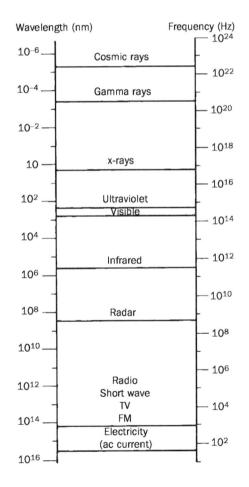

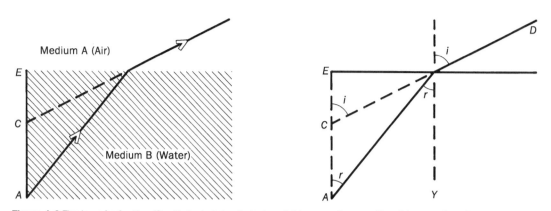

Figure 1.2 The law of refraction (Snell's law) states that when light passes from medium A into medium B the sine of the angle of incidence (*i*) bears a constant ratio to the sine of the angle of refraction (*r*).

prism as a fan of light, yielding all of the spectral colors (see color plate 2).

All electromagnetic radiation is similar. The physical difference between radio waves, infrared, visible light, ultraviolet, and x-rays is their wavelength. A *spectral color* is light of a specific wavelength; it exhibits deep chromatic saturation. *Hue* is the attribute of color perception denoted by what we call red, orange, yellow, green, blue, and violet.

THE EYE

A parallel is often drawn between the human eye and a camera. Yet visual perception involves much more than an optical image projected on the retina of the eye and interpreted "photographically" by the brain.

The human eye is primarily a device that gathers information about the outside world. Its focusing *lens* throws a minute inverted image onto a dense mosaic of light-sensitive receptors, which convert the patterns of light energy into chains of electrical impulses that the brain will interpret (figure 1.3).

The simplest way to form an image is not with a lens, however, but with a pinhole. In figure 1.4, a ray from each point of the object reaches only a single point on the

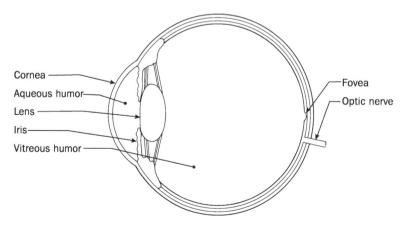

Cornea
Aqueous humor
Lens
Iris
Vitreous humor

Fovea
Optic nerve

Figure 1.3 Cross section of the human eye.

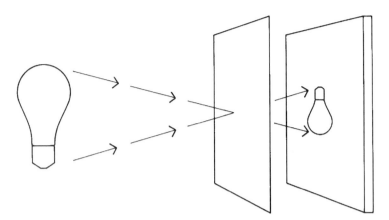

Figure 1.4 Forming an image with a pinhole.

screen, the two parts being connected by a straight line passing through the pinhole. Each part of the object illuminates a corresponding part of the screen, so an upside-down image of the object is formed. The pinhole image is dim, however, because the hole must be small (allowing little light to pass through) if the image is to be sharp.

A lens is able to form a much brighter image. It collects a bundle of light rays from each point of the object and directs them to corresponding points on the screen, thus giving a bright image (figure 1.5).

The lens of the human eye is built up from its center, with cells being added all through life, although growth gradually slows down. The center is thus the oldest part, and as the cells age they become more compact and harden. As a result, the lens stiffens and is less able to change its shape to accommodate varying distances (*presbyopia*) (figure 1.6).

Lenses work well only when they fit properly and are adjusted correctly. Sometimes the lens is not suited to the eye in which it finds itself: (1) the lens focuses the image in

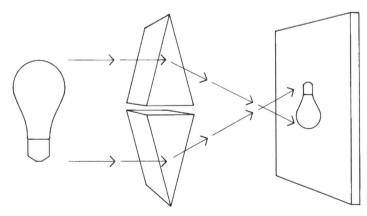

Figure 1.5 Forming an image with a lens. The lens shown is a pair of prisms; image-forming lenses have curved surfaces.

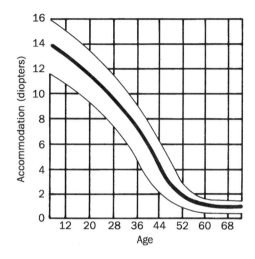

Figure 1.6 Loss of accommodation of the lens of the eye with aging.

front of or behind the retina instead of on it, giving "short" sight (nearsighted or *myopic*) or "long" sight (farsighted or *hyperopic*); (2) the lens is not truly spherical, giving distortion and, in some directions, blurring of the image (*astigmatic*); or (3) the cornea is irregular or pitted.

Fortunately, almost all optical defects can be corrected by adding artificial lenses, which we call *eyeglasses*. Eyeglasses correct for errors of focus (called *accommodation*) by changing the power of the lens of the eye; they correct for distortion (called *astigmatism*) by adding a nonspherical component. Ordinary glasses do not correct damage to the surface of the cornea, but *corneal lenses*, fitted to the eye itself, serve to give a fresh surface to the cornea.

The *iris* is the pigmented part of the eye. It is found in a wide range of colors, but the color has no impact on vision as long as it is opaque. The iris is a muscle that forms the *pupil*. Light passes through the pupil to the lens which lies immediately behind it. This muscle contracts to reduce the aperture of the lens in bright light and also when the eyes converge to view near objects.

The *retina* is a thin sheet of interconnected nerve cells, which include the light-sensitive cells that convert light into electrical impulses. The two kinds of light-receptor cells—*rods* and *cones*—are named after their appearance as viewed under a microscope (figure 1.7).

Until recently, it was assumed that the cones function in high *illuminance*, providing color vision, and the rods function under low illuminance, yielding only shades of gray. Color vision, using the cones of the retina, is called *photopic*; the gray world given by the rods in dim light is called *scotopic*.

Recent research, however, suggests that both rods and cones are active at high illuminance, with each contributing to different aspects of vision. When both rods and cones are active, vision is called *mesopic*.

THE BRAIN

The eyes supply the brain with information coded into chains of electrical impulses. But the "seeing" of objects is determined only partially by these neural signals. The brain searches for the best interpretation of available data. The perception of an object is a hypothesis, suggested and tested by sensory signals and knowledge derived from previous experience.

Usually the hypothesis is correct, and we perceive a world of separate solid objects in a surrounding space. Sometimes the evaluation is incorrect; we call this an *illusion*. The ambiguous shapes seen in figures 1.8 and 1.9 illustrate how the same pattern of stimulation at the eye gives rise to different perceptions.

BRIGHTNESS PERCEPTION

We speak of light entering the eye, called *luminance*, which gives rise to the sensation

LIGHT

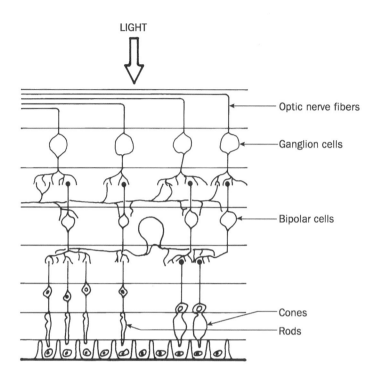

Optic nerve fibers

Ganglion cells

Bipolar cells

Cones

Rods

Figure 1.7 The retina.

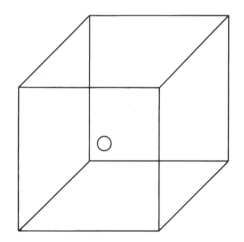

Figure 1.8 Necker cube. When you stare at the dot, the cube flips as the brain entertains two different depth hypotheses.

Figure 1.9 Ambiguous shapes. Is it a vase or two faces in profile?

of *brightness*. Illuminance, which is the density of light received on a surface, is measured by various kinds of photometers, including the familiar photographer's exposure meter.

Brightness is a subjective experience. We hear someone say, "What a bright day!" and we know what is meant by that. But this sensation of brightness can be only partly attributed to the intensity of light entering the eyes.

Brightness is a result of: (1) the intensity of light falling on a given region of the retina at a certain time, (2) the intensity of light that the retina has been subject to in the recent past (called *adaptation*), and (3) the intensities of light falling on other regions of the retina (called *contrast*).

Figure 1.10 demonstrates how the intensity of surrounding areas affects the perception of brightness. A given region looks brighter if its surroundings are dark,

and a given color looks more intense if it is surrounded by its complementary color.

If the eyes are kept in low light for some time they grow more sensitive, and a given quantity of light will seem brighter. This "dark adaptation" is rapid for the first few seconds, then slows down. As the eye becomes dark adapted, it loses *acuity* while it gains sensitivity. With a decrease of intensity and the compensating dark adaptation, the ability to make out fine detail is lost.

The cone and rod receptor cells adapt at different rates: cone adaptation is completed in about seven minutes; rod adaptation continues for an hour or more. This is demonstrated by the difference between leaving a dark movie theatre and emerging into bright daylight (cone or light adaptation), and its reverse: entering a dark theatre from a bright, sunny day (rod or dark adaptation).

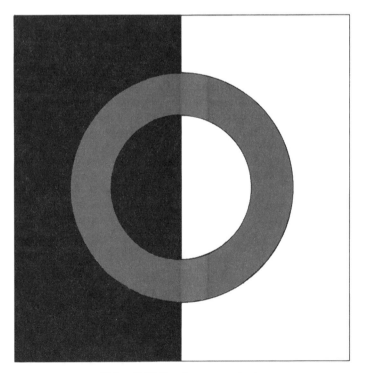

Figure 1.10 Simultaneous contrast.

COLOR PERCEPTION

Brightness is also a function of color. For a given intensity, the colors at the middle of the spectrum look brighter than those at the ends. The sensitivity curves for rods and cones are different. Their shape is similar, but the cones are most sensitive to yellow, and the rods are most sensitive to green. This change with increasing intensity is known as the *Purkinje Shift* (figure 1.11).

The visible spectrum is comprised of five colors of light (see color plate 3) (not of pigment [see color plate 4]): violet, blue, green, yellow, and red. These colors can be mixed: for example, yellow is obtained by combining red with green light.

Mixing colors of light is achieved by using filters, prisms, or diffraction gratings. By mixing two colors of light, a third color is formed in which the two mixed colors cannot be identified.

By mixing three colors of light and adjusting their intensities, any spectral hue can be produced. White can be made, but not black or nonspectral colors such as brown (see color plate 3).

When speaking technically about color vision, we do not refer to "colors" but rather to "hues." This is to avoid difficulty with the term colors, which is descriptive of the physiological sensations to which we give specific names, such as "red" or "blue." We therefore speak technically of spectral hues rather than spectral colors.

Another important distinction is to be found between color as a *sensation* and color as a *wavelength* (or a set of wavelengths) of light entering the eye. Technically, light itself is not colored: it gives rise to sensations of brightness and color, but only in conjunction with a suitable eye and nervous system. When we speak of "yellow light," it means light that gives rise to a sensation described by the majority of people as "yellow."

All the colors of the spectrum are interpreted by the brain from only three kinds of receptors in the eyes: violet, green, and red. These three kinds of color-sensitive receptors (cones) respond to blue-violet, pure green, and orange-red; all colors are "seen" by a mixture of signals from the three systems.

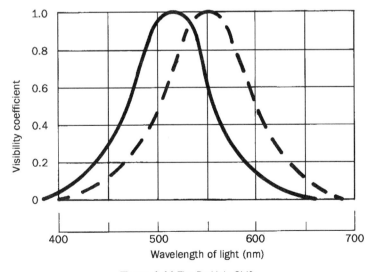

Figure 1.11 The Purkinje Shift.

What we perceive as white is not a particular mixture of colors, but rather the general illumination, whatever this is. A candle or lamplight that looks white by itself appears yellow when "white" electric light or daylight is present for comparison.

The reference for what is taken as white shifts. Knowledge of the normal color of objects is called *color constancy*; it leads us to expect that a tomato will be red. The brain's stored knowledge and expectations exert a strong influence on color perception: objects such as oranges and lemons, for example, take on a richer color because they are recognized as orange and yellow.

Grass is a plant found on lawns and we call the sensation of color it gives "green," but we identify grass by characteristics other than its color: its presence as a lawn, the form and density of the blades, and so forth. If we do confuse the color, sufficient additional evidence is available to identify it as grass. We know it is supposed to be green and we call it green, even when this is doubtful as in the dim light of dusk.

In 1992, neurophysiologists discovered that an alignment of brain cells forms the basis of visual memory. The cells are stacked in columns; depending on which columns are excited by an object, the brain is able to instantly recognize complex images such as faces, even when presented at odd angles or when only part of the face is visible.

Yet it remains a mystery how the contributions from separate channels for brightness, color, shape, and movement—with their own locations in different regions of the brain—come together to form consistent perceptions.

THE SENSE OF SIGHT

We do know that perception is independent of the quantity of light entering the eye; it is based on the quantity of contrast: the differences between light and dark. A certain quantity of light is necessary for a person to see, yet the eye responds not to the total intensity, but to the average intensity in the field of view.

The sense of sight, therefore, is contrast sensitive. It is a mechanism for the detection of differences: of figures on a ground, of objects in a surround. Subjective impressions of space are a function of the degree of contrast present in the environment.

Psychology

2

Because the sense of sight is contrast sensitive, the brightness contrast of a space determines its emotional impact.

EMOTIONAL IMPACT

Subjective impressions of space are a function of brightness contrast: the relationship of surfaces that are lighted (the focus or foreground) to those that are left in comparative darkness (the surround or background). It is possible, of course, to simply introduce general illumination into a room to permit vision. But establishing the emotional impact of an interior through the manipulation of brightness contrast is the real challenge for the creative designer.

Reliance on published standards for illuminance on the *workplane* leads unintentionally to environments that are sterile and unstimulating. Proper attention to the manipulation of brightness contrast as a principal technique for the design of lighting systems results in environments that are inviting, inspiring, and supportive of the tasks to be performed.

If all objects and surfaces in a room receive equal emphasis from light, contrast is lost. Over time, the lack of contrast causes people to feel listless and depressed. Without contrast, the environment produced has the quality of a cloudy, overcast day.

People feel more alert, energetic, and positive on a sunny day, which is marked by bright highlights and crisp shadows. By providing brightness contrast, an environment may be created that has the attributes of a sunny day. In truth, the significant difference between a "dull, dreary day" and a "bright, cheerful" one is the quality of light.

DEGREES OF STIMULATION

Some activities and tasks benefit from a high degree of stimulation to encourage participation and increase enjoyment. Other activities and tasks benefit from a minimum of contrast to help a person feel contented, comfortable, focused, and relaxed. Although individuals react differently to the same environment, there is a high degree of similarity in people's reactions to light.

Environmental psychologists use the terms *high-load* and *low-load* to describe degrees of stimulation or arousal. The more stimuli that must be processed by a person, the higher the load. Environments that are complex, crowded, asymmetrical, novel, unfamiliar, surprising, or random are high load. Environments that are simple, uncrowded, symmetrical, conventional, familiar, unsurprising, or organized are low-load.

If the task to be performed is complex or unusual—studying technical material, preparing for an exam, or writing an essay—the load is great enough that our degree of arousal is fairly high; additional load from the environment will increase stimulation to such a point that the task is avoided. We become distracted, annoyed, or frustrated, and performance falls off sharply.

Tasks that are simple or routine—writing checks, making a shopping list, or other familiar chores—benefit from a mildly stimulating environment. Daydreaming or dozing may result without increased stimulation. This is why such work often fails to be performed in home offices or studies designed for paperwork; instead it is done in kitchens, dining rooms, or living rooms, which have a higher degree of stimulation.

The lower the load of the task, the more it requires a high-load setting for optimum performance. Boring tasks are boring because they are unstimulating (simple or overly familiar) and often unpleasant. Within reason, the more stimulation provided, the more pleasant the task becomes. For many, basic housework is monotonous; playing background music increases stimulation, enabling us to complete "boring" domestic chores.

DEGREES OF BRIGHTNESS CONTRAST

The degree of brightness contrast evokes emotions in the same way as background music. It affects the performance of tasks, influences the behavior of people at work and at play, and impacts the amount of con-

tentment and pleasure we experience. The degree of brightness contrast establishes the emotional setting, which either reinforces or undermines the intended activity.

The first step in the lighting design process is to identify the activity that will occur in a space. The second step is to determine a degree of stimulation that will reinforce that activity. The third step is to establish the degree of brightness contrast that will yield the necessary level of stimulation.

Brightness contrast is established by developing patterns of light and shade—by selecting specific surfaces and objects to receive lighting emphasis while leaving others in comparative darkness. This emphasis creates the relationship between foreground and background (figure 2.1).

Low-Contrast Environment

If everything is to receive equal emphasis, no hierarchy is established between foreground and background. The result is a *low-contrast* environment. Low-contrast spaces are low in stimulation: few stimuli exist to respond to. These spaces are behaviorally neutral (figure 2.2).

A large proportion of *diffuse* light and a small amount of *focused* light produce this low-contrast environment. Low-contrast lighting systems are intended to provide easy seeing for visual tasks, to allow random circulation, or to permit flexible relocation of work surfaces. The diffuse lighting technique provides a uniformly illuminated working environment, an area suitable for difficult and sustained visual tasks (figure 2.3).

Lighting systems that flood a space with diffuse light from overhead reduce contrast. Highly diffuse light produces a shadowless environment; forms are ill-defined and textural perception is poor. Although this is adequate for task vision, it ignores the problem created by the bland psychological reaction to a cloudy day.

Figure 2.1 Patterns of light and shade establish brightness contrast.

Figure 2.2 Low-contrast lighting.

Figure 2.3 Low-contrast lighting.

High-Contrast Environment

A small proportion of diffuse light and a large amount of focused light produce a *high-contrast* environment. High-contrast lighting systems render patterns of light and shade; they intentionally establish a hierarchy between foreground and background. High-contrast spaces increase stimulation; they are intended to evoke specific moods or emotions (figure 2.4).

A single spotlight on a stage is an extreme example of the influence of brightness contrast in creating focal points. A room lighted in this way dominates the people in it; the brightness contrast directs their attention and holds their interest, producing visual direction and focus (figure 2.5).

Attention is involuntarily drawn toward areas of brightness that contrast with the visual background. When a person approaches an unfamiliar space or activity, brightness contrast and color contrast help to establish an initial response. High-contrast environments are useful for guiding the circulation of people entering an unfamiliar room.

THE THREE ELEMENTS OF LIGHT

The three fundamental elements of light are: ambient light, focal glow, and sparkle. The ratio of ambient light to focal glow establishes the degree of brightness contrast in a space; sparkle adds the highlights that contribute to feelings of well-being. The proportions of these three elements yield the desired emotional setting.

The late lighting designer Richard Kelly poetically defines the three elements of light. To Kelly, ambient or general light is

> a snowy morning in open country . . . twilight haze on a mountain top or a cloudy day on the ocean . . . the light in a white tent at noon . . . moonlight coming through the fog.

Figure 2.4 High-contrast lighting.

Figure 2.5 High-contrast lighting.

Ambient luminescence is shadowless illumination. It minimizes form and bulk. It dematerializes. It reduces the importance of things and people. It fills people with a sense of freedom of space and suggests infinity. It is usually reassuring and restful.

The best example is a foggy day on a mountain top. There is an even glow without incidence all around; there are no shadows, nothing to tell you what to look at. In that sense it's confusing, but it is also relaxing and restful, as there is no excitement, no interest. It minimizes man—think about a figure moving through that fog—and destroys form [figure 2.6].

Focal glow or task light, for Kelly, is

the campfire of all time, the glowing embers around which stories are told, or the football rally bonfire. Focal glow is the limelight, the follow spot on the stage, and an aircraft beacon. . . . It is the light burning at the window or the welcoming gleam of the open door.

Focal glow is the sunburst through the clouds and the shaft of sunshine that warms the far end of the valley. It is the pool of light at your favorite reading chair, your airplane-seat light, or match-light on a face. Focal glow is the end of the rainbow; it commands attention, creates interest, fixes the gaze, and tells people what to look at. Focal glow is the focus. It separates the important from the unimportant, establishes precedence, can induce movement, and can control traffic.

Focal light is directive, creates a bright center; it tells us what to look

Figure 2.6 Ambient luminescence.

at, organizes, marks the most important element. It creates a sense of space; you can organize depth through a sequence of focal centers [figure 2.7].

To Kelly, sparkle or glitter is:

a play of brilliants . . . the sensation of a cache of diamonds in an opened cave or the Versailles Hall of Mirrors with its thousands of candle flames . . . a ballroom of crystal chandeliers. Play of brilliants is Times Square at

Figure 2.7 Focal glow.

night . . . sunlight on a tumbling brook . . . the heaven full of stars . . . birch trees interlaced by a motor car's headlights.

Play of brilliants excites the optic nerves . . . stimulates the body and spirit and charms the senses. It creates a feeling of aliveness, alerts the mind, awakens curiosity, and sharpens the wits. It quickens the appetite and heightens all sensations. It can be distracting or it can be entertaining.

Sparkle is scintillation. It is a tiny microscopic bombardment of points of light—the most exciting kind of light there is. It stimulates and arouses appetites of all kinds; chandeliers in dining rooms, sequins on dresses, and lights on theatre marquees all take advantage of the fact[1] [figure 2.8].

Outdoors, during daytime, the sky provides the ambient light. Objects and surfaces that are illuminated by the sun, such as a meadow, trees, or the side of a building, are the focal glow. The reflection of the sun from *specular* surfaces, such as moving water, dew on leaves, or polished metal on a building, supplies the sparkle.

At the beach, the ambient light provided by the sky is balanced by the diffuse,

---

[1]John Marsteller, "A Philosophy of Light: Recalling Richard Kelly's Three Functional Elements," *Interior Design* February 1987: 78–80.

Figure 2.8 Sparkle.

reflected light from the sand. Objects that are lighted by the sun, such as sandcastles, people, bright beach blankets, and bathing suits, become the focus. The glistening of the sun on the agitated water or on wet stones at the water's edge is the sparkle.

Indoors, the proportions of these same elements—ambient light, focal glow, and sparkle—always and everywhere determine the emotional setting.

SUBJECTIVE IMPRESSIONS

The late professor John Flynn documents that as patterns of brightness contrast change, the strength of visual stimuli also changes, altering our impressions of space.

While looking for evidence that lighting changes alone elicit significantly different reactions, Flynn tested six lighting schemes without making other changes in the room (figures 2.9 to 2.14). These changes in lighting condition evoke consistent responses in three areas of impression: spaciousness, perceptual clarity, and pleasantness.

Impressions of spaciousness

The impression of a room's largeness or smallness is affected by the intensity and uniformity of the lighting at the room perime-

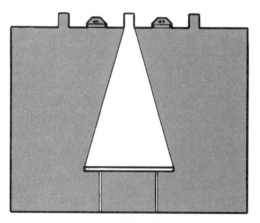

Figure 2.9 Overhead downlighting, low intensity.

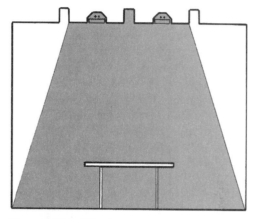

Figure 2.10 Peripheral wall lighting, all walls.

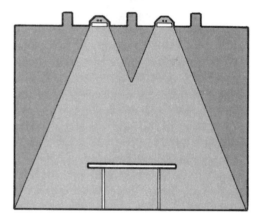

Figure 2.11 Overhead diffuse lighting, low setting.

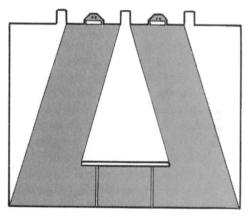

Figure 2.12 Combination: overhead downlighting + end walls.

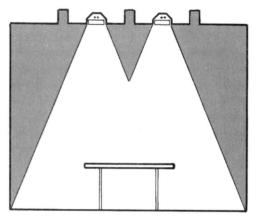

Figure 2.13 Overhead diffuse lighting, high intensity.

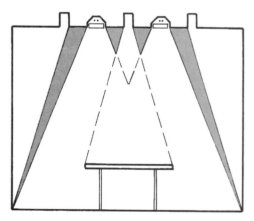

Figure 2.14 Combination: overhead downlighting, overhead diffuse lighting, + end walls.

Figure 2.15 Impressions of spaciousness (large-small).

ter. Flynn found that differences in quantity of horizontal illuminance significantly alter impressions of spaciousness and perceptual clarity. Higher illuminance values are described as "clear," "bright," "distinct," "large," and "more spacious"[2] (figure 2.15).

[2]Improvement in visual contact continues to approximately 25 footcandles (fc) of ambient horizontal illuminance, beyond which it stabilizes.

Impressions of perceptual clarity

Nothing is more important than how people's faces appear. Flynn demonstrated that lighting schemes rated high in facial clarity are considered more public; schemes that are rated low in facial clarity are considered more private.

Public space implies intermingling and bringing people together. The potential for visual contact improves as the intensity of

Figure 2.16 Impressions of perceptual clarity—public space.

Figure 2.17 Impressions of perceptual clarity—private space.

general illuminance is increased. Increasing intensities reduce anonymity and bring people together because facial expressions and gestures are more clearly perceptible (figure 2.16).

Private space suggests separating people and keeping them apart. Shadow and silhouette reinforce feelings of detachment and privacy because these lighting techniques inhibit the ability to perceive precise facial detail; even nearby individuals become more anonymous (figure 2.17).

In a crowded space, when it is impossible to separate people physically by distance, it is possible to separate them visually by lighting. This technique is often used in cocktail lounges, fine restaurants, and reception rooms.

Impressions of pleasantness

Flynn also found that the nonuniform brightness produced by a downward concentrating lighting system rates more favorably than the uniform brightness produced by a diffuse system. The nonuniform brightness is rated as more "friendly," "pleasant," "sociable," and "interesting" (figure 2.18). Differences in the quantity of horizontal illuminance from overhead systems exert negligible influence on impressions of pleasantness.

Figure 2.18 Impressions of pleasantness.

Vertical Surface Illumination

When wall lighting is added, Flynn discovered that ratings shift to the positive for all three categories of impression. Lighted vertical surfaces reinforce feelings of spaciousness, clarity, and pleasantness.

VARIATION

Lack of variation in the built environment is an obstacle that lighting helps to overcome. Monotony results in boredom and depression: even a string of bright, sunny days will become boring through overfamiliarity. Variation increases stimulation and impressions of pleasantness.

One way to increase the load of office or factory environments is to introduce stimuli that vary over time; otherwise, workers quickly become accustomed to the setting. For example, areas for coffee and lunch breaks that have greater contrast and sparkle than the workplace introduce variety through a change of the lighting condition, while also encouraging sociability and conversation.

People using a library, as those in the office and factory, benefit from more stimulating lighting systems in areas used for taking breaks, socializing, or simply daydreaming, for relief from the fatigue caused by concentrated work. The typical library has quiet stacks and cubicles conducive to study, and other areas for relaxed reading and scanning periodicals. People prefer less loaded settings for difficult, complex materials, and more loaded spaces for casual, pleasant reading.

If workers are performing complex and dangerous tasks, however, a pleasant low-load lounge lowers their degree of stimulation. Conversely, performance of low-load tasks in dull settings benefits enormously from pleasant and mildly stimulating diversions. If you must wade through low-load paperwork, such as reading reports, reviewing dull proposals, or composing routine correspondence, productivity is increased when offices are provided with a means of altering the lighting condition.

A fixed, ideal lighting solution that will increase performance while a person is doing a monotonous task is unattainable. Changing all the lamps in a factory to an improved-color light source is insufficient, for example; in time, such a static modification loses much of its stimulating value. A controllable variability of the lighting environment is necessary and beneficial.

In addition to the lighting system, surface finishes, textures, and colors also contribute to the environmental load. In practice, they all must be considered at the same time.

Brightness

3

Specifying the direction and distribution of light in a space yields the desired brightness contrast.

Brightness versus luminance

Brightness is the subjective sensation that occurs in the consciousness of a human observer. *Luminance* is the objective measurement of intensity per unit of projected area.

DIRECTION AND DISTRIBUTION OF LIGHT

A *luminaire* (lighting fixture) emits light in one of three directions—downward, upward, or multidirectional—and in one of two distributions—concentrated or diffuse (figure 3.1).

Downward light from a properly designed luminaire has a restricted angular spread; *direct glare* is prevented by both this restricted spread and the shape of the human eyebrow. *Upward* light usually covers a large area of the ceiling; the light reflected from the ceiling is of low luminance and is unlikely to cause distracting glare. *Multidirectional* light is emitted in all directions, but it cannot emit much of its output sideways without causing objectionable glare.

Upward and downward light is emitted in patterns that vary from narrow to wide. *Con-* *centrated* distribution focuses light in a narrow pattern; *diffuse* distribution disperses light in a wide pattern.

Luminaires with narrow *beam-spreads* that lack an upward component of light produce a *concentrated downward* (also called *direct*) distribution (figure 3.2). When located in low ceilings, concentrated downward beams—with spreads of 30° or less—create areas of high luminance on the floor with dark areas in between. To avoid this unevenness, luminaires would need to be placed inordinately close to each other. Low ceilings require the use of diffuse downward luminaires.

When located in high ceilings, concentrated downward beams overlap and avoid such light and dark areas, yet only horizontal surfaces and the tops of objects are lighted; faces and walls receive little light and appear in shadow. This yields a high-contrast space, one of low ambient brightness with high brightness accents (figure 3.3).

Luminaires with diffuse beam-spreads and a downward distribution produce *diffuse downward* (*direct*) light (figure 3.4). Diffuse downward beams—with spreads from 80° to

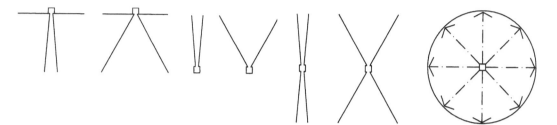

Figure 3.1 The seven directions and distributions of light.

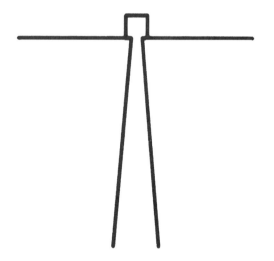

Figure 3.2 Concentrated downward (direct) distribution.

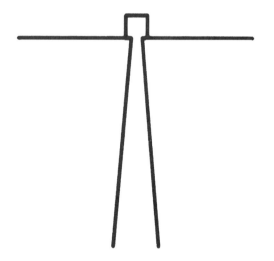

Figure 3.3 An example of concentrated downward distribution.

120°—offer a more practical light distribution for many purposes. A luminaire with a 100° beam-spread, emitting most of its light below a *cutoff* angle of 40° from horizontal, is offered by most well-designed *downlights*. This greater percentage of light at higher angles increases incident light on vertical surfaces, *models* faces, and reduces the concentration of brightness within the space. Diffuse downward luminaires yield a low-contrast setting (figure 3.5).

A *concentrated upward* (*indirect*) distribution directs light toward the ceiling (figure 3.6). With light directed upward and the downward component removed, the ceiling becomes visually prominent. It also becomes a *secondary light source* because of its reflective properties.

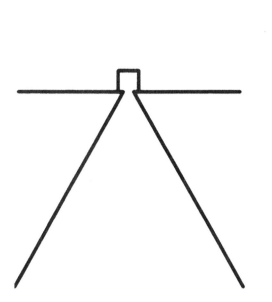

Figure 3.4 Diffuse downward (direct) distribution.

Figure 3.5 An example of diffuse downward distribution.

When mounted in close proximity to the surface being lighted, concentrated upward beams create isolated areas of high luminance. The nonuniformity of concentrated upward distribution reduces the strong contrast that results from a concentrated downward system by adding visual interest through brightness variation (figure 3.7).

If this is the main source of room illumination in areas with low ceiling heights, the "spots" of high brightness on the ceiling become uncomfortable and cause glare. When placed farther from the surface to be lighted, however, concentrated upward beams produce uniform brightness: each beam covers a wider area and multiple beam patterns overlap. In areas with higher ceiling heights, the concentrated beam has sufficient distance to spread; thus the ceiling is lighted uniformly, reducing brightness and glare (figure 3.8).

A *diffuse upward* (*indirect*) distribution directs light toward the ceiling and the upper side walls (figure 3.9). This technique is used to create uniform ceiling luminance for the prevention of glare in areas with video display terminals (VDTs) and to emphasize structural form or decorative detail on or near the ceiling plane (figure 3.10).

Because each point on the ceiling reflects light in every direction, diffuse upward distribution produces a flat, low-contrast environment: the reflected light reduces contrast and shadow; objects and faces have the washed-out appearance similar to that caused by an overcast day.

Multidirectional diffuse (*general diffuse*) distribution is produced by luminaires that deliver both upward and downward components of light (figure 3.11). These luminaires emit light in several directions at the same time—toward the ceiling and walls as well as toward the floor. The reflected light from the ceiling and the interreflection of light in the space diffuse the downward distribution, reducing shadow and contrast and creating a uniform, high-brightness interior (figure 3.12).

Luminaires that deliver both direct and indirect components of diffuse light, but no side lighting, are called *direct/indirect* (figure 3.13).

Figure 3.6 Concentrated upward (indirect) distribution.

Figure 3.7 An example of concentrated upward distribution.

Figure 3.8 An example of concentrated upward distribution with the light source placed farther from the illuminated surface.

Figure 3.9 Diffuse upward (indirect) distribution.

Figure 3.10 An example of diffuse upward distribution.

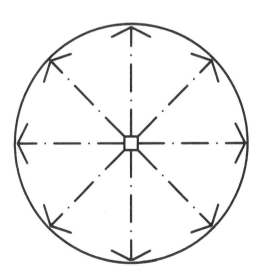

Figure 3.11 Multidirectional diffuse (general diffuse) distribution.

Figure 3.12 An example of multidirectional diffuse distribution.

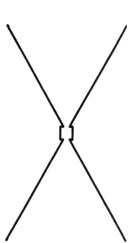

Figure 3.13 Direct/indirect distribution.

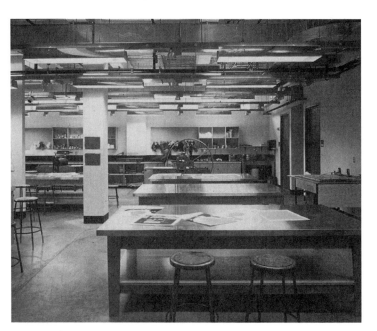

Figure 3.14 An example of direct/indirect distribution.

Figure 3.15 Multidirectional concentrated (semidirect or semi-indirect) distribution.

Figure 3.16 An example of multidirectional concentrated distribution.

They provide efficient use of light on work surfaces while relieving contrast by reflecting light from the ceiling plane (figure 3.14).

Multidirectional distribution created with concentrated beam-spreads is called *multidirectional concentrated* (figure 3.15). It is also called *semidirect* if 60% to 90% of the *lumens* (light emanating from the luminaire) are directed downward, and *semi-indirect* if 60% to 90% of the lumens are directed upward.

A higher contrast, nonuniform brightness condition is produced with concentrated distributions present in both the upward and downward components. The upward component reduces excessive contrast in a space; however, the nonuniform light reflected from wall or ceiling surfaces is insufficient to "wash out" all shadow and contrast. This lack of diffusion yields moderate contrast (figure 3.16).

Vertical Surface Illumination

Wall lighting is sometimes a substitute for indirect ceiling lighting: it lightens shadow and reduces excessive contrast. It works especially well when the walls are high in relation to the size of the room. Another substitute is direct downlights in combination with a light-colored floor: the floor reflects light back to the ceiling as though indirect lighting were being used. The floor must be kept clean for this technique to be successful.

The ideal lighting arrangement is often a combination of direct and indirect light, where the direct light takes the place of the sun, casting shadows and modeling shapes, and the indirect light softens the shadows, acting as a blue sky or a photographer's fill light. Direct/indirect lighting designs are produced either with separate systems for downward and upward light or with one system that provides both downward and upward distribution.

SURFACE FINISHES AND REFLECTANCES

What is perceived as brightness is not the incident light on a surface, but the light that is *reflected* from that surface toward the eyes. Brightness results from the intensity of light that initially strikes a surface *and* the reflecting or transmitting properties of that surface.

Whether it is of high or low intensity, some amount of incident light from luminaires or from interreflection falls on all room surfaces. The relative size of these surfaces and the intensity of light reflected from them determine their visual prominence in an interior composition.

Reflected light is usually diffuse and multidirectional, causing interreflection between all surfaces and objects. This interreflection fills in shadows, reduces contrast, and yields more uniform brightness.

The overall brightness results from the distribution of reflected light, which, in turn, depends on the reflectance properties of the surfaces in the space. Dark-colored, low-reflectance finishes absorb much of the light that strikes them, reflecting only a small amount toward the eye. This gives an impression of a dark, high-contrast space regardless of the amount of illuminance (figures 3.17 and 3.18).

Light-colored and high-reflectance finishes reflect much more of the incident light, contributing to a higher brightness and a greater diffusion of light (figures 3.19 and 3.20). This interreflection is independent of the initial distribution of light, whether that distribution is concentrated or diffuse.

The choice of surface finishes augments or negates the initial distribution of light from luminaires. This influence of reflected light must be accounted for: understanding the relationship between lighting equipment and room surfaces is critical to successful lighting design.

Secondary Light Sources

Any object or surface that reflects or transmits light becomes a secondary light source. The moon is an example: it is incapable of producing light. The moonlight we see is produced by a primary source—the sun—which is reflected by the moon's surface.

Similarly, a lighted wall or ceiling becomes a secondary light source that illuminates a room through reflection. The result is then dependent on the reflected light from the lighted surface, rather than on the initial distribution of light from the luminaires (see color plate 5).

THREE-DIMENSIONAL FORM

In addition to altering our perception of space, the direction and distribution of light affect the perception of surfaces and objects in a room.

All three-dimensional form is seen as a pattern of brightness contrasts, often con-

Figures 3.17 and 3.18 If all the room surfaces are dark, there is little interreflection; contrast is high.

Figures 3.19 and 3.20 If all of the room surfaces are light-colored, interreflections will fill in shadows and reduce contrast.

Figures 3.21 and 3.22 Grazing illumination.

sisting of highlights and shadows. A change in this pattern, caused by a change in the direction and distribution of light, alters visual impressions of form and surface.

Lighting alters perception of texture. *Grazing light*, from luminaires located close to a surface being lighted, strengthens highlights and shadows. It enhances the perception of depth by emphasizing the natural textures and sculptural relief of the surface. Grazing light is also used for inspection to detect surface blemishes and errors in workmanship (figures 3.21 and 3.22).

Grazing light is appropriate for lighting heavily textured surfaces such as rough plaster, masonry, or concrete. It is disastrous for "flat" walls of smooth plaster or gypsum board, however, because such walls are not

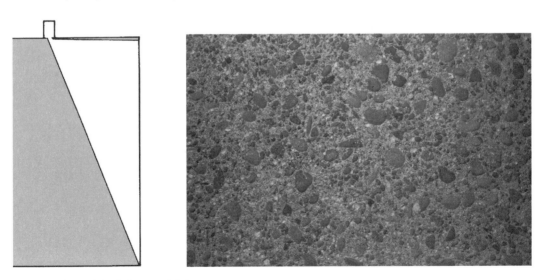

Figures 3.23 and 3.24 Diffuse wash light.

Figure 3.25 Sculpture lighted with concentrated direct lighting from below.

Figure 3.26 Sculpture lighted with diffuse lighting from above.

truly flat: minor surface imperfections such as trowel marks, tape, and nail-head depressions are magnified by the shadows that result from grazing light.

Conversely, diffuse *wash light* reduces the likelihood that surface flaws will be noticed and strengthens an impression of surface smoothness. This is more suitable for a gypsum board wall or an acoustical tile ceiling. Diffuse wash light from the front is particularly successful at reducing or removing shadows and small variations in brightness (figures 3.23 and 3.24).

Concentrated direct lighting on objects produces drama and emotional excitement. Yet the same sharp shadows that contribute to the dramatic impact also reduce visibility of detail. This diminishes the ability to study and appreciate all aspects of the object accurately (figure 3.25).

A diffuse lighting distribution, on the other hand, illuminates the entire object, reducing shadows and facilitating study of workmanship and detail. Although it is often desirable, this kind of lighting sacrifices the

dramatic impact and visual excitement (figure 3.26).

Sharp highlights and dark shadows create a dramatic setting and strengthen impressions of texture and form; however, they are distracting in a working environment. Some shadows on a work surface are mildly irritating, such as those cast by a hand or pencil while one is writing under a concentrated light source.

Other shadows are extremely distracting and even hazardous, such as those on an assembly line. During a period of sustained visual activity, the extreme concentration and constant reädaptation required by workers in high contrast settings result in visual fatigue, errors, and accidents.

Sometimes highlight and shadow are desirable in a work environment. Just as the highlights and shadows of a sunny day are emotionally stimulating, carefully placed highlights and shadows in an interior provide visual relief and interest. Office and factory workers benefit from the stimulation and variation provided by greater brightness con-

Figure 3.27 Bust of Lincoln lighted from above.

Figure 3.28 Bust of Lincoln lighted from below.

trast in corridors, washrooms, lunchrooms, lounges, and other meeting places. On most *work* surfaces, however, diffuse light distribution is desirable to minimize highlights and shadows.

Experience and memory also influence our perception of objects. Through the course of time, people have come to expect midday sunlight to emanate from a concentrated source overhead, at an angle less than 45° from nadir (straight down), and skylight to be a diffuse, multidirectional source.

When a lighting system alters the expected direction of light, it changes the normal relationship between highlights and shadows. An unnatural impression results, inducing mystery or anxiety (figures 3.27 and 3.28).

In practice, objects being exhibited or photographed are often lighted from two sides to reduce excessive shadows. One side has a concentrated beam-spread to enhance drama and function as the sun's directional rays; the other side receives diffuse illumination to soften shadows and replicate the sky's diffusing quality. The background may be lighted separately to distinguish the object from its surround and to add visual depth.

GLARE AND SPARKLE

Excessive contrast or luminance is distracting and annoying. This negative side of brightness is called *glare*. In the extreme, glare cripples vision by reducing or destroying the ability to see accurately.

Glare is often misunderstood as "too much light." In fact, it is light coming from the wrong direction, the result of an extreme luminance within the normal field of view. The difference between the high and low beams

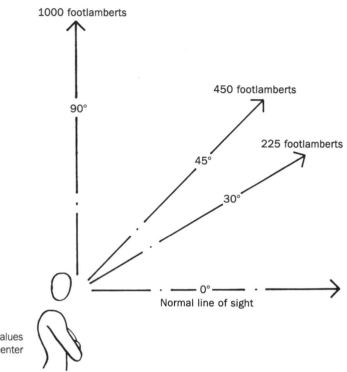

Figure 3.29 Acceptable luminance values decrease as the source approaches the center of the visual field.

of automobile headlights at night demonstrates that glare for the approaching driver is a function of direction as well as intensity. It also demonstrates that glare may be present in an environment with little light.

Glare is also a function of luminance area. Although a small area of luminance is tolerable, a larger area of the same intensity becomes uncomfortable. It is desirable to reduce luminance intensities as the area of luminance becomes more dominant in the field of view.

In addition, glare is a function of location. Within limits, the human eyebrow conceals glare from overhead luminaires, but not from poorly shielded, wall-mounted luminaires or high-luminance wall surfaces, as these elements are directly in the field of view (figure 3.29).

Direct Glare

The late afternoon sun and an unshielded electric light source are examples of the distracting influence of direct glare in the environment. *Direct glare* is caused by the lighting system; it is defined as excessive light misdirected toward the eye.

Usually, the uncontrolled luminance of an exposed light source produces glare. For this reason, bare *lamps* (the technical word for light bulb) are rarely used in architectural applications (figure 3.30).

When direct glare occurs in the normal field of view, three main control techniques are available. One is to limit the amount of light emitted in the direction of the eye (figure 3.31). Shielding devices such as the hand, used instinctively, and sun visors improve visibility and restore visual comfort in this way.

Electromagnetic Spectrum

Wavelength in Nanometers (10 Angstroms = 1 Nanometer)

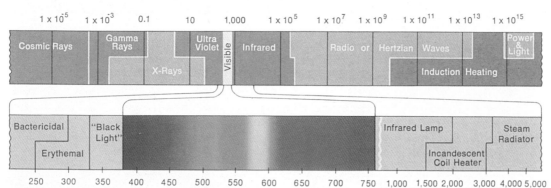

Plate 1

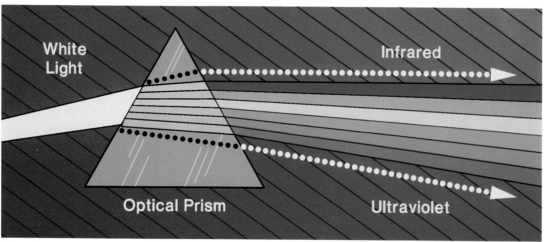

Plate 2

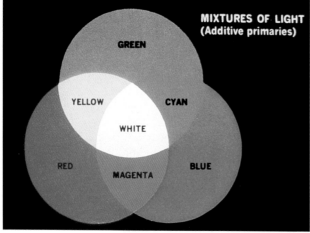

Plate 3

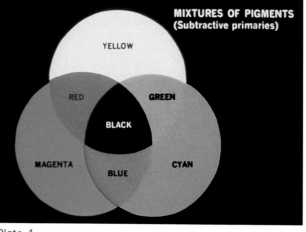

Plate 4

Plate 5

Plate 6

Plate 7

Plate 8

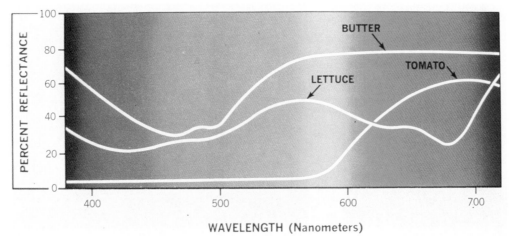

Plate 9

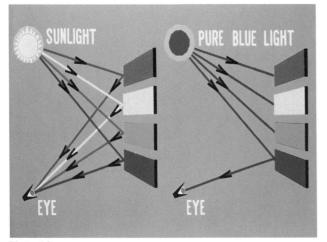

Plate 10

Plate 11

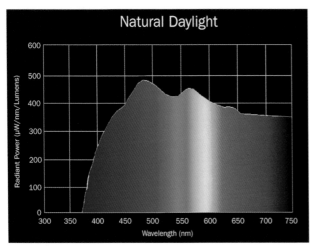

Plate 12

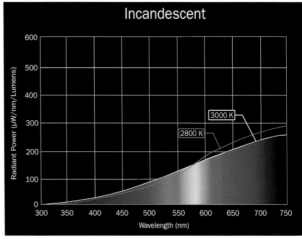

Plate 13

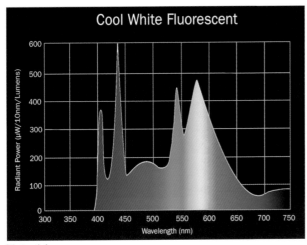

Plate 14

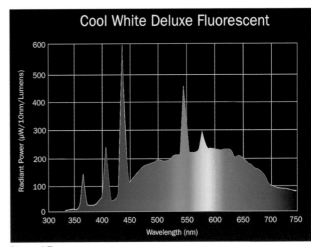

Plate 15

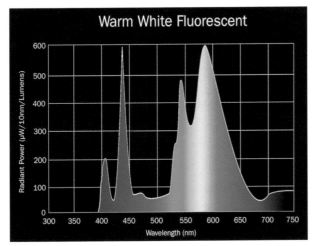

Plate 16

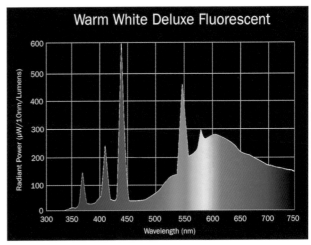

Plate 17

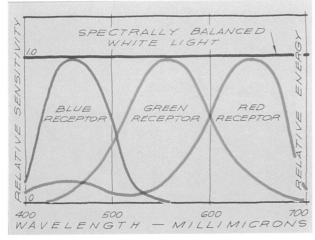

Plate 18

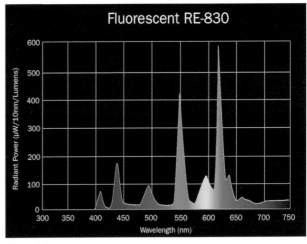

Plate 19

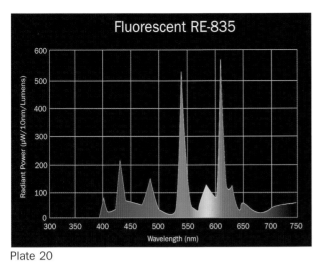

Plate 20

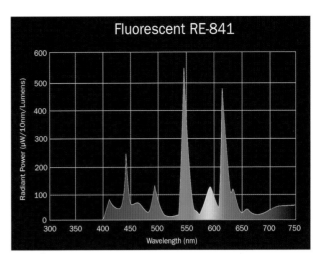

Plate 21

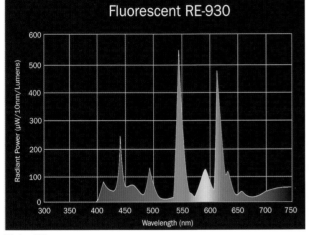

Plate 22

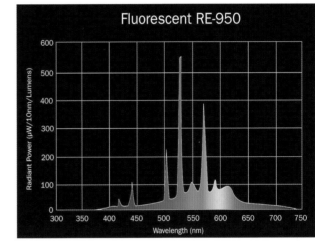

Plate 23

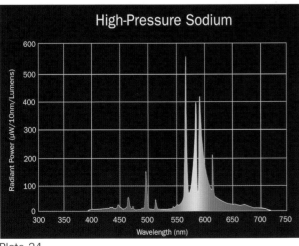

Plate 24

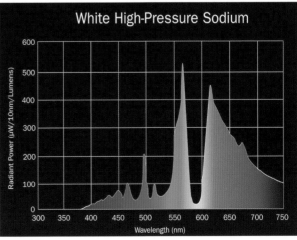

Plate 25

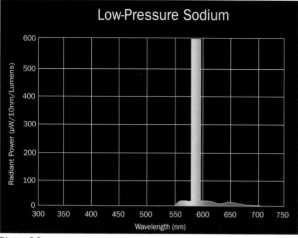

Plate 26

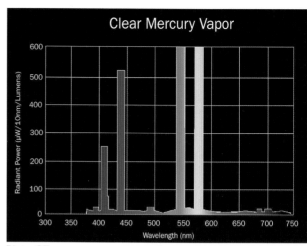

Plate 27

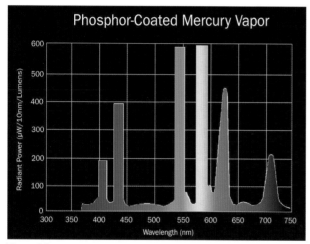

Plate 28

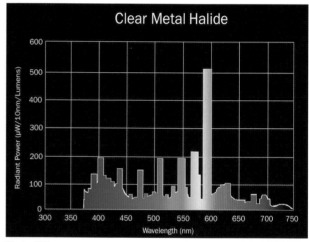

Plate 29

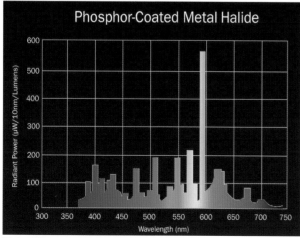

Plate 30

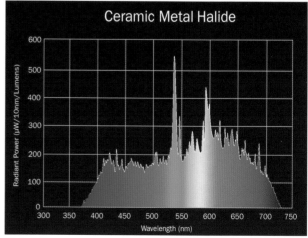

Plate 31

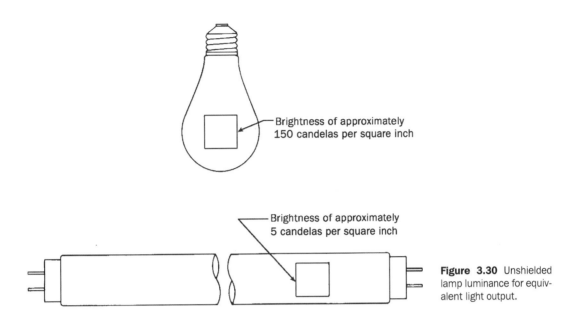

Brightness of approximately
150 candelas per square inch

Brightness of approximately
5 candelas per square inch

Figure 3.30 Unshielded lamp luminance for equivalent light output.

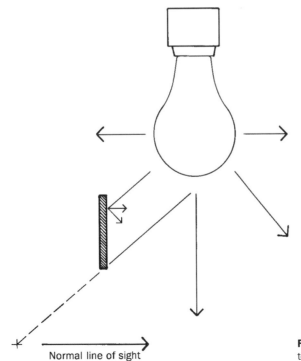

Normal line of sight

Figure 3.31 Limiting the amount of light emitted toward the eye.

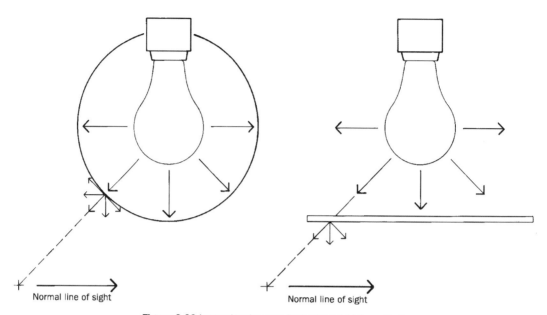

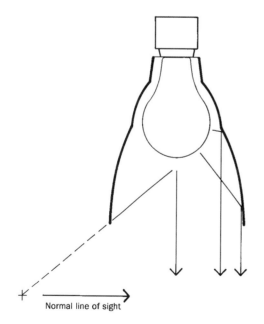

Figure 3.32 Increasing the area from which light is emitted.

Figure 3.33 Change in the direction of the beam to control direct glare.

The second is to increase the area from which light is emitted (figure 3.32). A white glass globe and diffusing panels of white glass or plastic are examples.

The automobile headlights redirected below the line of sight demonstrates the third technique whereby directional control and change in the direction of the beam (figure 3.33) aid visual comfort. This third method is more efficient; it uses accurate control devices to redirect light in the desired direction. Typical devices are reflectors and refracting lenses that limit the distribution of stray light emitted toward the eye.

Visual comfort results from the reduction of glare and distracting luminance in the field of view. Excessive luminance is physiologically disconcerting and reduces the ability to see detail accurately. The quality and comfort of vision depend upon the avoidance of distracting or disabling luminances.

Visual Comfort Probability (VCP)

A *visual comfort probability (VCP)* rating is defined as the percentage of people who, if seated in the least desirable location in an office work space, will find a lighting installation comfortable. VCP depends on the size and shape of the room, the reflectances of room surfaces, and the location and light distribution of the luminaires.

A VCP of 70 or more is recommended for general office use, and 80 or more for office areas using video display terminals (VDTs). Originally tested and validated using lensed fluorescent direct luminaires, VCP is applicable only for direct lighting systems.

Reflected Glare

Visual comfort is achieved by limiting not only direct glare but also reflected glare. *Reflected glare* is excessive uncontrolled luminance reflected from objects or surfaces in the field of view. This includes the reflected luminance from interior surfaces as well as the luminance of the lighting system.

Specular surfaces have reflecting properties similar to those of a mirror. The luminance reflected is the mirrored image of the light source, or of another lighted surface within the reflected field of view.

These properties make specular surfaces useful as reflectors for light control in luminaires, but polished or specular interior surfaces such as desks, countertops, floors, walls, and ceilings introduce problems of reflected glare. *Diffuse surfaces* prevent highlights and are uniformly bright from all angles of view.

Reflected images on glass and other transparent materials form a visual barrier. At night, large areas of glass may become black mirrors. If surfaces viewed through the transparent material are higher in luminance than the reflected images, a sense of transparency is achieved.

Most work surfaces reflect light both diffusely and specularly. Diffuse reflectance is dependent on the quantity of illuminance on the surface. Specular reflectance is dependent on the luminance of the source: the reflected image of the lamp or luminaire. This reflected image causes a veiling image on the work surface that obscures surface detail.

In the visual task area, remove glossy surfaces wherever possible. A glass-covered or highly polished desk top is quite specular; reflected images become distracting. Matte (low-gloss) finishes should always be used for work surfaces.

It is helpful to think of the work surface as a mirror when orienting task luminaires (figure 3.34). Proper luminaire location reduces reflected glare from the task (figure 3.35). When luminaires are located on either side of the desk, shadows cast by the luminaires are filled in and light is reflected away from the worker's eyes (figure 3.36).

Video Display Terminals (VDTs)

VDTs are glossy *vertical* work surfaces. Screen reflections are caused by variations in luminance being "seen" by the screen surface and reflected into the worker's eyes. Screens that are convex and inclined upward, in particular, reflect into the eyes large areas of ceiling, walls, windows, and the surrounding space.

Positioning the screen, adjusting its angle, low-reflectance screens, blinds on windows, and dark clothing for workers are techniques that relieve many reflection problems. Reflections caused by the lighting system can be controlled with properly designed, deep-cell parabolic louvers to prevent lamp images from appearing on the VDT screen.

In addition to reflections on the screen surface, which make viewing the screen images difficult, two additional lighting problems that cause concern for VDT users are: (1) proper lighting for the non-VDT tasks the

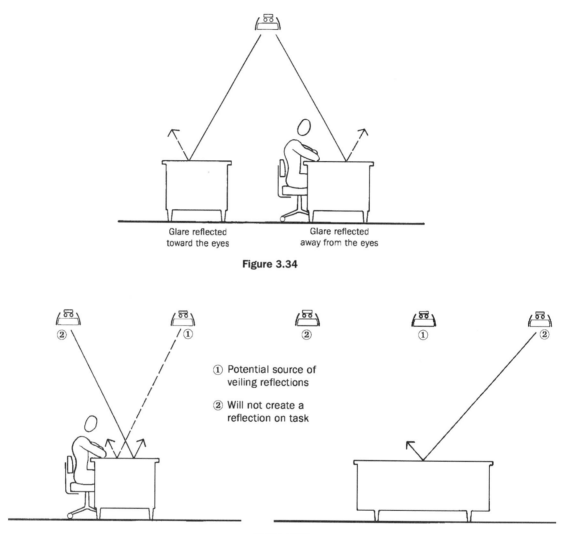

Glare reflected
toward the eyes

Glare reflected
away from the eyes

Figure 3.34

① Potential source of
veiling reflections

② Will not create a
reflection on task

Figure 3.35

worker must also perform, and (2) lighting of the area in the worker's field of view.

Sometimes the ambient room illuminance in VDT areas is set low in the belief that this improves screen visibility. The opposite is true. While low quantities of ambient light reduce screen reflections, the room appears visually gloomy; there will also be areas of high contrast between the bright

screen and the dark surround. Furthermore, low ambient illuminance is unstimulating, especially when contact with the outdoors via windows is missing.

Indirect uplighting systems are sometimes used to avoid luminaire reflections in the screen. The ceiling must be high enough to allow pendant- or floor-mounted luminaires to distribute light evenly (see figure 13.21) or

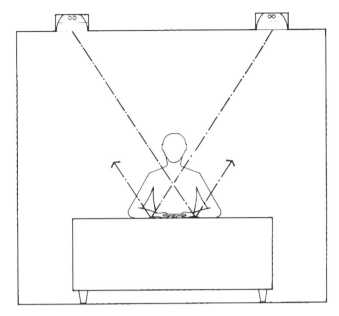

Figure 3.36 Proper desk lighting.

excessive contrast is created in a different way. Even when uniform ceiling luminance is achieved, the diffuse reflected light may have a "washing out" effect that reduces the visibility of the screen. Moreover, because all of the light in the space is diffuse, indirect systems also create a bland interior.

It is the *variation* in room luminance that is extremely critical, however. All surfaces and objects reflected by the VDT screen into the worker's normal line of sight—especially room surface finishes such as system divider panels, vertical surfaces of filing cabinets, and the ceiling plane—must be of more or less equal luminance if distracting images are to be prevented.

Many high-quality VDTs are now furnished with integral low-reflectance screens; newer, flat-screen monitors have liquid crystal displays (LCDs), which reflect very little light from all directions except perpendicular to the screen. In time, VDTs may cease to be a lighting challenge.

Sparkle

The principal difference between glare and sparkle is the relationship between the area and magnitude of luminance in the field of view. Large areas of luminance are distracting and disconcerting; relatively small areas of similar or higher intensity are points of sparkle and highlight that contribute to emotional excitement and visual interest.

• **Direct sparkle**. Examples include Christmas tree lights; small, exposed, clear filament lamps; and perforated shielding materials (see color plate 6).

• **Reflected sparkle**. Examples include textured metal and pebbled surface finishes (see color plate 7).

• **Transmitted sparkle**. Examples include crystal chandeliers and sandblasted- or etched-glass (frosted) *diffusers* around clear filament lamps. Clear filament lamps combined with crystal glass, particularly when that glass is faceted, introduce subtle color

INTERIOR LIGHTING FOR DESIGNERS

highlights via the dispersion of "white" light into the rainbow of colors that comprise it (see color plate 8).

The presence of sparkle, highlight, and shadows constitutes the chief visual attrib-utes that make a sunny day interesting and stimulating; their absence makes a cloudy, overcast day flat and dull. The emotional stimulation provided by carefully controlled sparkle, highlight, and shadows is equally significant in interiors.

Color

Color is not a physical property of the things we see—it is the consequence of light waves bouncing off or passing through various objects.

The color of an object or surface is determined by its reflected or transmitted light. Color is not a physical property of the things we see—it is the consequence of light waves bouncing off or passing through various objects. What is perceived as color is the result of materials reflecting or transmitting energy in particular regions of the visible spectrum.

Green glass transmits the green portion of the spectrum, absorbing almost all of the other regions; yellow paint reflects the yellow portion, absorbing almost all other wavelengths (figure 4.1). White or neutral gray materials reflect all wavelengths in approximately equal amounts.

Pure spectral colors are specified by their wavelength, which is usually expressed in nanometers. A nanometer (nm) is one billionth of a meter or about thirty-nine billionths of an inch.

The reflectance chart (color plate 9) shows that butter absorbs blue light and reflects a high percentage of all other colors; these other colors combine to produce what we call yellow. Green lettuce reflects light with wavelengths primarily in the 500–600-nm region and absorbs all of the energy at other wavelengths. A tomato is red only because it reflects visible energy at 610 nm while absorbing almost all of the other wavelengths.

A light source that emits radiant energy comparatively balanced in all visible wavelengths appears "white" in color. Passing a narrow beam of this white light through a prism separates and spreads the individual wavelengths, allowing the eye to distinguish among them. The resulting visual phenomenon is called a *color spectrum* (color plate 2).

"White" light sources emit energy at all or almost all visible wavelengths, but not always in an ideal proportion. Almost all sources are deficient at some wavelengths yet still appear to be white. This deficiency influences the perception of colors; the effect is known as *color rendition*. It causes the graying of some colors while enhancing the vividness of others.

To provide accurate color perception, a light source must emit those wavelengths that a material reflects. Lighting a tomato's surface with a white light source makes the

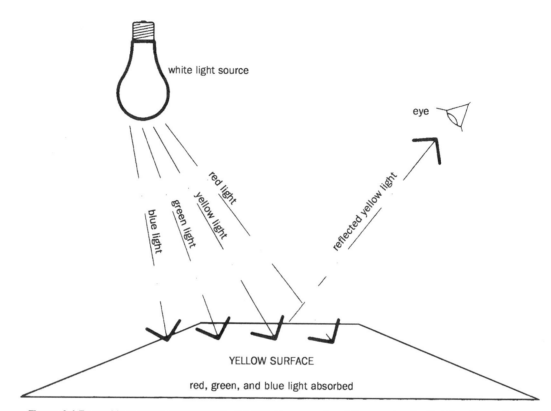

white light source

eye

red light

yellow light

green light

blue light

reflected yellow light

YELLOW SURFACE

red, green, and blue light absorbed

Figure 4.1 To provide accurate color rendition, the light source must emit the wavelengths that the object reflects.

surface appear red, because only red wavelengths of light are reflected toward the eye. All other wavelengths are absorbed.

If the tomato is lighted with a green source, however, it will appear dark gray because no red energy is available to be reflected. The eye can see only the colors of a surface that are present in the source of illumination (color plate 10).

Because the proportion of colors in "white" light varies, what we call white light is a broad category. Within this category, the most common variations are described as "warm" or "cool." A warm white light emphasizes the long (high nm) end of the spectrum, with hues of yellow through orange to

red. Warm light sources that emphasize these hues include the sun and *incandescent, tungsten-halogen,* and *high-pressure sodium* lamps. Conversely, a cool white light source emphasizes the short (low nm) end of the spectrum, with hues of blue through green to yellow. Cool light sources that emphasize these hues include north skylight and many *fluorescent* and *metal halide* lamps.

Spectral distribution charts, available from lamp manufacturers, express the relative color composition of light sources (color plates 13–17 and 19–31). Because these charts are of limited practical value in predicting how colors will appear, simplified systems of color notation and color rendition have been developed.

COLOR TEMPERATURE

Color temperature describes how a lamp appears when lighted. Color temperature is measured in kelvin (K), a scale that starts at absolute zero (−273°C).

At room temperature, an object such as a bar of steel does not emit light, but if it is heated to a certain point it glows dull red. Instead of a bar of steel, physicists use an imaginary object called a *blackbody radiator*. Similar to a steel bar, the blackbody radiator emits red light when heated to 800 K; a warm, yellowish "white" at 2800 K; a daylight-like white at 5000 K; a bluish, daylight white at 8000 K; and a brilliant blue at 60,000 K. The theoretical blackbody is necessary because the bar of steel would melt at these higher temperatures.

Color temperature is not a measure of the surface temperature of an actual lamp or any of its components. Color temperature refers to the absolute temperature of the laboratory blackbody radiator when its visible radiation matches the color of the light source.

Incandescent lamps closely resemble blackbody radiators in that they emit a continuous spectrum of all of the visible colors of light (color plate 13). Consequently, the incandescent spectrum is accurately specified by color temperature in kelvin. Fluorescent and *high-intensity discharge* (HID) lamps produce a discontinuous spectrum with blank areas punctuated by bands at specific frequencies (color plates 14–17 and 19–31). These bands combine to give the impression of "white" light; fluorescent and HID lamp color appearance is specified by its *apparent* or *correlated color temperature* (CCT).

Incandescent lamps used in architectural lighting have color temperatures in the 2600 K to 3100 K range; fluorescent lamps are available with apparent color temperatures from 2700 K to 7500 K; north skylight is arbitrarily called 10,400 K.

Unfortunately, the apparent color temperature of discontinuous spectrum light sources fails to provide information about its spectral energy distribution. For example, warm white and RE-930 fluorescent lamps have the same apparent color temperature, yet their spectral distribution curves and their color rendition of objects and materials are vastly different. This same limitation applies when using color temperature notations for high-intensity discharge sources, including *mercury vapor*, metal halide, and high-pressure sodium lamps.

COLOR RENDERING

To remedy this limitation, *color rendering* expresses how colors appear under a given light source. For example, a shade of red will be rendered lighter or darker, more crimson or more orange, depending on the spectral-distribution properties of the light falling on it.

The most accepted method to determine the color-rendering ability of a light source is a rating system called the *Color Rendering Index* (CRI).

The CRI first establishes the real or apparent color temperature of a given light source. Then, it establishes a comparison between the color rendition of the given light source and of a reference light source. If the color temperature of a given source is 5000 K or less, the reference source is the blackbody radiator at the nearest color temperature. If the given color temperature is above 5000 K, the reference source is the nearest simulated daylight source.

The comparison is expressed as an R_a factor, on a scale of 1 to 100, which indicates how closely the given light source matches the color-rendering ability of the reference light source. Since the reference for CRI changes with color temperature, the

CRIs of different lamps are valid only if they have similar correlated color temperatures. Therefore, it is inappropriate to compare two light sources unless their color temperature is similar—within 100 K to 300 K.

For example, a 3000 K RE-70 fluorescent lamp and a 6500 K "daylight" fluorescent lamp render objects differently, despite the fact that they both have a CRI of 75. This occurs because the CRI for the 3000 K lamp was compared to a blackbody radiator and the CRI for the 6500 K lamp was based on comparison to actual daylight.

R_a is an average of the color rendering ability of eight test colors; better performance at some wavelengths is concealed when averaged with poorer performance at other wavelengths. As a consequence, two lamps that have the same color temperature and CRI may have different spectral distributions and may render colored materials differently.

Some typical CRIs appear in table 1 in the appendix.

The color properties of the light source significantly alter the appearance of people. Because incandescent sources are rich in red wavelengths, they complement and flatter complexions, imparting a healthy, ruddy, or tanned quality to the skin. Cool fluorescent and HID sources that emphasize the yellow or blue range produce a sallow or pale appearance.

SUBJECTIVE IMPRESSIONS

The color of light has a profound effect on subjective impressions of the environment. The Amenity Curve indicates that warmer light is desirable for low luminance values (figure 4.2). It also shows that a room uniformly lighted to 20 footcandles (fc) will be unpleasant with either kerosene lamps (about 2000 K) or lamps that simulate daylight (about 5000 K).

With the warm-toned kerosene source, the quantity will seem too high and the space too greatly lighted. With the simulated daylight source, the same quantity of light will seem dark and dingy. Both warm fluorescent (2700 K or 3000 K) and standard incandescent lamps (2600 K to 3100 K) fall within the acceptable range on the chart.

In addition, a warm atmosphere suggests friendliness or coziness. A cool atmosphere implies efficiency and neatness. Flynn evaluated subjective responses to colors of white light that are produced by electric light sources in interior spaces at intermediate illuminance values.

Flynn's subjects categorized their impressions of visually warm versus visually cool space as follows: cool colors (4100 K) stimulate impressions of visual clarity; warm colors (3000 K) reinforce impressions of pleasantness, particularly when a feeling of relaxation is desirable.

Flynn found that diffuse light plus warm (orange-red) hues intensify impressions of tension and anxiety. Diffuse light plus cool (violet-blue) hues reinforce impressions of somberness; at low luminance values, they create an impression of gloom.

He also found that patterns of sparkle plus saturated warm (orange-red) hues strengthen impressions of playfulness and merriment; this is particularly strong with random patterns of light and color. Patterns of sparkle plus saturated cool (violet-blue) hues reinforce impressions of enchantment; this is particularly strong with rhythmic or regimented patterns of light and color.

SURFACE FINISHES AND COLOR OF LIGHT

To reiterate: light does not have color, and objects do not have color. Color resides in the eye/brain system.

The relationship between the spectral distribution of light and the colors of fabrics, walls, and other elements in the interior is, therefore, pivotal. Some objects appear to

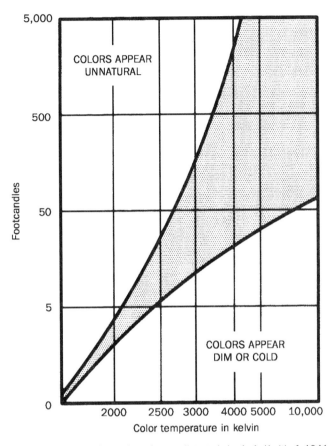

Figure 4.2 Amenity Curve, based on a pilot study by A. A. Kruithof, 1941.

be the same color under a certain light source although they are different in spectral composition. If the light source is changed, however, the object color differences become apparent (color plate 11).

It is advisable to appraise, match, and specify colored materials using light sources identical in color to those that will be used in the completed installation. When the lighting system that will be installed is unknown, two light sources of different spectral character may be used to examine the samples: one of the sources should be predominantly blue in

spectral distribution, such as a daylight fluorescent lamp, and the other predominantly red, such as an incandescent lamp.

Incandescent Sources
Incandescent lamps emit energy in a smooth curve beginning with a small amount of deep-blue radiation in the near ultraviolet range and increasing into the deep-red portion of the spectrum (color plate 13). The color of incandescent light is warm in tone, with most of the energy concentrated in the red and yellow range. Although this "white" light is

deficient in blue and green, and tends to gray these colors, it complements the appearance of warm colors and human faces.

Incandescent lamps enjoy one slight advantage over other lamps in color rendering—not because they render colors more naturally, but because more than a century of use has established them as a norm. Incandescent lamps also produce light as a by-product of heat, similar to other sources of light that have been familiar for thousands of years: the sun, open fire, candles, oil lamps, and gas lamps. All of these give warm-colored light and all are *point* sources.

Good color rendition is usually interpreted to mean the familiar appearance of familiar objects: things assume familiar colors by frequently being seen under certain kinds of light sources, such as incandescent lamps or daylight.

Tungsten-halogen lamps (3000 K) have more blue and less red energy than standard incandescent lamps; they appear whiter than the slightly yellowish standard incandescent lamps (2700 K). All incandescent and tungsten-halogen lamps are assigned a CRI of 100.

Fluorescent Sources

Fluorescent lamps produce a discontinuous spectrum: peaks of energy at specific wavelengths. Variations in the composition of the *phosphors* that coat the inside of the lamp produce differences in the color of emitted light. Three principal color temperatures are available with fluorescent lamps: (1) warm (3000 K) lamps are compatible with incandescent lamps, (2) cool (4100 K) lamps are compatible with daylight, and (3) 3500 K lamps are compatible with both.

Fluorescent lamps also fall into three groups with regard to *efficacy* and color rendition: standard, deluxe, and rare-earth. Standard white lamps—both cool and warm kinds—produce high efficacy and poor color

rendition (color plates 14 and 16). Warm white fluorescent lamps have CRIs of 52 to 53; cool white fluorescent lamps have CRIs of 60 to 62.

Deluxe white lamps produce improved color rendering with an approximately 25 percent sacrifice in lighting efficacy. The reduction in light quantity is often imperceptible, however, because of the vivid and accurate colors that improve contrast and portray tones that are grayed with standard lamps (color plates 15 and 17). Deluxe fluorescent lamps have CRIs between 84 and 89.

For both high color rendering and high luminous efficacy, rare-earth lamps are used. Three kinds of rare-earth (RE) lamps are available: triphosphor RE-70, triphosphor RE-80, and quad-phosphor RE-90.

Triphosphor rare-earth lamps produce light in accordance with the theory that the human eye reacts to three *prime colors*— blue-violet, pure green, and orange-red (color plate 18). When these three prime (not primary) colors are combined in a triphosphor lamp, only those wavelengths are emitted; the brain fills in the remainder of the spectrum. This yields more colorful interiors because the three narrow-emission, prime-color phosphors compress all hues into the eye's color response system, increasing color contrast (color plates 19, 20, and 21).

Because the eye/brain system can be fully stimulated with these three monochromatic wavelengths, all pigment colors can be rendered by adjusting the relative intensities of the three prime-color phosphors. The key is to choose the components that maximize the visual system responses. For maximum effect, the three wavelengths must correspond to the peak spectral sensitivities of human vision, which are near 450 nm, 530 nm, and 610 nm.

RE-70 lamps use a coat of conventional phosphors and a thin coat of narrow-emission, rare-earth phosphors, producing CRIs of 70 to 78. *RE-80* lamps use a thick coat of the narrow-emission, rare-earth phosphors, producing CRIs of 80 to 86.

Quad-phosphor *RE-90* lamps do not use the narrow-emission phosphors; they contain four wider-emission phosphors that produce CRIs of 95 at 3000 K and 98 at 5000 K (color plates 22 and 23). RE-90 rare-earth lamps with CRIs of 95 to 98 are the highest color-rendering fluorescent lamps available.

High-Intensity Discharge (HID) Sources

As with fluorescent lamps, high-intensity discharge (HID) lamps produce a discontinuous spectrum. The different metals in the arc of the various HID sources yield different color-rendering abilities.

If you were to throw salt on a barbecue, the sodium chloride would make the flames appear yellow. Similarly, the sodium in high-pressure sodium lamps makes their color appear yellow. If you were to throw mercury on a barbecue, although this is not recommended because it would cause mercury poisoning, the mercury would make the flames appear blue. Similarly, the mercury in mercury vapor lamps makes their color appear blue.

High-pressure sodium lamps produce predominantly yellow light at 2100 K, which creates a shift in how we perceive almost all observed colors. Reds, greens, blues, and violets are muted (color plate 24). High-pressure sodium lamps have CRIs of 21 and 22.

By further increasing the gas pressure inside the lamp, *white high-pressure sodium* lamps produce incandescent-like color at 2700 K with good color-rendering properties and a CRI of 85 (color plate 25).

Low-pressure sodium lamps emit all visible energy at 589 nm, which means that they render only materials that reflect light at that wavelength. All other colors appear gray (color plate 26). Low-pressure sodium lamps are assigned a CRI of 0.

The clear mercury vapor lamp produces a cool, "white" light of predominantly blue and green energy. The lack of energy at the warm (red) end of the spectrum results in poor color rendering; people appear ghastly. Clear mercury vapor lamps exhibit particularly poor rendering of red. Rendering of other colors is fair, but blues appear purplish (color plate 27). Clear mercury vapor lamps have CRIs between 15 and 20.

Applying a phosphor coating to the inside surface of a mercury lamp's outer bulb slightly improves the color-rendering properties, but also reduces its efficacy. The phosphors convert invisible ultraviolet energy into visible light (color plate 28). Phosphor-coated mercury vapor lamps have CRIs of 45 to 50.

Metal halide lamps are similar in construction to mercury vapor lamps, except that various metal halides have been added. These halides add missing wavelengths that improve the mercury lamp's spectral distribution, yielding a more uniform spectrum and better color rendering, but reds are slightly muted (color plate 29). The addition of phosphor coatings on the inside of the bulb provides diffusion and some additional color improvement (color plate 30). A broad range of color-rendering quality exists in the different metal halide lamps; many experience lamp-to-lamp color inconsistency and color shift over the lamp life. The majority of metal halide lamps have CRIs of 65 to 70.

New *ceramic metal halide* lamps combine the ceramic arc tube technology of high-pressure sodium lamps with existing metal halide chemistry. The ceramic arc tube minimizes color variation between lamps and limits color shift during lamp life.

Because it can withstand higher operating temperatures, color rendering is also improved; ceramic metal halide lamps have CRIs of 81 to 96 (color plate 31). These are the highest color-rendering HID lamps available.

A "best" lamp color is nonexistent, as is "true" color. Each spectral distribution results in different object colors, whether that distribution comes from natural sources, such as sunlight or skylight, or from electric sources, such as incandescent, fluorescent, or HID lamps. The "right" color source for a given application depends upon an evaluation of trade-offs, including directional control, familiarity, color rendition, efficacy, absence of glare, maintenance, and cost.

Daylight

The goal of daylight design is to provide visual variety with controlled brightness contrasts.

A principal characteristic of daylight is its variability. The color of daylight changes with the time of day, the cleanliness of the atmosphere, and the interreflection of surrounding objects. The intensity of the sun changes with the time of day, the time of year, and the latitude of the site. The luminance of the sky depends on whether the light is coming from an overcast sky, from a clear sky only, or from a clear sky and direct sunlight.

Daylight has two components: sunlight and skylight. *Sunlight* is the directional beam emitted by the sun; *skylight* is the diffuse reflection of light from particles in the atmosphere.

Direct sunlight is usually an impractical source for interiors unless it is shielded. Just as electric luminaires are designed to reduce glare, direct sunlight entering interior spaces requires careful control. For critical seeing tasks, sunlight often causes excessive luminance differences that result in discomfort and poor visibility. This high contrast in the field of view inhibits the eye's ability to adjust, leading to visual fatigue and disturbing the accommodation needed for clear vision.

Skylight, on the other hand, is a useful source without shielding. Although special building configurations or controls are necessary to make skylight acceptable for horizontal tasks at the workplane or for displaying art, it is used with less control to light noncritical seeing areas such as corridors, stairwells, cafeterias, and seating areas.

People require changing stimuli to remain sensitive and alert. For example, gazing out the window at distant objects provides relief for the muscles of the eye. And the constantly changing nature of daylight satisfies our biological and psychological needs for change—a view of the sky provides information about the time of day, which helps maintain our biological cycles, and the varying light intensity as a cloud passes in front of the sun provides respite or stimulation, which helps reduce monotony.

The proper introduction of daylight into the interior is the simplest way to provide this change. The goal of daylight design is to provide visual variety with controlled brightness contrasts.

Comfort requires moderate changes. Monotony will cause fatigue, but so will overstimulation. Excessive contrast provides emotional appeal but also impairs visual performance. The sudden appearance of a beam of sunlight on a task will provide momentary change and relief; if it remains it will soon cause visual fatigue and stress.

Daylight and view do not necessarily go together and often are achieved through different building openings. The criteria for producing a view to the exterior are different from the criteria for producing good interior daylight.

The more complex the view and the more frequent the changes, the greater will be our satisfaction. Although large windows are sometimes desirable, people's basic need for a view of the outside can be satisfied with comparatively small openings.

DAYLIGHT DESIGN

Window size and height above the work surface are factors in daylighting design. Of course, as the window becomes larger in size, the amount of daylight increases. But the height of the window is the more significant factor.

The higher the window opening, the deeper the daylight can penetrate into the room, and if it is high enough, it may prevent exterior brightness from causing glare. This high-entry light is softened and spread by proper design of the room surfaces. Interreflections between these surfaces cause the brightness patterns to become more uniform; visibility and seeing comfort are increased.

Windows and other daylight openings that are set flush in a wall or ceiling produce excessive contrasts between exterior brightness and the immediately adjacent interior surfaces. This contrast is often harsh and uncomfortable.

A softer transition is achieved with the use of splayed jambs, rounded jambs, and deep window wells. Instead of the sharp contrast between adjacent surfaces, these designs provide a zone of intermediate luminance to soften the change (figure 5.1). The jambs of the window become light-reflecting shelves that reflect the light indirectly into the interior. Other solutions include using white paint around the windows or hanging draperies or blinds.

For comfortable seeing, the luminance ratio between *fenestration* and adjacent surfaces ought to be less than 20:1. This ratio is also desirable for the surface luminance of

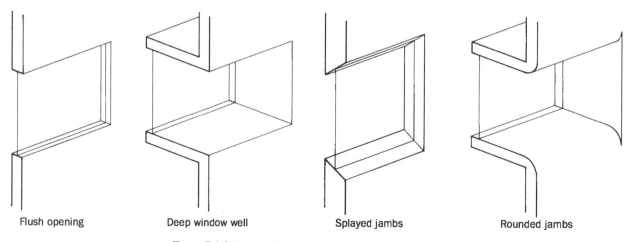

Flush opening   Deep window well   Splayed jambs   Rounded jambs

Figure 5.1 Splayed and rounded window jambs soften contrasts.

luminaires and adjacent surfaces. It is advisable to limit luminance ratios anywhere in the field of view to less than 40:1.

Fenestration Sections

Windows placed on a single side of the room (figure 5.2) are the usual method of fenestration. To achieve useful work surface illuminance throughout the room, limit the depth of the room to twice the height from the floor to a full-room-width window head. For example, if the window head height is 10 ft, the optimum room will be no more than 20 ft deep. Somewhat narrower windows provide slightly lower illuminance values, but the difference is minor.

This ratio of 1:2 may be increased to 2:5 as long as the reflectances of interior surfaces are high and carefully controlled. If these ratios are exceeded, people seated in the deepest part of the room will feel as if they are receiving insufficient light, even if they are provided with adequate electric lighting.

Windows placed on opposite sides double the feasible room depth for daylighting. The opposite windows need only occupy the upper part of the wall; the quantity of interior light will be almost the same as if the windows were full height, with the added benefit of reducing the possibility of glare (figure 5.3).

Skylights are tools for delivering daylight deep into interior areas of one-story buildings or into the top floors of multistory buildings. They also bring daylight into the lower floors of multistory buildings through light wells and reflective devices.

Figure 5.2 Unilateral section.

Figure 5.3 Bilateral section.

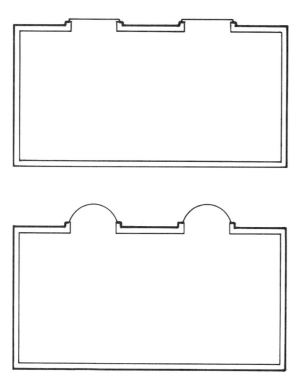

Figure 5.4 Skylight sections.

Skylights come in a variety of shapes and sizes. They are made of clear, patterned, or translucent glass or various kinds of plastic. Clear, gray-tinted, or milk-white acrylics are best for this purpose; their optical properties are similar to glass, and they are easier to maintain.

Flat skylights have both drainage and dirt-accumulation problems. Domed or slanted skylights mitigate these drawbacks (figure 5.4). Although a domed skylight is "self-cleaning" on the outside, dirt still collects on the inside, making a program of periodic cleaning as important with skylights as it is with electric luminaires.

Depending on the shape of the room and the location and size of the skylight, brightness control will be necessary in areas with demanding visual requirements. If directly exposed to view from below, at angles in the *glare zone*, skylights often produce excessive luminance and cause disabling veiling reflections on tasks. Light from skylights is controlled with the use of deep wells, splayed wells, and louvers, preventing any view of the skylight at unsuitable angles and minimizing veiling reflections.

Diffuse (milk-white) plastic or glass skylights diminish the biological benefits of daylight by obscuring the view of the weather. Clear glass or plastic skylights, however, produce more heat gain for a given unit of illuminance at the work surface below and may admit direct sunlight in undesirable ways.

An exterior shield that shades the skylight from direct sun but allows daylight to penetrate reduces the heat load. For colder climates, *double glazing*—two thicknesses of glass or plastic with an air space between—reduces conductive heat loss in winter.

Clerestories have all the attributes of skylights; because they occur in the vertical rather than the horizontal plane, they can be oriented to prevent the penetration of direct sun (figure 5.5). When built in combination with a light shelf, a clerestory reflects great quantities of daylight against the upper ceiling yet blocks the view of the glaring sky from below (figure 5.6).

When facing the same (or opposite) direction as the main windows, the clerestory extends the room-depth limitations (figure 5.7). When clerestories are located on walls opposite each other, as was often the case in early church buildings, these vertical glazing sections are called *roof monitors* (figure 5.8). A series of parallel clerestories is suited for large, low-roofed structures such as factories and warehouses; this is called a *sawtooth* section (figure 5.9).

To maximize the light delivered by the clerestory, it is recommended that the roof directly below the clerestory and the adjacent interior ceiling area be diffuse and highly reflective.

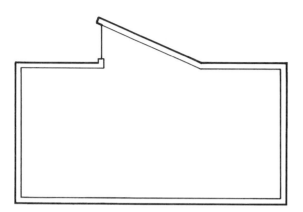

Figure 5.5 Clerestory section.

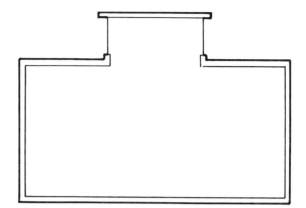

Figure 5.8 Roof monitor section.

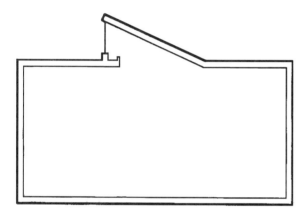

Figure 5.6 Clerestory section with light shelf.

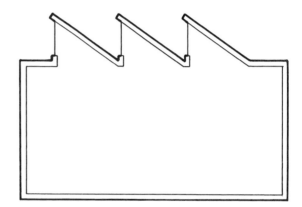

Figure 5.9 Sawtooth section.

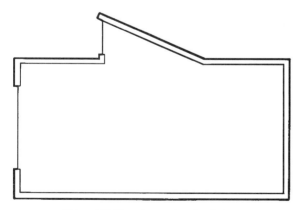

Figure 5.7 Clerestory and main window.

Tubular skylights deliver natural light to a room where a traditional skylight or vertical glazing is impractical. They consist of three components: (1) a small, clear acrylic dome located on the roof, which allows sunlight to enter; (2) an adjustable cylindrical aluminum shaft that has been treated with a highly reflective coating; and (3) a translucent diffuser lens located on the interior ceiling, which disperses light throughout the room (figure 5.10).

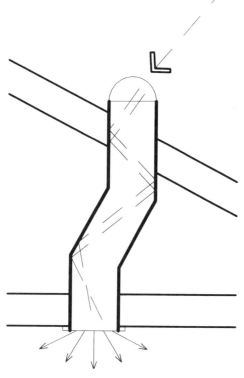

Figure 5.10 Tubular skylight.

The dome is typically installed between rafters and joists on the roof, and the adjustable aluminum tube extends from the roof to the ceiling of the interior. Sold in kits, tubular skylights minimize heat gain and loss: the aluminum tube radiates any collected exterior heat into the attic, and the sealed shaft allows very little interior heat to escape up. Also, little UV is transmitted to the interior; almost all of the UV rays are absorbed by the dome, shaft, and diffuser materials.

Heat Gain

When buildings use glazing to admit daylight, a single layer of ordinary glass exposed to the sun also admits warming radiant energy—heat. This helps in cold winters but poses a problem in hot summers.

If buildings are properly designed to use daylight, they reject most of the direct light from the sun yet still admit an ample supply of skylight. Just as the sun's light can be controlled, there are many ways to control the sun's radiant heat; it may be admitted or excluded as seasonally required without eliminating the benefits of daylighting.

Orientation is a primary method for managing solar heat radiation because the sun strikes differently oriented surfaces with widely varying intensity. The size and placement of glazed areas are also factors in capturing the sun's energy for cold-weather heat gain.

For example, a house benefits if its walls and roof are oriented to receive heat from the sun in the winter and shed it in the summer. If the principal façade of a house faces due south or within 30° of due south, the south-facing walls may be designed to absorb radiation from the low winter sun; the roof may be designed to reject the sun's heat by reflecting the high summer sun.

It is possible with any building orientation to achieve good quality daylighting indoors. North light is inherently softer, cooler, and more uniform; because of the sun, south light is more intense and variable. But the same high quality of illumination that comes naturally from the north sky can be achieved with any other orientation by the proper use of daylight controls.

SHADING DEVICES

Shading devices used on the inside of the building reflect some of the radiant heat energy back outdoors, reducing the energy gain from the sun by as much as 60 to 70 percent. Exterior shading devices can reduce that energy penetration even more—by 90 to 95 percent. Exterior shading devices are more expensive to build and maintain, but with hot climates or high energy costs or both, air-conditioning savings often give quick paybacks.

A variety of shading devices are employed to deliver daylight to where it is needed and to reduce glare by limiting excessive luminance in the field of view. Shading devices are divided into two categories: movable and stationary.

Movable controls adjusted in response to varying sky conditions are the most efficient, but they require a human operator or an automatic device. Stationary (static) controls are less expensive but are also less efficient, because they are unresponsive to daily and seasonal changes.

Movable Controls

Draperies, shades, and screens are available with a wide range of materials that vary in their openness of weave and surface reflectivity. They provide almost any desired degree of light transmission or a complete blackout. Greater flexibility is achieved with two separately tracked draperies over a window area—one used to reduce light and the second to block it completely.

Light-colored *venetian blinds* (interior horizontal louvers) can be adjusted to exclude direct sunshine but reflect light to the ceiling, increasing its penetration into the space while still allowing a view of the outdoors (figure 5.11). Or they can be closed completely, blocking both light and view.

But for venetian blinds to function appropriately under changing sky conditions, they must be operated with an understanding of their potential by someone who has the opportunity and the incentive to perform the task. Venetian blinds collect dirt easily and are tedious to clean; they are subject to mechanical failure of support straps and control strings.

Double-glazed windows are available with a narrow venetian blind positioned between the inner and outer glass, which eliminates the dirt-collection problem. These blinds are fully operable and reject heat

more efficiently than interior blinds or other shading devices such as roller shades or draperies.

Motorized controls allow convenient adjustment of sun-filtering and light-blocking fabrics on windows and skylights. They permit one-touch adjustment of blinds and draperies for changing activities or changing sun, or they can be programmed to move fabrics with the sun automatically.

Motorized controls may be linked to home or building automation systems, so that shades move at preset times or at specific illuminance values. They can also combine control of daylight with electric light so that sun-filtering or light-blocking fabrics and electric lights are adjusted at the same time.

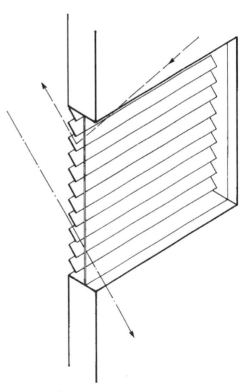

Figure 5.11 Properly adjusted venetian blinds reflect daylight to the ceiling and do not prevent a view outside.

Exterior motorized shades place the sun-filtering fabrics on the exterior of a window, providing solar protection by stopping excessive glare, UV rays, and heat before they enter a building. Movable shading devices on building exteriors are difficult to maintain, however, and they deteriorate rapidly unless made of a copper alloy or stainless steel. Awnings are highly reliable, but their aesthetic appeal is limited.

Stationary Controls

Fixed awnings and building overhangs serve to shade direct sunlight and reduce glare through the upper area of windows (figure 5.12). They also reduce the daylight entering the room, decreasing the illumination close to the window and the penetration into the room. The maximum depth of useful light penetration is calculated from the outer edge of the awning or overhang instead of the vertical plane of the window.

Although they reduce the quantity of skylight entering the building, overhangs can collect light from a light-colored exterior surround and reflect it into the interior. This results in a more even distribution of light.

An overhang located on the southern side of a building is especially efficient at controlling both light and heat from the sun (figure 5.13). In the summer, the overhang shields the glass from the sun's direct rays yet allows daylight to enter from the lower sky and by reflection from the ground. In the winter, the overhang allows the low-angle sun to penetrate for warmth, but seating must be oriented to avoid direct sun glare.

Exterior horizontal louvers may pick up direct sun, causing excessive luminance and discomforting or disabling glare (figure 5.14). Exterior or interior vertical louvers are useful for low sun angles that occur in the early morning or late afternoon, particularly on building walls oriented toward the east or

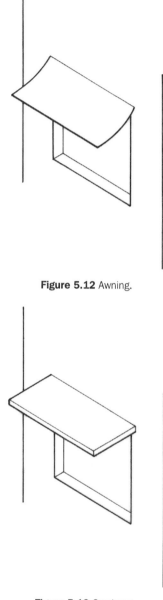

Figure 5.12 Awning.

Figure 5.13 Overhang.

west (figure 5.15). When it is necessary to control both high sun and low sun, "egg-crate" louvers are used because they combine horizontal and vertical shielding.

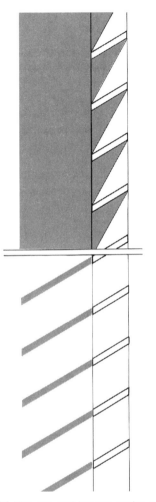

Figure **5.14** High sun and low sun angles at exterior louvers.

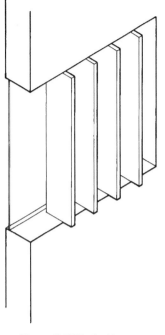

Figure **5.15** Vertical louvers.

Direct sunshine from flat skylights or from pitched skylights facing east, south, or west must also be controlled. Interior louvers or translucent shades will reduce glare and heat, but exterior controls provide superior shading.

Exterior sun shades can be oriented to shade light and heat from the sun during warm weather yet allow penetration during the cold seasons, or be designed to eliminate direct sun from the interior all year long (figure 5.16).

A difficulty with fixed overhangs and awnings is that the amount of shading follows the solar seasons rather than the climatic seasons. The middle of the summer for the sun is June 21, but the hottest days occur from the end of July to the middle of August. The overhang designed for optimal shading on September 21, when the weather is still warm and solar heat gain is unwelcome, causes the same shading on March 21, when temperatures are lower and solar heat gain is welcome (figure 5.17).

Vegetation, which follows the climatic seasons, provides excellent shading year-round. On March 21, many plants are without leaves and do not obstruct the passage of sunlight. On September 21, however, the leaves are still full and provide good shading. Deciduous trees or an overhanging trellis with a climbing vine that sheds its leaves in

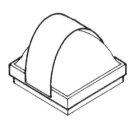 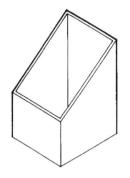 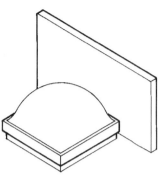

Figure 5.16 Skylight shades.

winter provide natural climatic control when placed in front of south-facing windows.

GLAZING MATERIALS

Glazing materials are available with a wide range of heat and light transmittance, color, and prismatic control. Because of its resistance to abrasion, glass is the preferred material; where breakage is a concern, acrylic or polycarbonate is substituted. Both glass and plastic can be tinted in warm, neutral, or cool gray tones to reduce the transmission of light and heat yet remain transparent to vision. Saturated colors are to be avoided except in carefully designed art ("stained") glass windows.

Translucent glazing materials that transmit diffused light but obscure vision include etched, sandblasted, opal, and patterned glass and plastic. Many translucent materials become excessively glary with exposure to the sun and will be distracting when seen from task areas. Because they prevent a view of the outside, their psychological value is minimal. As diffusion increases so does the area of luminance and the possibility that the window or skylight will become a source of glare.

Selectively transmitting materials allow the desirable wavelengths of the visible spectrum to pass but reflect or absorb the radiant heat energy. Directionally selective glass blocks and prismatic glass or plastics refract light for directional control.

When installed vertically, prismatic glass block walls are used to reflect daylight onto the ceiling of a room, increasing illuminance values deep in the interior and removing the glaring sky from view (figure 5.18). When installed horizontally, as with glass-block pavers, they transmit light yet maintain a low surface luminance even when exposed to direct sun.

QUANTITY

Because of the great variety of changing sun and sky conditions, it is impractical to predict precisely the interior illuminance patterns derived from daylighting. By knowing the size and position of windows and using tables of average daylighting conditions for various locations and orientations, the average amount of available daylight that will enter a space can be determined, but not the precise amount at any moment.

Interior daylight illuminance values are often expressed as a daylight factor. The daylight factor accounts for light received directly from the sky, light reflected from external surfaces, and interreflections within

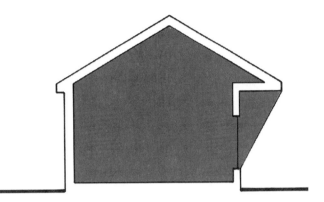

June 21

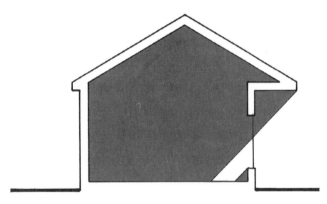

March or September 21

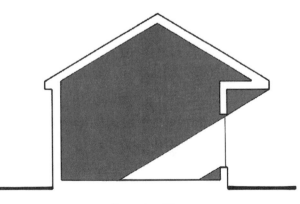

December 21

Figure 5.17 Shading a south window with a fixed overhang (at solar noon).

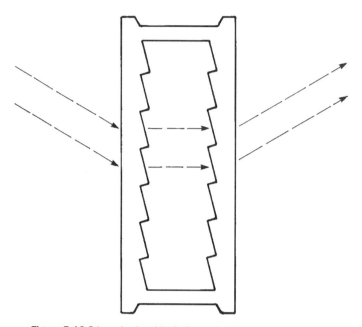

Figure 5.18 Prismatic glass block directs daylight toward the ceiling.

the room. It is a measure of the proportion of the outdoor illumination to the daylight illumination received indoors.

Average interior daylight illuminance is also calculated by graphic methods, such as the Libbey-Owens-Ford™ "Sun Angle Calculator," and by computer programs that consider geographic location, time of day, time of year, fenestration, room shape, and interior finishes. The most sophisticated programs produce a rendering of the interior showing the relative luminances of room surfaces.

The simplest, most versatile, and most reliable technique for studying the aesthetics of daylighting is simulation by construction of a scale model. Daylight behaves in the same way in a scale model as in an actual building. If studied under similar sky conditions, the interior of the scale model appears exactly as will the interior of the building. Miniature photo electric cells are placed inside the model to read illuminance values. But identical sky conditions are difficult to achieve by placing the model outdoors; this has led to the development of sky simulators that can reproduce almost any sky condition.

ENERGY CONTROL

Photosensors (light-sensing devices) automatically switch electric luminaires off when the daylight contribution at selected interior locations reaches prescribed levels. The luminaires are automatically switched on as the available daylight decreases. This kind of switching has the disadvantage of calling undue attention to the change; it may be abrupt and jarring.

Dimming systems that allow a gradual increase and decrease in light quantity are more satisfactory. This is more pleasant and may even go unnoticed. Sophisticated systems are designed with a built-in delay so that a cloud passing rapidly across the sun triggers no response.

Incandescent Lamps 6

The incandescent lamp is a simple device—a hot wire (the filament) sealed in a glass jar (the bulb).

An electric current passing through the wire heats it to incandescence, and the wire emits light. The filament wire diameter and length determine the amount of electrical current drawn by the lamp, regulating its light output (figure 6.1).

The incandescent lamps discussed in this chapter are commonly referred to as "large" lamps. This designation does not refer to large physical size, but has traditionally described lamps that operate on standard-voltage circuits. The "large lamp" category now includes lamps of many voltages commonly found in residential, commercial, and industrial use.

"Miniature" lamps, conversely, are not necessarily small, although many of them are. They are lamps that operate at less common voltages, powered by storage batteries or by transformers that reduce or increase the standard voltage to the voltage required by the lamp. Their predominant use is in transportation vehicles and instruments.

The family of large lamps contains about one hundred combinations of glass and quartz bulb shapes and sizes. These variations are designated by a two-part abbrevia-

tion: the first part, one or more letters, indicates the shape of the bulb; the second part, a number, indicates the diameter of the bulb in eighths of an inch. For example, an A19 lamp is an arbitrary-shaped lamp that is $\frac{19}{8}$ ($2\frac{3}{8}$) inches in diameter (figure 6.2).

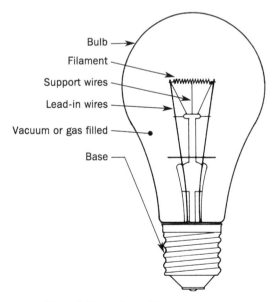

Bulb
Filament
Support wires
Lead-in wires
Vacuum or gas filled
Base

Figure 6.1 Incandescent lamp components.

A   arbitrary (with familiar teardrop shape)
AR   aluminum *reflector*
B   flame (smooth)
C   cone shape
CA   candle
F   flame (irregular)
G   globe shape
GT   globe–tubular
MR   multifaceted *mirror-reflector*
P   *pear* shape
PAR   *parabolic aluminized reflector*
PS   *pear*–straight neck
R   *reflector*
S   straight side
T   tubular

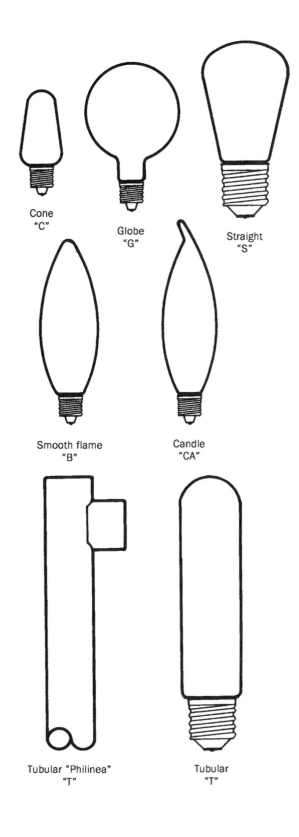

Cone
"C"

Globe
"G"

Straight
"S"

Smooth flame
"B"

Candle
"CA"

Tubular "Philinea"
"T"

Tubular
"T"

LAMP BASES

Incandescent lamps have a base at one end, although some tubular lamps have bases at both ends. All bases conduct current from the electrical supply into the lamp (figure 6.3); most bases also support the lamp physically, but many kinds of PAR lamps can be supported by their bulbs.

The most frequently used is the medium base; its name describes its size. Smaller lamps have smaller bases, including *bayonet, bipin, candelabra, intermediate, miniature, mini-candelabra ("mini-can"), twist-and-lock (TAL),* and *two-pin* bases. Larger lamps have larger bases, including *mogul* screw and medium and mogul *bipost* bases. The bipin and bipost bases orient the filament position, providing rotational alignment for optical control. Bayonet and *prefocus* medium and mogul bases also locate the filament in the exact predetermined position required for optical instruments and searchlights.

FILAMENTS

All incandescent lamps contain a filament, which is more or less centered within the bulb. A filament is a length of tungsten wire; tungsten is used because of its high melting

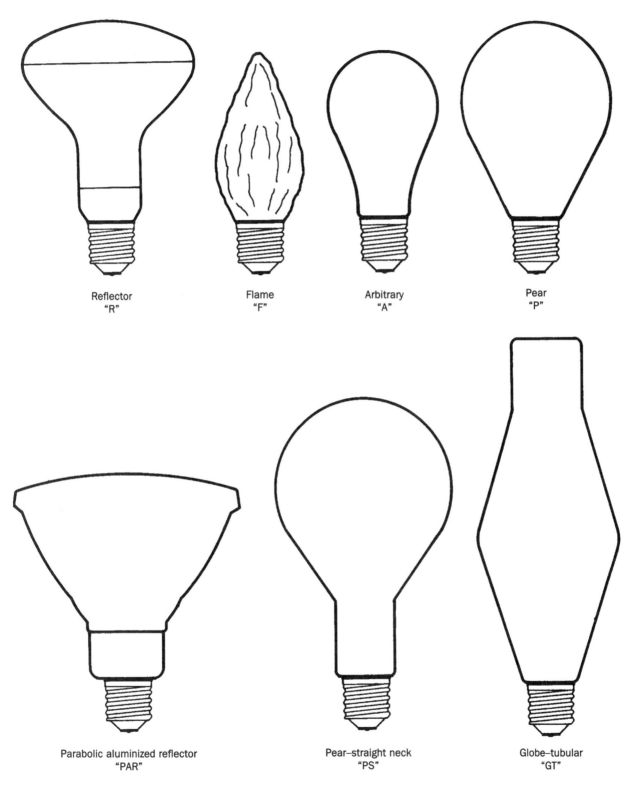

Reflector
"R"

Flame
"F"

Arbitrary
"A"

Pear
"P"

Parabolic aluminized reflector
"PAR"

Pear–straight neck
"PS"

Globe–tubular
"GT"

Figure 6.2 Incandescent bulb shapes at one-half actual size.

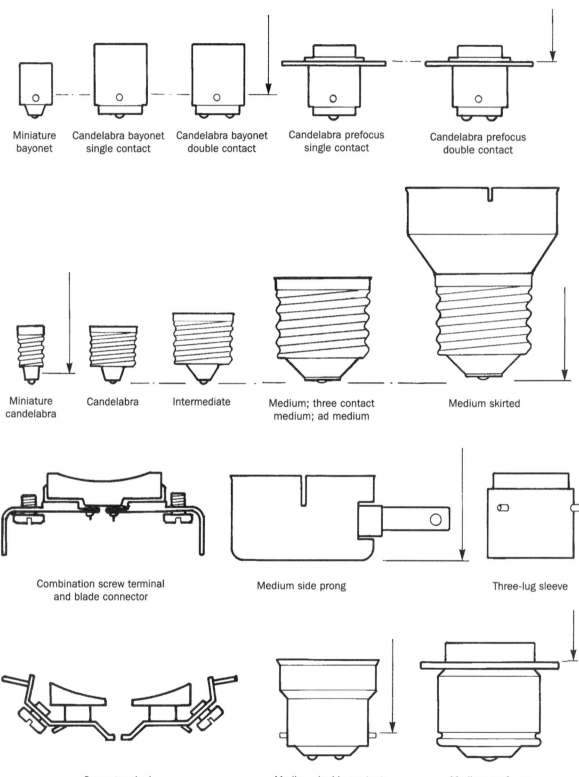

Miniature
bayonet

Candelabra bayonet
single contact

Candelabra bayonet
double contact

Candelabra prefocus
single contact

Candelabra prefocus
double contact

Miniature
candelabra

Candelabra

Intermediate

Medium; three contact
medium; ad medium

Medium skirted

Combination screw terminal
and blade connector

Medium side prong

Three-lug sleeve

Screw terminal

Medium double contact

Medium prefocus

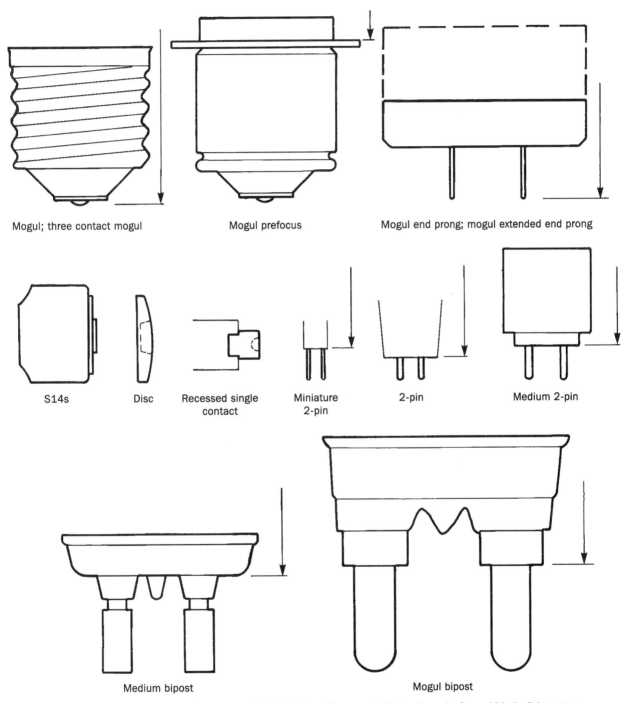

Mogul; three contact mogul

Mogul prefocus

Mogul end prong; mogul extended end prong

S14s

Disc

Recessed single contact

Miniature 2-pin

2-pin

Medium 2-pin

Medium bipost

Mogul bipost

Figure 6.3 Incandescent lamp bases at one-half actual size. The arrow indicates the point from which the light center length (LCL)—the dimension from the filament to a designated point that varies with different base types—is measured.

temperature. Occasionally the wire is straight, but usually it is coiled to pack more length into a small envelope, concentrating light and heat and increasing efficacy. Coiled filaments are designated by the letter *C*. Sometimes the coil itself is coiled and designated *CC* for "coiled coil."

Filament design is determined by striking a balance between light output and lamp life. It is a function of filament temperature: the higher the temperature at which the filament operates or "burns," the more light it emits and the shorter its life—the sooner it fails or "burns out." A long-life lamp of a given wattage produces less light than a standard-life lamp of the same wattage, which consumes the same current but is designed for a shorter life.

Lamp efficacy is the ratio of light produced (measured in *lumens* [lm]) to electricity consumed (measured in *watts* [W]). Lamp life is measured in hours (hr).

LIGHT OUTPUT

Lamp bulbs do not contain air, because the incandescent tungsten will react with the oxygen in the air and quickly evaporate. Originally this was prevented by creating a vacuum in the bulb. Today, filling the bulb with an inert gas slows bulb blackening, which is caused by condensation of evaporated tungsten particles on the inner bulb wall. Argon, nitrogen, and krypton gases are used for this purpose. (Some incandescent lamps, particularly those below 40 W, still use a vacuum.)

Although reduced by the inert gas pressure, the filament evaporation continues throughout life; the tungsten wire becomes thinner, consumes less power, and emits less light. This light loss combined with bulb blackening causes a steady decrease in light output throughout the life of the lamp.

A reciprocal relationship exists between light output and life. Over-voltage operation results in higher wattage, higher efficacy, and higher light output, but shorter lamp life. Under-voltage burning results in lower wattage, lower efficacy, and lower light output, but longer lamp life (figure 6.4). As a rule of thumb, a given percentage reduction in wattage is accompanied by double that percentage reduction in light.

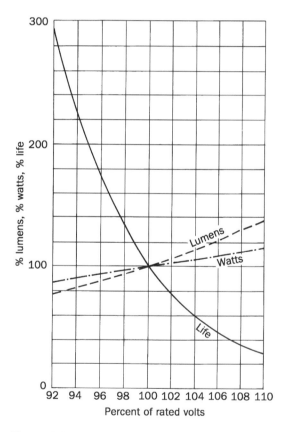

Figure 6.4 Incandescent lamp characteristics as affected by voltage (V). For example, operating a 120 V lamp at 125 V means approximately 16% more light (lm), 7% more power (W), and 42% less life (hr). Operating a 120 V lamp at 115 V means approximately 15% less light (lm), 7% less power (W), and 72% more life (hr).

Incandescent lamps are usually sold by wattage, but a watt is not a measure of light—it is a measure of power consumed. With electric light sources, it is a measure of how much electricity the lamp uses during operation. Lumens tell how much light a lamp emits.

Extended-service (2,500-hr) incandescent lamps achieve their longer life by a reduction in light output and efficacy. Lumen output is approximately 15 percent less than standard 750-hr and 1,000-hr life lamps. These lamps are more expensive than standard ones, but their longer life is useful in locations that are difficult to relamp.

Many energy-saving or "watt-saving" lamps are simply reduced-wattage lamps. The reduced power consumption is accomplished by a reduction in light output. Some energy-saving lamps have a more efficient filament design, gas fill, or reflector bulb shape to maintain light output.

LAMP TYPES

Incandescent lamps are divided into three categories according to their ability to direct light: (1) nondirectional sources emit light in all directions and require additional components to control their distribution, (2) semi-directional sources give a direction to their light output and require additional components to complete a spatial distribution, and (3) directional sources control the distribution of emitted light and require no additional components, being complete optical systems in themselves.

Nondirectional Sources

Nondirectional lamps emit light in all directions. They include A, C, G, P, PS, S, and T shapes and decorative lamps. These lamps require external elements in the form of a lens, reflector, or shield to modify their distribution and to control their brightness (figure 6.5).

To reduce the glare from an exposed filament, many nondirectional lamps have a coating applied to the inner surface of the clear bulb. A two-bath acid etch or a light coating of electrostatically applied white powder absorbs an insignificant amount of light, yielding a ball of light inside the bulb. This kind of lamp has lower luminance and less glare than the exposed filament. It is called an *inside-frost* lamp (figure 6.6).

Still greater diffusion, with a further reduction of glare and a sacrifice of about 2 percent of the light output, is achieved by a double coating of white silica powder. This gives a ball of light the size of the lamp, yielding a bulb of almost uniform brightness. It is called a *soft-white* lamp.

In both treatments, the outer surface of the bulb is left smooth, which makes it easy to clean. Inside-frost lamps are preferred for most luminaires to reduce the sharpness of shadows and the possibility of striations on nearby surfaces. Where the small point source contributes to glitter, as in the sparkle of crystal chandeliers, clear lamps are necessary.

Semi-Directional Sources

The category of *semi-directional* sources includes silver-bowl and white-bowl lamps. *Silver-bowl* lamps, usually used to direct light upward, have an opaque silver coating applied to the inside of the bowl (figure 6.7). This functions as a specular reflector that remains clean, and therefore efficient, throughout the life of the lamp. Silver-bowl lamps are available in both clear and inside frost.

When used indirectly in a suspended luminaire to light the ceiling, the upper part of the bulb must be concealed to prevent excessive brightness and glare. This is accomplished by an assemblage of circular rings around the lamps or by a shallow, diffusing glass bowl. When silver-bowl lamps

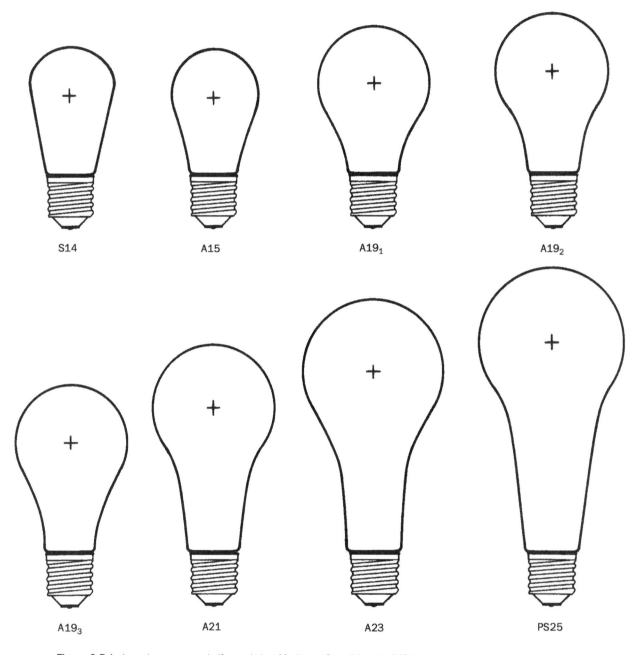

Figure 6.5 A-shape lamps at one-half actual size. Maximum Overall Length (MOL): maximum end-to-end length of the bulb within tolerances stipulated by the American National Standards Institute (ANSI). Actual length may be less. Light center length (LCL): the distance from the center of the filament to a designated point that varies with different base types.

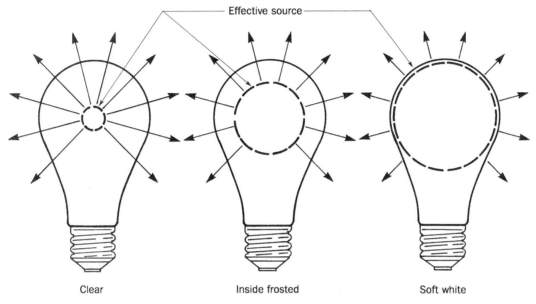

Effective source

Clear   Inside frosted   Soft white

Figure 6.6 Clear, inside-frosted (acid-etched), and soft-white (silica-coated) lamps.

Figure 6.7 Silver-bowl lamp.

are used in recessed luminaires, the upward light emitted by the lamp is redirected in a downward direction by a secondary reflector.

White-bowl lamps, also used for indirect lighting, have a translucent white coating on the inner surface of the bulb bowl, which reduces the direct filament glare. As with silver-bowl lamps, white-bowl lamps require additional control elements.

Directional Sources

Directional sources are lamps that are complete optical systems; they include a source (the filament), a reflector, and sometimes a lens or a filament shield. Lamps in this category are *r*eflector (R), *a*luminum *r*eflector (AR), multifaceted *m*irror-*r*eflector (MR), and *p*arabolic *a*luminized *r*eflector (PAR). These directional sources are available in a wide range of wattages and beam-spreads, as indicated in table 2 in the Appendix.

R lamps

In *reflector* (R) lamps, the bulb is shaped into a reflecting contour; the inner surface is coated with vaporized silver. The lamps are available in spot or flood beam-spreads. Spot lamps have a light frost on the inside front of the bulb; flood lamps have a heavier frosting to increase the spread of the beam.

As with nondirectional and semi-directional incandescent lamps, the glass bulbs of most R lamps are made of blown lime glass. This "soft" glass is intended only for indoor use. Some wattages are available in a "hard," heat-resistant glass for areas where contact with moisture is a possibility, but these lamps still require protection from rain.

All R lamps emit a substantial percentage of light outside the principal beam. Unless intercepted by an auxiliary reflector, this light is usually lost due to absorption within the luminaire; in most luminaires, R lamps are inefficient.

AR and MR lamps

See low-voltage lamps, pages 75 to 77.

PAR lamps

Parabolic aluminized reflector (PAR) lamps are made of low-expansion, heat-resistant borosilicate glass that is pressed rather than blown. This method of construction allows great precision in shaping the reflector of the bulb and in the configuration of the lens, as well as in the positioning of the filament. The combined precision of these factors accounts for the superior beam control and greater efficacy that are characteristic of PAR lamps (figure 6.8).

PAR lamps were originally designed for outdoor applications and are sometimes still referred to as "outdoor" lamps because they are weather-resistant. Over the years their use indoors has grown rapidly wherever efficacy and precise beam control are desired.

PAR lamps are available with beam-spreads that range from 3° (very narrow spot, or VNSP) to 60° (very wide flood, or VWFL). The initial beam is formed by the shape of the reflector and the position of the filament. The configuration of the lens modifies that beam: a light stipple smoothes the narrow beam for a spot lamp; "prescription" lenses similar to those of car headlights provide the wider beam distributions of flood lamps.

In *cool-beam* PAR lamps, a reflective dichroic coating replaces the bright aluminum used on the reflector surface of standard PAR lamps. Visible wavelengths (light) are reflected forward into the beam while infrared wavelengths (heat) pass through the back of the bulb. About two-thirds of the heat energy in the beam is removed; light output and distribution are unchanged. These lamps were originally developed to light perishable foods (figure 6.9).

EPACT

The U.S. Energy Policy Act of 1992 (EPACT) established minimum average efficacy standards for certain incandescent R and PAR lamps that operate at 115 to 130 V and have medium bases and diameters larger than 2¾ in. Most incandescent R30, R40, and PAR38 lamps do not meet the criteria; tungsten-halogen PAR lamps do. Colored lamps and rough- and vibration-service lamps are exempt from the efficacy standards. The act does not prescribe standards for other kinds of incandescent lamps.

As of 31 October 1995, the following lamps are prohibited from manufacture or sale in the United States: 75R30; 75-, 100-, 120-, and 150R40; and 65-, 75-, 85-, 120-, and 150PAR38. These efficacy standards, measured in lumens per watt, were established according to lamp wattage. This approach ignores the function of the luminaire, however: an inefficient, incandes-

Figure 6.8 R and PAR spot and flood lamp beam-spreads.

cent R lamp with a well-designed reflector can be more efficacious than the most efficient, tungsten-halogen PAR lamp in a light-wasting, multi-groove-baffle downlight.

TUNGSTEN-HALOGEN LAMPS

The *tungsten-halogen* (or *halogen*) lamp is an incandescent lamp with a selected gas of the halogen family sealed into it. As the lamp burns, the halogen gas combines with tungsten molecules that sputter off the filament and deposits the tungsten back on the filament, rather than on the bulb wall. This keeps the bulb wall clean and at the same time builds up the filament wire to compensate for the evaporative loss that reduces its diameter, thus maintaining relatively constant wattage. The result is a lamp that deliv-

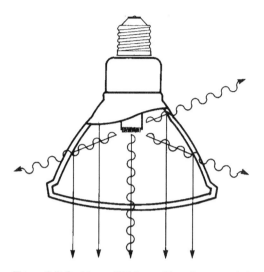

Figure 6.9 Cool-beam PAR lamp. Since the unwanted heat is transmitted from the back of the lamp, cool-beam lamps are to be used only in luminaires designed to allow the heat to escape.

ers almost its full light output throughout its life (figure 6.10).

In order for this self-cleaning cycle to occur consistently, the temperature of the lamp bulb must be a minimum of 500°C. The use of quartz rather than glass is dictated by this thermal requirement and the need for strength to resist high internal gas pressures. Although quartz is no longer the only material used for the enclosure of these

lamps, the lamps are still sometimes referred to as "quartz-halogen."

The high internal pressure may cause an explosive shattering of the bulb if it develops a fault and fails. Although this is a rare occurrence, halogen lamps must be enclosed because fragments of quartz glass are hot and can cause burns or start a fire. The halogen tube is either enclosed in an outer bulb or used in a luminaire equipped with a glass cover or fine mesh screen.

The higher the operating temperature of a filament, the higher the color temperature. Therefore, halogen lamps have a higher color temperature than conventional incandescent lamps. And, greater energy in the blue region of the spectrum makes them appear "whiter." They have longer life and greater efficacy; they are also more compact, permitting the use of smaller luminaires.

Halogen lamps are available in five configurations: (1) single-ended T; (2) double-ended T; (3) integral-reflector AR, MR, and PAR; (4) modified A-lamp CP, MB, and TB; and (5) modified decorative B and F shapes.

Single-ended halogen lamps have bayonet, bipin, miniature screw, mini-candelabra ("mini-can"), twist-and-lock (TAL), or two-pin bases in sizes that range from T3 to T24 and wattages from 5 W to 10,000 W.

Double-ended halogen lamps have recessed single contact (RSC) bases, one at

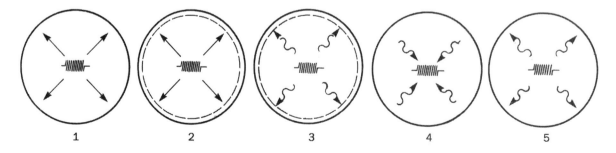

Figure 6.10 Halogen cleaning cycle.

each end of the lamp. Their bulbs are of small diameter: T2, T2½, T3, T4, T6, and T8. Wattages range from 45 W to 2,000 W.

Halogen Infrared (IR) Lamps

Of the energy radiated by standard incandescent and halogen lamps, 85 percent is invisible infrared (heat). *Infrared reflecting (IR)* halogen lamps have a thin, infrared-reflective coating applied to the inner filament tube that converts some of the infrared energy to visible light. The coating allows visible light to pass through the tube wall; the infrared energy is reflected back onto the lamp filament, further heating the filament and producing more visible light for the same amount of energy.

The operating temperature for the halogen cycle is maintained with less input power, resulting in increased efficacy: the efficacy of a standard 1750 lm, 100 W, A-lamp is 17.5 lm/W; conventional halogen lamps have efficacies of approximately 20 lm/W; halogen IR lamps have efficacies in excess of 30 lm/W.

LOW-VOLTAGE LAMPS

Low-voltage lamps are not of magical construction—they are simply incandescent and tungsten-halogen lamps that operate between 6 V and 75 V.

The wattage of all filament lamps is the product of the voltage delivered at the socket multiplied by the *amperes* (current) flowing through the filament. The lower the voltage of the lamp of a given wattage, the higher the amperes and the larger the diameter of the filament wire required to carry it.

The increased diameter of the filament wire of low-voltage lamps allows for a more compact filament. The more compact the filament, the more precise the beam control. The main advantage of low-voltage lamps is their precise beam control.

An increase in the diameter of a filament wire raises the temperature at which it can be operated without danger of excessive evaporation. High-wattage lamps, therefore, are more efficacious than low-wattage lamps of the same voltage and life rating. Lower-voltage lamps, because their filament wire is of greater diameter, are also more efficient than higher-voltage lamps of the same wattage; thus, a 120 V lamp (common in the United States and Canada) is more efficacious than the 250 V lamps used in much of the rest of the world.

Low-voltage reflector lamps with narrow beam-spreads are energy-saving when their concentrated distribution is used to light small objects or large objects at great distances because light is confined to the lighted object without spilling beyond it. Where wider beams are required, low-voltage lamps are often less efficient than standard lamps.

Low-voltage operation also means that the standard building current of 115 V to 125 V must be stepped down by the use of a *transformer*. Low-voltage luminaires with integral transformers are often larger, bulkier, and more expensive than line-voltage equipment.

The low-voltage lamps commonly used for architectural applications operate at 12 V. They include PAR, AR, and MR lamps. Low-voltage PAR lamps are manufactured in the same way as line-voltage PAR lamps; the shape and diameter of the lamps may differ, and the bases are always different to avoid wrong electrical connection (figure 6.11).

Many low-voltage PAR lamps are equipped with filament shields to minimize the stray light that comes directly from the filament. As a result, the lamps emit only the controlled beam from the reflector. These filament shields have the added benefit of providing glare control by preventing view of the filament.

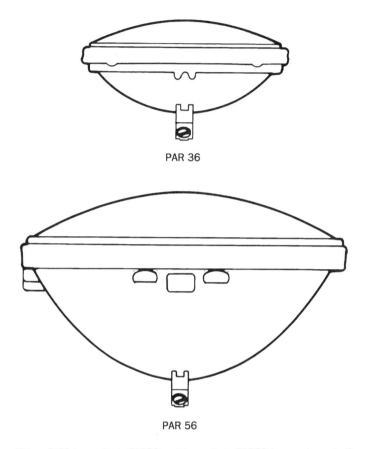

PAR 36

PAR 56

Figure 6.11 Low-voltage PAR36 and low-voltage PAR56 lamps at one-half actual size.

The *aluminum reflector* (AR) lamp consists of a prefocused axial filament lamp and faceted aluminum reflector that form an optical system. With some AR lamps the filament cap forms a grip for easy handling in addition to preventing direct glare from view. Other AR lamps have an integral diffusing glass lens to modify the beam-spread.

AR lamps are available without lenses in diameters of 70 mm and 111 mm (figure 6.12) and with lenses in diameters of 37 mm and 56 mm. The AR111 lamp is comparable to the PAR36 lamp size and base and is used interchangeably with sealed-beam

PAR36 lamps. AR111 lamps also have excellently designed reflector surfaces.

With *multifaceted mirror-reflector (MR)* lamps, a small halogen lamp is attached to a mirror with a surface composed of specular facets (flood) or a smooth plane (spot) (figure 6.13). The mirror is ellipsoidal in shape; the lamp's coiled filament is placed near its focus.

This combination acts as an optical condensing system in slide projectors, removing the need for lenses to control the light pattern. By changing the shape of the mirror or relocating the light source within the reflec-

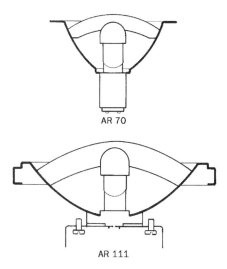

Figure 6.12 AR70 and AR111 lamps at one-half actual size.

tor, MR lamps are produced with beam-spreads from 7° (very narrow spot) to 60° (wide flood).

MR lamps are available in both 1⅜ in (MR11) and 2 in (MR16) diameters with either a miniature two-pin or turn-and-lock (50 W only) base. MR11 lamps are offered in 12 W, 20 W, and 35 W versions. MR16 lamps are offered in 20 W, 35 W, 42 W, 50 W, 65 W, 71 W, and 75 W versions. MR16 IR (infrared-reflecting) lamps are available in 20 W, 35 W, 37 W, 45 W, and 50 W versions.

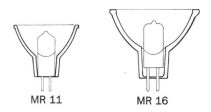

Figure 6.13 MR11 and MR16 lamps at one-half actual size.

Originally all MR11 and MR16 lamps had glass bulbs, two-pin bases, open fronts, and dichroic reflector coatings. These coatings remove two-thirds of the infrared heat from the projected beam and pass it through the back of the lamp, with the advantages described earlier for dichroic PAR38 cool-beam lamps.

The compact size of these lamps encouraged the design of compact luminaires. This often caused severe problems of heat build-up, however, because heat that is usually radiated from the front of a directional lamp now passes through the back and into the luminaire. To correct this problem, lamp manufacturers developed some MR11 and MR16 lamps with an aluminum-reflector coating that substitutes for the dichroic coating. This aluminum reflector coating also prevents "spill" light from the back of the lamp.

MR lamps are also available with a glass cover on the front of the lamp to protect against shattering of the halogen tube and, in some cases, to spread and smooth the beam. Other variations include reflectors made of aluminum instead of glass and turn-and-lock bases instead of the two-pin bases. Lamps with improved dichroic coatings provide constant color over lamp life, longer lamp life, and improved lumen maintenance.

COLORED LIGHT

Colored light is commonly described in terms of hue, saturation, and brightness. Hue is the quality that is called red or green. Saturation is the strength or depth of the color—the amount by which the light appears to differ from white. A deep red light, for example, is said to be of high saturation; pink is a red of low saturation. Brightness is the perceived quantity of light, without regard to hue or saturation.

A colored or filtered incandescent lamp produces colored light by starting with "white" light and filtering out the undesired portions of the spectrum. Yet most colored light sources, even those that appear highly saturated, are not truly monochromatic. They emit a fairly wide band of wavelengths, often including small amounts of energy in other hue regions. The less saturated the color, the greater the content of other hues.

Color Filters

The predominant method of producing colored light is the use of color *filters* with a "white" light source. The white source contains all of the colors of the spectrum; the filter absorbs the unwanted parts of the spectrum and transmits the wavelengths that make up the desired color.

Color filters are usually designed for incandescent lamps. Other types of light sources, lacking a truly continuous spectrum, are seldom used with color filters. The greatest use of colored light is in retail store windows and in theatre, television, and photographic lighting.

Gelatin filters ("gels") are thin, colored, transparent plastic sheets available in a wide variety of colors as well as multicolored and diffusing sheets. Deeper saturations are obtained by using more than one thickness. Gels have a short service life because their color fades rapidly when they are transmitting intense light and heat.

Colored plastic panels are available for use with fluorescent lamps but are unsatisfactory for use with hot incandescent filaments. Colored glass filters, which can withstand the heat of incandescent lamps, come smooth, stippled, prismatic, or split; they are highly stable.

Interference filters consist of one or more layers of ultrathin film coating on clear glass that reflect rather than absorb the unwanted wavelengths. The number and thickness of the film coatings determine the transmission (hue and saturation). Because unwanted wavelengths are not absorbed, interference filters remain cool.

Some interference filters are designed to reflect or transmit a portion of the spectrum: infrared or ultraviolet or both. Broadband interference filters are often called dichroic ("two-colored") because they transmit one color and reflect the complimentary color (figure 6.14).

It is advisable to determine the approximate spectral composition of the "white" light source before selecting a filter. If the desired wavelengths are not present in the original source, the filter will be ineffective. An extreme example is a red lamp with a green filter, which will transmit no visible light.

Colored Lamps

Incandescent colored sign and decorative lamps have outside ceramic enamels, sprayed finishes, or dip coatings applied to clear bulbs to obtain colored light by the subtractive method: by absorbing the light of those colors that are undesirable.

Transparent ceramic enamels are used to coat clear glass bulbs; the finely ground colored glass is fired into the bulb to fuse the coating into a hard, permanent finish. The coating is applied before the bulbs are made into lamps. This makes these lamps resistant to scuffing, chipping, and weather, but they are less transparent than lamps with lacquers or plastic coatings.

Sprayed finishes, usually shellacs or silicones, are applied to the completed lamp. Although these sprayed coatings have good adhesion, they lack the hardness of the ceramic enamels and have less resistance to scratches or scuffing. Sprayed lacquers are highly transparent and therefore often used when the sparkle of a visible filament is desired.

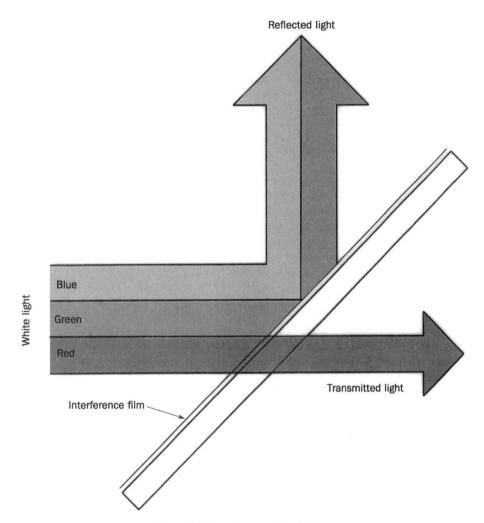

Figure 6.14 Interference (dichroic) filter.

Dip coatings of transparent colors that are given an overcoat of acrylic are an improvement over the sprayed lacquers; they yield a similar result with a higher resistance to abrasion and weather. These plastic-coated lamps offer more sparkle, greater brightness, and higher saturation for any given color.

Colored 50R20, 75R30, and 150R40 lamps are manufactured with fired enamel finishes. Colored 100PAR38 lamps have a coating of dye-impregnated silicone plastic, similar to the plastic-coated sign lamps.

Colored 150PAR38 lamps have dichroic interference filters that are vacuum-deposited on the inside of the cover lens. The filter produces its specific color by transmitting only the desired wavelengths of light, with minimal heat absorption; light of other wavelengths is reflected back into the lamp. It is often more efficient than passing light through color-absorbing materials, and it produces a more brilliant color than absorption methods.

Discharge Lamps 7

In electric discharge lamps, light is produced by the passage of an electric current through a vapor or gas, rather than through a tungsten wire as in incandescent lamps.

The light production by *discharge* sources is more efficient than the electric heating method used in filament lamps. Discharge lamps used in architectural lighting are more efficacious and have a longer life. See table 4 in the Appendix.

FLUORESCENT LAMPS

A *fluorescent* lamp is a low-pressure mercury arc discharge source. Its operation relies on an electrical arc passing between two cathodes, one at either end of a glass tube. Fluorescent lamps require a *ballast* to provide the proper starting voltage and regulate the lamp operating current.

When the voltage difference between the two cathodes is sufficient to strike an arc, an electric current passes through mercury vapor within the bulb. As the arc current passes through the vapor, it causes changes in the energy levels of electrons in the individual mercury ions. As the electrons change levels, they release several wavelengths of visible and ultraviolet energy. This radiation strikes the tube wall, where it causes phosphor material to fluoresce (become luminous) and emit light (figure 7.1).

Because light emanates from the phosphor, light from a fluorescent lamp is emitted from the surface of the bulb; the entire tube is the actual light source. Average luminance of the lamp is comparatively low because light is generated from a large area. See table 5 in the Appendix.

The selection of phosphors and additives determines the kind of light that is produced: ultraviolet light, colored light, or the more commonly numerous variations of "white" light.

Although operating principles are the same for all fluorescent lamps, two kinds of cathode exist: hot-cathode and cold-cathode. (These names are misleading, however, because the cold-cathode type dissipates more heat than the hot-cathode kind.)

Cold-Cathode

The *cold-cathode* lamp is a thimble-shaped cylinder of soft iron, sometimes coated with emissive materials (figure 7.2). This large-area source of electrons has an extremely long life. Voltage drop at the cathode is higher than with a hot cathode; therefore, the watt-

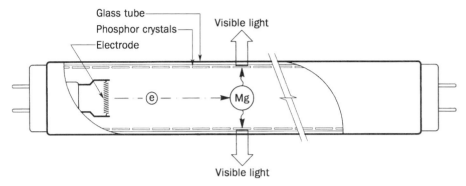

Figure 7.1 The fluorescent (hot-cathode) lamp consists of a glass tube, internally coated with phosphors that convert ultraviolet energy into light; cathodes supported by a glass structure and sealed at the ends of the tube; a filling gas to aid starting and operation—usually a combination of krypton, argon, and neon; a small amount of mercury, which vaporizes during lamp operation; and a base cemented on each end of the tube to connect the lamp to the lighting circuit.

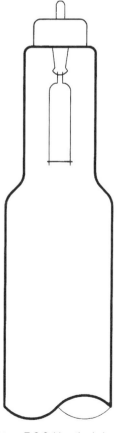

Figure 7.2 Cold-cathode lamp.

age loss is greater, more heat is developed, and lamp efficacy is lower.

Neon is a particular kind of small-diameter, cold-cathode lamp; it is easily bent to form signs and artworks. The operating principle is related to that of other cold-cathode lamps, but light is produced by excitation of the gas itself without the help of phosphors. All cold-cathode lamps provide instant starting and are easily dimmed.

Although lower in efficacy and output, cold-cathode lamps have a longer life. They are used for decorative applications and in places where inaccessibility makes lamp replacement difficult. Cold-cathode lamps are less frequently used than the hot-cathode kind.

Hot-Cathode

Hot-cathode lamps are used for virtually all fluorescent lighting. The cathode is a coiled tungsten filament at each end of the bulb impregnated with electron-emissive materials. Hot-cathode lamps are operated at a higher light output per unit length and with a higher overall efficacy than cold-cathode lamps, resulting in a lower cost for equal illuminance.

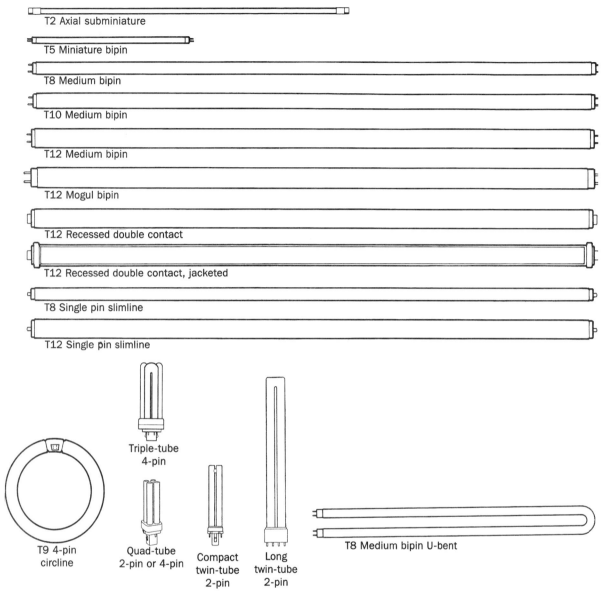

T2 Axial subminiature

T5 Miniature bipin

T8 Medium bipin

T10 Medium bipin

T12 Medium bipin

T12 Mogul bipin

T12 Recessed double contact

T12 Recessed double contact, jacketed

T8 Single pin slimline

T12 Single pin slimline

T9 4-pin circline

Triple-tube 4-pin

Quad-tube 2-pin or 4-pin

Compact twin-tube 2-pin

Long twin-tube 2-pin

T8 Medium bipin U-bent

Figure 7.3 Fluorescent lamp shapes and sizes at one-eighth actual size.

The superior efficacy and greater light output make the hot-cathode ("fluorescent") lamp more suitable in almost all lighting applications; hot cathode lamps are the principal light source for lighting building interiors. Fluorescent lamps are usually identified by an "F" followed by wattage, shape, bulb diameter in eighths of an inch, and color (phosphor kind and correlated color temperature). For example, F32T8/RE830 is a 32 W, 1-in-diameter, fluorescent lamp with rare-earth phosphors and a correlated color temperature of 3000 K (figure 7.3).

Lamp-ballast circuits

Fluorescent lamps require a ballast to regulate the electric current through the lamp. Three kinds of fluorescent lamp-ballast circuits are made: preheat, instant-start, and rapid-start.

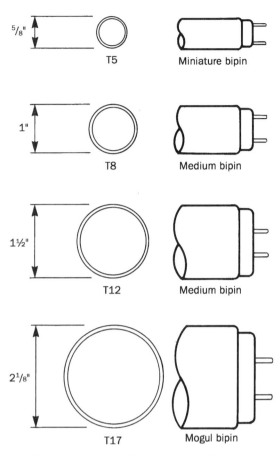

Figure 7.4 Preheat fluorescent lamp diameters and bases at one-half actual size.

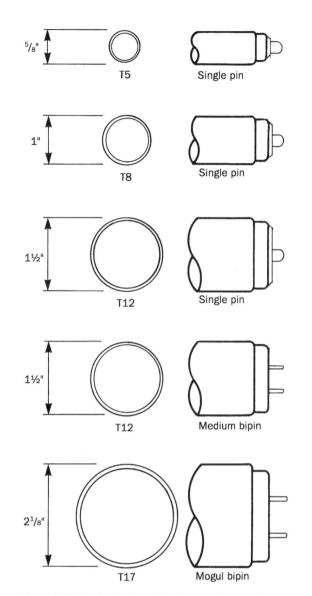

Figure 7.5 Instant-start lamp diameters and bases at one-half actual size.

The earliest fluorescent lamps were of the *preheat* kind (figure 7.4). Preheat lamps have cathodes that must be heated electrically in order to make them emit electrons and thus ionize the gas in the tube, making it more conductive and raising the voltage necessary to strike the arc. The current heats the cathodes; because this occurs before the arc strikes, it is said to preheat them.

The preheating process takes a few seconds. It is usually controlled by an automatic *starter*, which applies current to the cathodes of the lamp for a sufficient length of time to heat them; it then automatically shuts off, causing the voltage to be applied between the cathodes and striking the arc.

The preheating is sometimes accomplished by holding down a manual start button, as with some fluorescent desk luminaires. The button is held down for a few seconds while the cathodes heat; when the button is released, the arc strikes. Whether started manually or automatically, once the lamp is in operation, the arc maintains the cathode temperature.

Instant-start lamps are designed to operate without a starter (figure 7.5). This simplifies the lighting system and its maintenance. The ballast provides sufficient voltage

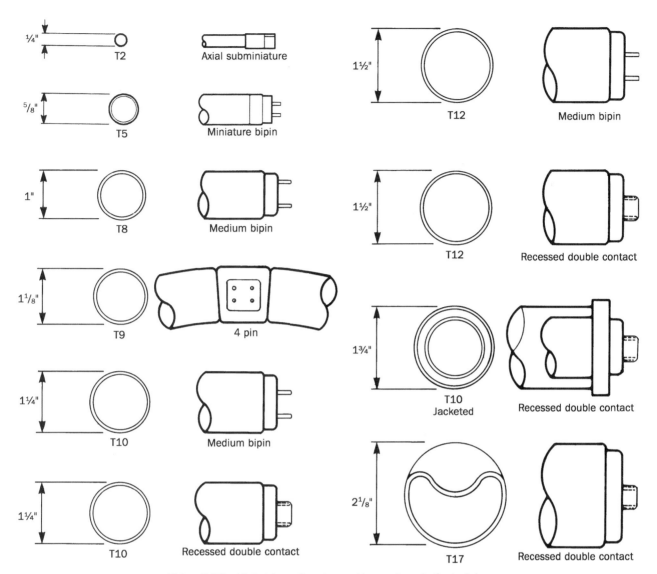

Figure 7.6 Rapid-start lamp diameters and bases at one-half actual size.

to strike the arc instantly. This is a violent action that requires cathodes able to withstand the jolt of instant starting.

Because preheating is unnecessary with instant-start lamps, only one external contact is located on each end of the lamp. Some instant-start lamps have bipin bases; lamps with single-pin bases are called *slimline* lamps. In these lamps, the pins are connected inside the base.

Slimline lamps can be operated at more than one current and wattage. For this reason, they are identified by length rather than lamp wattage. The number following the "F" in the designation is the nominal lamp length. For example, F96T12/RE830 is a 96 in (8 ft), 1½-in-diameter, slimline lamp with rare-earth phosphors and a correlated color temperature of 3000 K.

Rapid-start lamps combine the features of the preheat and instant-start circuits (figure 7.6). Starters are unnecessary. The ballasts have separate windings that heat the cathodes continuously; the lamps start almost instantly after being switched on, but less voltage is required for starting than with instant start lamps of comparable length. Rapid-start ballasts are less expensive, smaller, and have lower power loss than instant-start ballasts.

Rapid-start lamps are sometimes operated with instant-start ballasts. The instant-start ballasts provide higher voltage to start the lamps, but they do not supply current to the cathodes during lamp operation. The savings is approximately 2 to 3 watts per lamp.

Because the cathodes of rapid-start lamps are heated continuously during operation, these are the only fluorescent lamps that can be dimmed or flashed.

Trigger-start ballasts permit the operation of preheat fluorescent lamps up to 32 W without the use of starters. This circuit was developed prior to the rapid-start circuit and is similar in operation: it provides continuous heating of the cathodes, and starters are unnecessary. The lamps are made with bipin bases to permit the flow of current through the cathode filaments before the lamp starts.

For reliable starting, rapid-start and trigger-start lamps must be mounted within 1 in of a 1-in-wide grounded strip of metal, or within ½ in of a ½-in-wide grounded strip of metal, running the full length of the lamp. This is usually provided by a wiring channel or reflector in the luminaire housing.

T8 and T5 lamps

Good color-rendering fluorescent lamps require the use of rare-earth phosphors, which are more expensive than standard phosphors. For this reason, smaller-diameter *T8* and *T5* lamps are produced. (The T8 [1-in-diameter] bulb uses only two-thirds of the phosphor quantity required by the *T12* [1½-in-diameter] bulb, for example; it is therefore less expensive to produce.) The smaller diameter also gets the phosphors closer to the arc, increasing the efficiency of light generation.

In addition to better color rendering, the rare-earth phosphors provide a substantial increase in lighting efficiency. System efficacies up to 80 lumens per watt for T8 lamps on magnetic ballasts and up to 105 lumens per watt for T8 lamps on electronic ballasts compare with 65 to 75 lumens per watt with T12 lamps and ordinary phosphors. Due to their higher efficacies, T8 lamp-ballast systems have replaced conventional T12 lamps in many applications.

(Lamp manufacturers report *lamp efficacy:* lumens per watt when the lamp is operated under reference conditions. *System efficacy* is lumens generated by the lamp when operated by a given ballast divided by the input watts to the ballast.)

As tube diameter decreases in size, luminance is increased, requiring better methods of shielding the source. The smaller bulb diameter also increases the luminaire optical efficiency, however, yielding smaller luminaires with the potential for improved light-distribution patterns.

For T8 lamps, three kinds of rare-earth phosphors are available: RE-70, RE-80, and RE-90. Color temperature is varied according to the relative balance among the phosphors. RE-70 and RE-80 lamps have three narrow-emission phosphors that produce three "peaks" of visible energy: a blue, a green, and a red (see color plates 19, 20, and 21). RE-70 lamps contain a coat of conventional phosphors and a thin coat of the rare-earth triphosphors to produce a CRI of 70 to 79. RE-80 lamps contain a thick coat of the rare-earth triphosphors, increasing CRI to 80 to 89 with full light output and lumen maintenance.

RE-90 lamps do not use the three narrow-emission phosphors of the other two rare-earth lamps. These quad-phosphor lamps contain four wider-emission phosphors that produce CRIs of 95 at 3000 K and 98 at 5000 K (see color plates 22 and 23).

In addition to the four rare-earth phosphors, the RE-90 3000 K lamp has filters to reduce the quantity of blue light caused by mercury radiation, balancing the color. Light output of RE-90 lamps is reduced by one-third, but this is often imperceptible because of the vivid and accurate colors, which improve contrast and portray tones that are otherwise grayed with lamps of lower CRIs.

T5 ($\frac{5}{8}$-in-diameter) fluorescent lamps are only manufactured in metric lengths and with a miniature bipin base, and are designed to operate solely on electronic ballasts. Their smaller diameter provides even better optical control than T8 lamps. Additionally, T5 lamps produce optimum light output at an ambient temperature of 95°F (35°C) rather than the more typical 77°F (25°C) of other fluorescent lamps, allowing for the design of more compact luminaires that do not require added size to dissipate heat.

T5 lamps are also available in high-output versions providing almost twice the light output per length as their standard T5 counterparts. At the present time, all T5 lamps are available only with RE-80 phosphors.

Variations

Energy-saving or reduced-wattage lamps are interchangeable with standard lamps; they consume less power and deliver less light. Input wattage is reduced by 12 to 15 percent; lumen output is reduced by 10 to 20 percent. Energy-saving lamps are more sensitive to low temperatures than standard lamps: minimum starting temperature is 60°F, as opposed to 50°F for standard lamps.

T8 and T12 *U-bent* fluorescent lamps are regular 4-ft lamps bent into a "U" shape. This configuration allows two or three 4-ft lamps to be used in a 2-ft-square luminaire, with the further advantage of wiring and lampholders being conveniently located at one end of the luminaire.

T8 U-bent lamps are available in 1$\frac{5}{8}$-in and 6-in leg spacing, with the 6-in leg spacing more common. T12 U-bent lamps are available in 3$\frac{5}{8}$-in and 6-in leg spacing, with the 6-in leg spacing again more common.

Circular "circline" lamps are T9 (1$\frac{1}{8}$-in-diameter) tubes bent in a circle with the two ends adjacent to each other and a single, four-pin connector base. They are available in 6$\frac{1}{2}$-, 8$\frac{1}{4}$-, 12-, and 16-in outside diameters. Circline lamps are of the rapid-start design but operate equally well on preheat or trigger-start ballasts.

Circular T5 lamps are also available, in 9- and 12-in outside diameters. These lamps have a single base with a two-pin connector.

High-output (*HO*) T12 rapid-start lamps operate at 800 milliamperes (mA), compared with 425 mA for most standard rapid-start lamps. They produce about 45 percent more light than slimline lamps of corresponding physical size as a result of drawing considerably more current than the standard lamps.

High-output lamps are identified by lamp length, bulb diameter, color, and the letters *HO*. For example, F96T12/RE830/HO is an 8-ft, 1$\frac{1}{2}$-in-diameter, rare-earth, 3000 K, high-output lamp. HO lamps are available in lengths from 18 to 96 in, with a variety of phosphors and color temperatures, and in reduced-wattage, energy-saving versions.

Very-high output (*VHO*) T12 lamps also operate on the rapid-start principle at 1500 mA. They produce up to twice as much light as standard lamps of equal length, while using approximately three times more power. These are the most powerful fluorescent lamps available.

Reflector and *aperture* lamps contain an internal reflector on part of the inner surface of the tube to provide built-in directional light control. The un-reflectorized portion of the

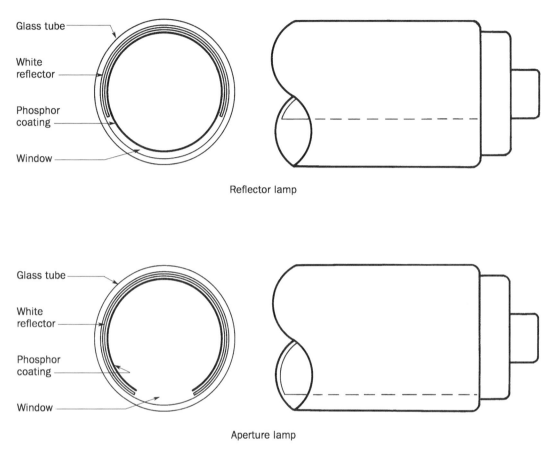

Reflector lamp

Aperture lamp

Figure 7.7 Reflector and aperture fluorescent lamps at one-half actual size.

tube is called the *window*. Intensity of light emitted through the window is significantly increased; total light output is reduced, however. Except in special applications, regular lamps in efficient luminaires perform better (figure 7.7).

Compact fluorescent lamps

Compact fluorescent lamps provide high efficacy, a CRI of 82, and 10,000- to 20,000-hr lives in a single-ended, multi-tube fluorescent lamp (figure 7.8). They operate in the preheat and rapid-start circuit modes; many have a starter built into the lamp base.

Compact fluorescent lamps have significantly higher lumen output per unit length than conventional small fluorescent lamps. This is the result of high phosphor loading, which is necessary because of their small diameter and sharp-cornered, multi-tube bulb shape. As with all fluorescent lamps, compact ones require a ballast in order to start and operate properly.

The compact lamps use the same high-color-rendering rare-earth phosphors as the T5 and T8 lamps mentioned earlier. Color temperature varies according to the relative balance among the phosphors. The 2700 K

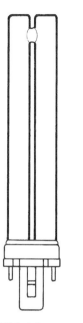

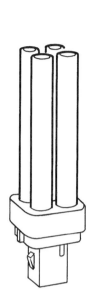

Figure 7.8 Twin-tube compact fluorescent lamp at one-half actual size.

Figure 7.9 Quad-tube compact fluorescent lamp at one-half actual size.

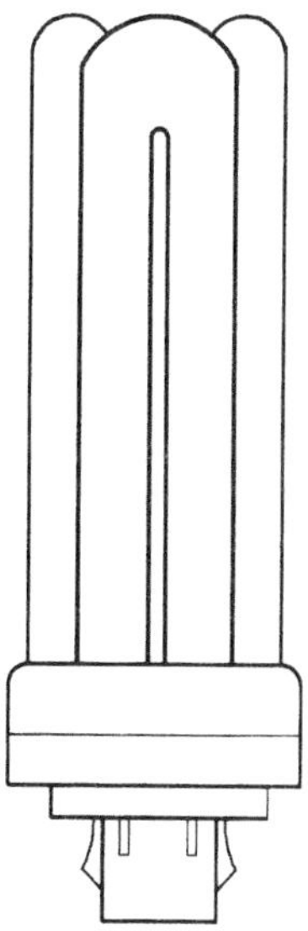

Figure 7.10 Triple-tube compact fluorescent lamp at one-half actual size.

color temperature is often used to simulate the color of standard incandescent lamps; 3000 K is compatible with tungsten-halogen and linear, straight-tube 3000 K fluorescent lamps; 3500 K and 4100 K are compatible with straight-tube 3500 K and 4100 K fluorescent lamps, respectively.

There are six families of compact fluorescent lamps:

1. T4 (½-in-diameter) *twin-tube* preheat lamps have starter devices in the two-pin plug base of the lamp. These lamps operate on inexpensive reactor ballasts and are available from 5 W to 13 W (figure 7.8).

2. T4 or T5 (⅝-in-diameter) *quad-tube* preheat lamps have two-pin plug bases and integral starters; they are available from 13 W to 26 W (figure 7.9). Some of these

lamps use reactor ballasts; others require autotransformer/reactor ballasts. Designed to be a more compact, higher lumen output variation of the twin-tube kind, they provide a substantial increase in light output compared to twin-tube lamps.

3. T4 *quad-tube* electronic lamps are similar to the quad-tube preheat lamps, except that they have four-pin plug bases and no integral starters; they are available from 13 W to 26 W (figure 7.9). Designed for operation with electronic rapid-start ballasts, they also operate on preheat circuits. These lamps can be dimmed with an electronic dimming ballast.

4. T4 *triple-tube* rapid-start/preheat lamps have four-pin plug bases without starters; they are available from 18 W to 70 W (figure 7.10). Designed to deliver high

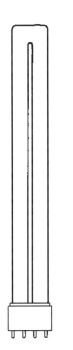

Figure 7.11 "Long" compact fluorescent lamp at one-quarter actual size.

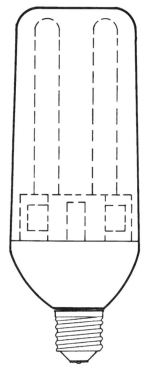

Figure 7.12 Non-modular, self-ballasted, compact fluorescent lamp.

lumen output from a small package, they are frequently used in recessed luminaires that resemble familiar incandescent downlights and wall-washers. These lamps can be dimmed with an electronic dimming ballast.

5. T5 twin-tube "*long*" rapid-start/preheat lamps have a four-pin in-line base without a starter; they are available from 18 W to 80 W (figure 7.11). These are higher-output lamps, designed to provide the lumen output of conventional fluorescent lamps in smaller packages. These lamps can be dimmed with an electronic dimming ballast.

6. *Self-ballasted* compact fluorescent lamps are designed to directly replace incandescent lamps, providing savings in energy and maintenance. They are a complete system, containing a double-folded compact fluorescent lamp, an instant-start electronic ballast, an outer diffuser, and a medium screw base (figure 7.12). They are available in two kinds: modular (replaceable lamp) and non-modular. The lamps consume one-fourth to one-third as much energy as their incandescent counterparts and last up to ten times longer. These compact fluorescents with medium screw bases are less efficacious than other compact

fluorescent lamps, but offer a means of easily increasing the efficiency of an incandescent luminaire.

Light output

During the first one hundred hours of burning a new fluorescent lamp, the initial lumen output drops by about 5 percent; lumen reduction thereafter is less rapid. Consequently, the published "initial lumens" for fluorescent lamps is the value obtained after the first hundred hours of burning.

The depreciation in light output during the life of the lamp is approximately 15 percent of the initial lumens. This is the result of the gradual deterioration of the phosphor powders and the evaporation of electron-emissive material from the cathodes, which causes blackening of the glass bulb adjacent to the cathodes.

The end of life is reached when the emission material on either cathode is depleted. Failed preheat lamps flash on and off or extinguish; instant-start and rapid-start lamps extinguish, flicker, or operate at reduced luminance.

Lamp life

Lamp life varies with the different kinds of fluorescent lamps. Rated average life of fluorescent lamps is based on the average life of a large representative group of lamps tested in a laboratory under controlled conditions; it is expressed in "burning hours." Preheat lamps have rated average lives of 7,500 to 9,000 hrs, slimline lamps 7,500 to 12,000 hrs, rapid-start lamps 14,000 to 24,000 hrs, high-output lamps 9,000 to 12,000 hrs, and very-high-output lamps 10,000 to 12,000 hrs.

The starting of all fluorescent lamps is affected by the ambient temperature. Low temperatures require higher voltages for reliable starting. The majority of ballasts provide voltages that start standard lamps down to 50°F. Ballasts are available for certain kinds of lamps that can start lamps down to 0°F and down to –20°F.

Because each start further depletes the tungsten cathodes, the average life of fluorescent lamps is affected by the number of lamp starts. Frequent starting shortens life; life is lengthened as the number of burning hours per start is increased. Published lamp-life ratings are based on an arbitrarily assigned three hours of burning per start. The life of cold-cathode lamps is unaffected by the number of starts.

EPACT

The U.S. Energy Policy Act of 1992 (EPACT) established minimum efficacy standards for certain kinds of fluorescent lamps. The efficacy standards are a combination of minimum average lamp efficacy, measured in lumens per watt, and minimum color rendering index (CRI). No full-wattage F40, F40/U, F96, or F96/HO lamps can be manufactured or imported unless the lamp has a CRI of 69 or higher and meets the minimum-efficacy requirement.

Full-wattage CW, D, W, WW, and WWX lamps are now unavailable; energy-saving D and WWX lamps are unavailable. CW, D, LW, W, WW, and WWX F96T12 and F96T12/HO lamps have been prohibited from manufacture or sale in the United States since 30 April 1994. CW, D, LW, W, WW, and WWX F40T12 and F40T12/U lamps have been prohibited from manufacture or sale in the United States since 31 October 1995. See table 3 in the Appendix.

Lamps with a CRI of 82 or higher are exempt from these efficacy standards. In addition, aperture, cold-temperature, colored, impact-resistant, plant growth, reflector, and ultraviolet lamps are exempt from the standards.

Until 1992, most fluorescent lamps used for architectural lighting in the United

States were T12 bulbs with less expensive phosphors and poorer color rendering. The combination of high efficacy and good color rendering has made the T8 lamp the current standard.

Colored Lamps

Colored fluorescent lamps emit only a particular portion of the spectrum; the color is determined by the selection of the phosphors used. Different mixtures of phosphor composition produce different colors of light.

In a few cases, additional filtering is required to absorb mercury radiations that will otherwise desaturate the color. For red and deep blue lamps, a filter coating is applied to the outside bulb wall.

The gold fluorescent lamp achieves its color by subtraction, because no phosphors emit mainly yellow light. A yellow filter coating on the inside of the tube absorbs the unwanted wavelengths from a warm-white phosphor. Whenever subtractive filtering is used, luminous efficacy is reduced.

Black light fluorescent lamps use a special phosphor that emits primarily near-ultraviolet energy, plus a small amount of visible blue light.

Colored fluorescent lamps vary widely in lumen output. For example, twenty-five red lamps are required to equal the lumen output of one green lamp. See table 6 in the Appendix.

Different colors of light have different degrees of effectiveness in attracting attention; this is independent of brightness intensity. See table 8 in the Appendix.

Flicker and Stroboscopic Effect

The mercury arc in a fluorescent lamp operated on a 60 Hz alternating current goes on and off 120 times per second. The light from the lamp remains visible because the phosphors have some phosphorescent or "carryover" action: they emit a reduced quantity of

light for a short period of time after the arc is extinguished.

The cyclic variation in light output is known as *flicker*. With 60 Hz operation, the flicker rate over the length of the lamp is 120 cycles per second. At the ends of the lamp each alternate flash is relatively weak, occurring at a rate of 60 flashes per second.

The 120-cycle flicker is too fast to be visible. The 60-cycle flicker can be detected, but only by the peripheral vision of the retina. For this reason, lamp flicker is seldom noticed except when seeing the ends of lamps out of the corner of the eye.

When rapidly moving objects are observed under discharge lighting systems, blurred "ghost" images are sometimes observed. This is known as *stroboscopic effect*. Because of this phenomenon, an object moving at a uniform speed will appear to move in jerks. Under extreme conditions, a rotating object will seem to be standing still or even rotating in reverse direction depending on its speed of rotation and its configuration.

Stroboscopic effect rarely causes difficulty because modern phosphors have relatively long carryover periods. If a problem occurs, operating multiple ballasts on all three phases of a three-phase circuit will reduce stroboscopic effect because only one-third of the lamps operate at reduced output at a given time.

HIGH-INTENSITY DISCHARGE (HID) LAMPS

The term "high-intensity discharge" applies to arc-discharge sources with a high power density. In HID lamps, light is produced by passing an electric current through a gas or vapor under high pressure, as contrasted to the low pressure in fluorescent or low-pressure sodium lamps. HID lamps used for illumination belong to three principal families:

(1) mercury vapor, (2) metal halide, and (3) high-pressure sodium lamps.

HID lamps consist of an arc tube enclosing two electrodes and one or more metals that are vaporized and ionized to conduct current in an electric arc from one electrode to the other. When a lamp is energized, an electric field is established between the starting electrode and the main electrode, causing individual particles of the starting gas to become electrically charged (figure 7.13). With most HID lamps, the arc tube is enclosed in an outer glass bulb.

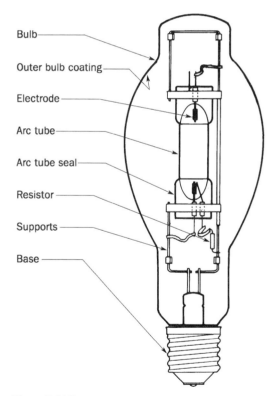

Bulb

Outer bulb coating

Electrode

Arc tube

Arc tube seal

Resistor

Supports

Base

Figure 7.13 Typical high-intensity discharge lamp. With all HID lamps, the light-producing element is the arc tube; it contains metallic vapors, gases, and the electrodes at the ends of the arc tube, where the arc originates and terminates. The base connects the lamp mechanically and electrically to the luminaire.

The electrons that comprise the current stream, or arc discharge, are accelerated to tremendous speeds. When they collide with the atoms of the gas or vapor, they temporarily alter the atomic structure, and light results from the energy given off in the form of radiation as the atoms return to their normal state. The lamp warm-up process takes three to seven minutes, depending on ambient temperature conditions.

Each kind of HID lamp is unique. With *mercury vapor* lamps, light is produced by an electric discharge through mercury vapor. The electrodes are made of tungsten, in which an emission material is embedded within the turns of an inner tungsten coil protected by an outer tungsten coil. The electrodes are heated to the proper electron-emissive temperature by bombardment energy received from the arc. After the arc strikes, its heat begins to vaporize the mercury, which results in poor color quality of a greenish hue: 15 to 20 CRI (color plate 27). The addition of phosphor coatings on the inside of the bulb improves color rendering: 45 to 50 CRI (color plate 28).

In *metal halide* lamps, the electric discharge is through the combined vapors of mercury and metal halides, which are introduced into the arc tube as compound iodides. When the lamp attains its full operating temperature, the metal halides in the arc tube are partially vaporized and the metals radiate their spectrum. The metal halides radiate a wider spectrum than the mercury lamp, yielding greater efficacies and better color rendering: 65 CRI (color plate 29). The addition of phosphor coatings on the inside of the bulb provides diffusion and some additional color improvement: 70 CRI (color plate 30).

Pulse-start metal halide lamps use an arc tube with substantially higher fill pressure than standard metal halide lamps. This reduces tungsten evaporation from the electrodes, which lessens the darkening of the arc tube. As a result, pulse-start lamps provide better lumen maintenance, longer lamp life, and improved color stability compared with standard metal halide lamps.

With *high-pressure sodium (HPS)* lamps, the electric discharge is through combined vapors of mercury and sodium, with the latter dominating. This produces the orange-tinted color familiar to us in street lighting: 21 to 22 CRI (color plate 24). In HPS lamps, the inner arc tube is constructed of polycrystalline alumina (PCA), a ceramic material that is resistant to sodium attack at high temperatures and has a high melting point. By further increasing the gas pressure inside the lamp, *white high-pressure sodium* lamps produce incandescent-like color at 2700 K with good color-rendering properties and a CRI of 85 (color plate 25).

Ceramic metal halide lamps combine the ceramic arc tube technology of high-pressure sodium lamps with existing metal halide chemistry. Instead of the quartz arc tube used in conventional metal halide lamps, ceramic metal halide lamps have an arc tube made of polycrystalline alumina (PCA). PCA permits the lamp to operate at higher internal temperatures, increasing color rendering, output, and efficacy. PCA resists interaction with the chemicals inside the tube, which stabilizes the chemical mix over the life of the lamp, improving color consistency and lumen maintenance. The PCA tube is smaller than quartz tubes, which prevents the chemical mix from dispersing and further improves color consistency.

Many high-color-rendering HID lamps have shorter lives and produce lower light output than standard HID lamps, but their superior color makes them the best choice for areas inhabited by people. White high-pressure sodium lamps offer 10,000-hr lives and a CRI of 85, and some have prefocus bases to provide precise location of the source in optical systems. Ceramic metal halide lamps offer 6,000- to 15,000-hr lives and CRIs of 81 to 96; some have bipin, recessed single-contact, or mogul bipost bases to ensure accurate alignment of the light source with the optical system of the luminaire.

Bulb shapes

HID bulbs are produced in several incandescent bulb shapes. In addition, four shapes have been specially designed for HID service: B, BT, E, and ED. Bulb shapes (figure 7.14) include

A	Arbitrary
B	Bulged
BT	Bulged-tubular
E	Elliptical
ED	Elliptical-dimpled
PAR	Parabolic aluminized reflector
R	Reflector
T	Tubular

The descriptive abbreviation of an HID lamp includes a multi-letter code that identifies the lamp kind or trade name and a number that identifies the lamp's wattage, followed by suffixes that may include lamp shape, a number that represents the maximum diameter of the bulb in eighths of an inch, outer bulb finish, operating position, base, and color. The American National Standards Institute (ANSI) code for description of HID lamps provides suggested standardized nomenclature among manufacturers.

Example: CMH100/C/U/MED/830

CMH	ceramic *m*etal *h*alide lamp, also CDM (for ceramic *d*ischarge *m*etal halide) and MHC for *m*etal *h*alide ceramic)

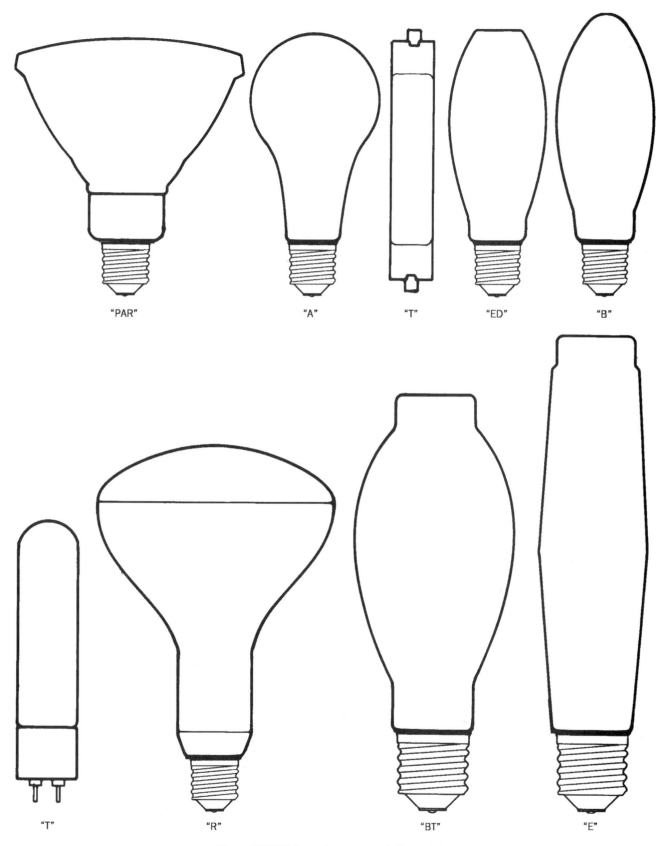

"PAR" "A" "T" "ED" "B"

"T" "R" "BT" "E"

Figure 7.14 HID lamp shapes at one-half actual size.

95

H   mercury vapor lamp (*H* stands for for *hydrargyrum*, the Greek word for mercury and the source of its chemical symbol Hg)

M   *m*etal halide lamp

S or LU   high-pressure sodium lamp (*LU* is short for the trademarked name of several manufacturers' HPS lamps)

SB   self-*b*allasted mercury lamp (for incandescent retrofit)

T   self-extinguishing mercury or metal halide lamps (these stop operating if the outer bulb is broken to protect people from exposure to excessive UV radiation; the designation is omitted with non-self-extinguishing lamps.[1]

39   with mercury lamps, two-digit numbers denote electrical properties and kind of ballast required; lamps with the same numbers are electrically interchangeable (double numbers such as 43/44 indicate that the lamp will operate from more than one ballast).

100   with metal halide and HPS lamps, the number specifying nominal lamp wattage.

/C   phosphor-coated (metal halide)

/D   *d*iffuse-coated (HPS)

/U   manufacturer-designated symbols appear after the next slant line; these commonly identify color or burning position (e.g., U = *u*niversal burning position).

/BD   base *d*own to horizontal ± 15°

/BU   base *u*p to horizontal ± 15°

/DX   *d*eluxe white phosphor

/HOR   base *hor*izontal ± 15°

/MED   *med*ium screw base

/T   *t*ubular bulb

/U   *u*niversal burning position

For optical control, clear lamps offer a relatively small "point source" of 2⅛ in to 9½ in in length. The phosphor-coated lamps enlarge the optical size of the source to the outer bulb wall; although the phosphor coating enhances the lamps' color-rendering abilities, the increased optical size dictates the use of large reflectors for useful optical control.

Lamp Operation

As with fluorescent lamps, HID lamps require ballasts to regulate the arc current flow and to deliver the proper voltage to strike the arc. Electronic ballasts are more efficient and provide more precise control of the arc tube voltage over the lamp's life, resulting in more consistent color and longer life.

Extinction of a lamp occurs in one of three ways: (1) a power interruption of more than half a cycle, (2) a severe voltage dip of more than a few cycles, or (3) insufficient voltage maintained from the ballast.

Before the lamp will relight, it must cool sufficiently to reduce the vapor pressure to a point where the arc will restrike. The time required to cool depends partly on a luminaire's ability to dissipate heat. Typically in a luminaire, mercury vapor lamps will relight in three to ten minutes. Metal halide lamps require ten to twenty minutes to restrike; pulse-start metal halide lamps relight in four to eight minutes. High-pressure sodium lamps usually restrike in approximately one minute. "Instant-strike" HPS lamps have a second arc tube that produces light instantly after a momentary power interruption.

[1]Mercury and metal halide lamps will cause serious skin burn and eye inflammation from shortwave ultraviolet radiation after only a few minutes when the outer envelope of the lamp is broken or punctured if adequate shielding is not used.

Light Output

Depreciation in light output during life occurs mainly because of the escape of electron-emissive material and tungsten from the cathodes to the walls of the arc tube. This depends in part on the frequency of starting; therefore, long burning cycles increase lamp life and lumen maintenance. Other factors affecting lumen maintenance are operating current and the current wave form produced by the ballast design.

The light output of metal halide lamps declines more rapidly than either mercury vapor or HPS lamps. With ceramic metal halide lamps, lumen maintenance is improved approximately 30 percent. Frequent starting is most harmful to metal halide, less harmful to HPS, and least harmful to mercury vapor lamps.

Lamp Life

Lamp life varies considerably depending on the kind of HID lamp and its burning orientation. The rated average life of HID lamps is the point at which approximately 50 percent of the lamps in a large group have burned out and 50 percent remain burning. Published lamp-life ratings are based on ten hours per start.

The normal mode of failure of a mercury vapor lamp is its inability to light. Almost all mercury vapor lamps have rated average lives of 24,000+ hrs (the plus sign indicates that in 50 percent of such lamps "burnout" occurs in excess of 24,000 hrs). It is wise to relamp before reaching the point of failure, however, because the lamps continue to operate long after they are a useful light source.

Metal halide lamps have rated average lives of 7,500 to 20,000 hrs, depending on lamp wattage. Lives of metal halide lamps are shorter than those of other HID lamps because of inferior lumen maintenance and

the presence of iodides in the arc tubes. The normal mode of failure is the inability to light because of an increased starting voltage requirement. Metal halide lamps are particularly sensitive to frequency of starting. As with all lamps, over-wattage operation also shortens life.

Almost all HPS lamps have rated average lives of 24,000 hrs. Normal end of life occurs when the lamp begins to cycle on and off, the result of lamp voltage having increased to the point where the ballast voltage is insufficient to keep the lamp lighted. Over-wattage operation causes voltage to rise faster; slight under-wattage does not affect lamp life.

As with fluorescent lamps, the initial lumen rating for HID lamps is measured after the first one hundred hours of operation. This "seasoning" is necessary because the lamps depreciate rapidly during these first hundred hours, when cleanup of impurities takes place.

Dimming

It is possible to dim some HID lamps using special ballasts, but operating HID lamps at less than full output will produce color shifts and reduced lamp efficacy. As wattage decreases, the color-rendering properties of metal halide lamps approach the color of mercury vapor; HPS lamps approach the yellow-amber color of low-pressure sodium. mercury vapor lamps will retain their already inferior color properties reasonably well, but lumen maintenance and length of life are reduced.

LOW-PRESSURE SODIUM (LPS) LAMPS

Low-pressure sodium (LPS) lamps, although technically not high-intensity discharge sources, are used in limited applications. They have high efficacies—up to 200 lumens per watt—but their extremely narrow spectral range makes these lamps unsuitable for use in interiors (color plate 26).

The lamp, consisting of two tubes, one inside the other, has a mixture of neon and argon gas, plus sodium metal in the inner tube and an evacuated outer bulb. Initially, the arc discharge is through the neon and argon gas and, as the sodium metal heats up and vaporizes, the yellow-amber color of sodium is produced (figure 7.15).

The light produced by the LPS arc, consisting only of radiation in the yellow region of the visible spectrum, is monochromatic. No mercury is present in the discharge; UV radiation emission is not a concern if the outer bulb breaks. The LPS lamps require specific ballasts; no retrofit lamps exist.

In contrast to HID sources, LPS systems maintain constant lumen output over life and light output is unaffected by changes in ambient temperature. Normal end of life occurs when the lamp fails to start or warm up to full light output.

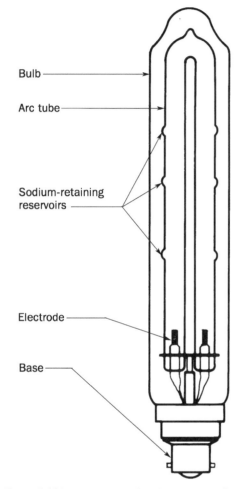

Figure 7.15 Low-pressure sodium lamp construction.

Auxiliary Equipment 8

All discharge sources and low-voltage incandescent sources require the use of auxiliary equipment to supply the correct current or voltage or both to the source.

Auxiliary equipment falls into two categories: transformers and ballasts. This auxiliary equipment consumes a small amount of electrical power, adding to the total amount of wattage used by the lighting system.

TRANSFORMERS

Low-voltage light sources require the use of a *transformer* to step down the standard building service of 120 V to 12 V. The nominal 120 V building service can vary between 115 V and 125 V; some low-voltage light sources operate at 6 V or 24 V. Transformers are placed either within (*integral* to) the luminaire or in a *remote* location.

The smaller size of many low-voltage light sources allows for the design of smaller luminaires. With recessed luminaires the transformer is hidden above the ceiling and out of view. With surface- or pendant-mounted luminaires that have their transformers enclosed within the housing, however, the bulk of the luminaire is increased. Where ceiling conditions permit, surface- and pendant-mounted luminaires can be designed with the transformer recessed in the ceiling and out of view.

Track-mounted luminaires usually contain their transformers. It is also possible to provide low-voltage service to a length of track, locating the transformer in the ceiling or in an ancillary space. The high amperage of low-voltage lamps strictly limits the number of track luminaires per transformer (W ÷ V = A): a 50 W, 12 V lamp draws the same amperage as a 500 W, 120 V lamp; therefore, a 20-ampere-rated track can service only four 50 W lamps (50 W × 4 ÷ 12 V = 16.7 A). This problem is reduced by the use of 50-amp track, which permits ten 50 W, 12 V lamps to be installed on a single track circuit (50 W × 10 ÷ 12 V = 41.7 A).

If remote transformers are used to maintain the compactness of the lighting element, the increased distance between the source and its transformer requires larger wire sizes to prevent a *voltage drop* from occurring over the longer wiring run. See table 9 in the Appendix.

Two kinds of transformers are manufactured for low-voltage lighting: magnetic (core-and-coil) and electronic (solid-state).

Magnetic transformers use copper wound around a steel core, which is *induc-*

tive by nature. Magnetic transformers are relatively large and heavy. Properly sized for the lamp load, they have a long life expectancy. They sometimes cause a noise problem by producing an audible 60-cycle "hum." *Toroidal* (doughnut-shaped) magnetic transformers are quieter, but they also hum when controlled by some kinds of electronic dimmers. The hum grows with the number of luminaires in a room, and the luminaires, if improperly designed, will resonate with their transformers.

Electronic transformers use electronic circuitry, which is *capacitive* by nature. Electronic transformers are compact, lightweight, and quiet. But their life is shorter than magnetic units, premature failures are common, and they are incompatible with some dimmers. The small dimensions of electronic transformers outweigh many of these flaws, however. The designer must consult the dimmer manufacturer to ensure the compatibility of transformers and dimmers.

BALLASTS

All lamps, except incandescent ones, require a *ballast*. Every discharge source has negative resistance characteristics. If the arc discharge is placed directly across a non-regulated voltage supply, it will draw an unlimited amount of current almost instantly and will be quickly destroyed. Therefore, a current-limiting device called a ballast is inserted between the discharge lamp and the power supply to limit the electric current flow through the arc discharge (figure 8.1).

Besides limiting the current flow, the ballast also provides the correct voltage to start the arc discharge. It transforms the available line voltage to that required by the lamp.

Traditionally, ballasts have not been interchangeable. Most ballasts are designed to provide the proper operating characteristics for only one kind of lamp. For example, 175 W M57 metal halide lamps are inoperable on ballasts intended for 175 W H39 mercury vapor lamps, and vice versa.

Newer electronic ballasts are designed to operate more than one connected load. For example, several manufacturers offer ballasts that can operate either one, two, or three fluorescent lamps.

Lamp wattage is controlled by the ballast, not by the lamp. If a 100 W HPS lamp is operated on a 400 W ballast, it will operate at 400 W, to the detriment of the lamp's performance. This may also lead to premature ballast failure.

Unlike incandescent lamps, the rated wattage of a discharge lamp is the wattage

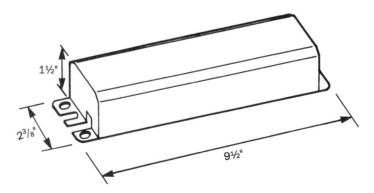

Figure 8.1 Typical F32T8 120 V ballast.

at which it is designed to operate, not the wattage at which it will operate. Therefore, it is impossible to reduce the wattage of a discharge system simply by changing the wattage of the lamps. The ballasts must also be changed.

Two-lamp fluorescent ballasts are used frequently to reduce ballast cost and installation cost per unit of light. They are available for two-lamp series operation or two-lamp parallel operation.

Two-lamp *series* designs are more common because they offer the lowest cost and the minimum size and weight. Only two lamp leads are supplied from the ballast. Both lamps go out when one lamp fails; the good lamp remains undamaged.

Two-lamp *parallel* designs have two independent ballast circuits and therefore are more expensive than two-lamp series designs. Three or six lamp leads are supplied from the ballast. Failure of one lamp leaves performance of the second lamp unaffected.

Electromagnetic Ballasts

Until the 1980s, all discharge ballasts were of the *electromagnetic* kind. The electromagnetic ballast consists of two copper or aluminum wire coils around a common core of steel laminations. This assembly converts electrical power into a form appropriate to start and regulate the lamp.

The ballast usually consists of a transformer, inductance coils, and a capacitor. The transformer converts the service voltage of the lighting circuit to the starting voltage required for the lamp. The *inductance coil* limits the current that can be drawn by the lamp, but in so doing introduces *inductive reactance* into the circuit. The *capacitor* realigns the phase relationship between voltage and current; it is a controlling device that consumes no electrical power.

The capacitor improves the ballast's *power factor* so that it uses energy more efficiently. An electromagnetic ballast that is equipped with a capacitor is called a *high-power-factor* ballast.

Power Factor

The *power factor* of a ballast is the measurement of how effectively the ballast converts the voltage and current supplied by the electrical distribution system to the power delivered by the ballast to the lamp. Perfect phase relationship would result in a power factor of 100 percent.

$$\text{Power factor} = \frac{\text{Input watts (W)}}{\text{Line volts (V)} \times \text{Line amps (A)}}$$

The power factor of an inductive circuit is lagging (figure 8.2) and that of a capacitive circuit is leading. When discharge lamps are operated in conjunction with simple

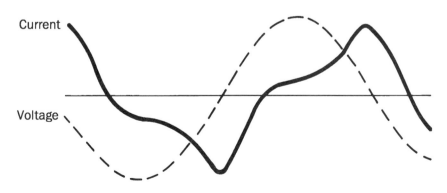

Figure 8.2 Power factor.

inductive ballasts, the overall power factor is 50 to 60 percent. With a capacitor, the leading current drawn by the capacitor compensates for the lagging current in the remainder of the circuit, improving the power factor.

Ballasts are classified according to one of the following three categories:

High power factor: 90% or greater

Power factor corrected: 80 to 89%

Low (normal) power factor: 79% or less

High-power-factor ballasts use the lowest level of current for the specific amount of power needed; this reduces wiring costs by permitting more luminaires on branch circuits. Low-power-factor ballasts use higher levels of current—approximately twice the line current needed by high-power-factor ballasts—allowing fewer luminaires per branch circuit and increasing wiring costs.

Power factor is not an indication of the lamp-ballast system's ability to produce light; power factor measurements pertain only to the ballast's ability to use the power that is supplied. Thus, power factors are invalid as a multiplier in determining light output values.

Lamp-Ballast System Efficacy

The initial lumen and mean-lumen ratings published by lamp manufacturers are based on the operation of the rated lamps by a *reference ballast*. This is a laboratory instrument that is used to establish a baseline, or reference conditions, so that commercially available ballasts can be compared against the same reference. Some commercially available ballasts operate lamps more efficiently than the reference; others operate lamps less efficiently.

In practice, when a lamp is operated by a commercially available ballast, it usually provides fewer lumens than the rated amount. Because of the electrical resistance created by the passage of a current through the core-and-coil of an electromagnetic ballast, some power is converted to heat. This lost power, called *ballast loss*, is unusable for producing light from the lamp.

The disparity between light provided by the reference ballast and the commercially available ballast is called the *ballast factor*. The ballast factor is the ratio of light output produced by lamps operated by a commercially available ballast to that which is theoretically supplied by lamps powered by a laboratory-reference ballast.

$$\text{Ballast factor} = \frac{\text{Lamp lumen output when operated with commercial ballast}}{\text{Lamp lumen output when operated with laboratory-reference ballast}}$$

The term "ballast factor" implies that this is a property of the ballast; it is actually a property of the lamp-ballast system. Some ballasts have different factors for different lamps. That is, they have one ballast factor for operating standard lamps and another for operating energy-saving lamps.

Ballast factors can be greater than 1.0. A commercial ballast can operate a lamp in a way that produces more lumens than when the lamp is operated under reference conditions.

The *ballast efficacy factor* is a ratio of the ballast factor to the input watts of the ballast. This measurement is used to compare the efficiency of various lamp-ballast systems. Ballast efficacy factors are meaningful only for comparing different ballasts when operating the same quantity and kind of lamp.

$$\text{Ballast efficacy factor} = \frac{\text{Ballast factor}}{\text{Ballast input watts}}$$

For a given lighting system, the ballast factor is an indication of the amount of light produced by the lamp-ballast combination; the input watts are an indication of the power consumed.

For example, a ballast with a ballast factor of 0.88 using 60 W of input power has a ballast efficacy factor of 1.47 (0.88 × 100 ÷ 60 = 1.47). Another ballast using the same input power with a ballast factor of 0.82 has a ballast efficacy of 1.37 (0.82 × 100 ÷ 60 = 1.37). The first ballast therefore offers greater efficacy because it has a higher ballast efficacy factor (1.47 versus 1.37).

An electromagnetic ballast operating from an alternating current source produces a sound called "hum." The degree of hum varies depending on the kind of ballast. To aid in the selection of ballasts, manufacturers give their ballasts a sound rating that ranges from *A* (the quietest, at 20 to 24 decibels) to *F* (the loudest, at 49 decibels and above).

Electronic Ballasts

The *electronic* ballast, based on an entirely different technology from the electromagnetic ballast, starts and regulates lamps with electronic components rather than the traditional core-and-coil assembly. The lighting systems they operate convert power to light more efficiently than systems run by electromagnetic ballasts.

Rather than produce more light output, electronic ballasts are usually designed to produce the same quantity of light as electromagnetic ballasts, but they use less power and thereby reduce energy costs.

HID electronic ballasts provide better output regulation (current and power), independent of input voltage variations or lamp wattage variations. This keeps color output (CCT and CRI) consistent and lumen output more uniform. Compared to electromagnetic systems, HID electronic ballasts provide improved performance in starting, normal, and restrike operations.

The humming sound associated with electromagnetic ballasts results from the vibration of the steel laminations in the core and coil. Because electronic ballasts do not have the laminated core and coil, they are 75 percent quieter than comparable A-rated electromagnetic ballasts.

Electronic ballasts operate fluorescent lamps at higher frequencies than electromagnetic ones, with the advantages that flicker is eliminated and lamp efficacy is increased. Both of these advantages occur because the lamp phosphors are under more constant excitation with high-frequency operation.

Electronic ballasts are also smaller and lighter in weight than electromagnetic ones, typically weighing less than half as much because the electronic components are lighter than the metal components of the core-and-coil assembly. Because electronic ballasts consume fewer watts than electromagnetic ballasts, they also produce less heat. This cooler operation yields significant savings in air-conditioning costs.

Air-Conditioning

The air-conditioning load caused by electric lighting derives from the total lighting system, including lamps and ballasts. Each *kilowatt* (kW) of electric power used by the lighting system adds 3,412 British thermal units (BTUs) to the air-conditioning load.

One ton of air-conditioning = 12,000 BTU. Therefore, every 3.5 kW of lighting requires one-ton of air conditioning.

$$\frac{12,000}{3,452} = 3.5 \text{ kW}$$

Fluorescent Dimming Ballasts

Electronic fluorescent *dimming* ballasts will dim T5, T5 high-output, T8, and T12 fluorescent lamps to 1 percent of measured light output (10 percent of perceived light). (Light output as it is measured is different from light perceived by the eye. See page 143.) For four-pin compact fluorescent lamps (T4 quad-tube, T4 triple-tube, and T5 long twin-tube), electronic dimming ballasts will dim to 5 percent of measured light output (22 percent of perceived light). New lamps must first be operated ("seasoned") for one hundred hours at full power prior to dimming to achieve proper dimming performance and ensure average rated lamp life.

Fluorescent Heater-Cutout Ballasts

Heater-cutout electromagnetic ballasts have an electric circuit that removes the voltage supplied to the electrode heaters in rapid-start fluorescent lamps after the lamps are ignited and operating. Heater-cutout ballasts consume approximately 20 percent less input power than do standard electromagnetic energy-efficient ballasts; lumen output is reduced by approximately 12 percent.

Other Ballasts

In addition to standard ballasts, several kinds of *energy-saving* ballasts are made. These fall into two categories: (1) ballasts that save energy by reducing wattage con-

sumed as well as reducing light output, and (2) ballasts that, because of refinements in design, save energy chiefly by reducing wattage loss in the ballasts themselves.

Class P ballasts are equipped with automatically resetting thermal protectors. These turn off the power when the operating temperature exceeds the limits specified by Underwriters Laboratories (UL) to prevent overheating. When the ballast cools, the protector resets, restoring operating power to the ballast.

The UL symbol applied to luminaires indicates that Underwriters Laboratories has examined a sample unit and determined that it complies with appropriate safety standards. It indicates that when properly installed, such a luminaire will operate safely. The UL label is also applied to components, such as transformers and ballasts, to signify that the components meet safety requirements. (The UL label indicates overall luminaire safety when applied to the luminaire and component safety when applied to the components. Different labels and markings are used for various applications, but all make use of the trademark UL circle.)

COMPARATIVE FLUORESCENT LAMP-BALLAST SYSTEMS

Ballast kind	Typical input power (W)	Typical ballast factor	System efficiency (Lumens/W)
Two F32T8/RS lamps, 32 W each			
electromagnetic energy-efficient	70	0.94	78
electromagnetic heater-cutout	61	0.86	82
electronic ballast rapid-start	62	0.88	82
electronic ballast instant-start	63	0.95	87
Two F40T12/RS/ES lamps, 34 W each			
electromagnetic energy-efficient	72	0.87	68
electromagnetic heater-cutout	58	0.81	78
electronic ballast rapid-start	60	0.85	79

Light Control

9

Directional sources, commonly called reflector lamps, such as AR, MR, PAR, and R lamps, have built-in optical systems. All other electric light sources require external devices to modify their distributions in order to be useful in architectural applications.

These modifications have two purposes: (1) to direct light to where it is wanted and (2) to block light from where it is unwanted—to shield the lamp from viewing angles that would otherwise cause glare. The control of light direction is accomplished by three methods: reflection, transmission, and refraction.

REFLECTION

Reflection is the return of light from a surface; it occurs when a portion of the light falling on the surface is thrown back by that surface just as a ball bounces back from the floor. Three kinds of reflection are involved in the control of light: specular, semi-specular, and diffuse.

Specular reflection

A smooth, highly polished surface, such as a mirror, alters the direction of a beam of light without changing its form. The angle of reflection is equal to the angle of incidence—a property that makes specular materials ideal where precise beam control is desired (figure 9.1).

Because *specular* surfaces are virtually mirrors, their own surfaces are almost invisible; they may appear dark or bright, depending on the observer's position and on the luminance of the reflected image.

Semi-specular (spread) reflection

Irregular surfaces, such as those that are corrugated, hammered, brushed, sandblasted, or etched, partially disperse or "spread" the reflected beam. The greatest intensity, however, is still reflected at an angle near the angle of incidence (figure 9.2).

Semi-specular materials appear with highlights or streaks of higher brightness on a background of lower brightness. In interiors, they are often used as elements of sparkle. In luminaires, semi-specular materials produce a moderately controlled beam that is smooth and free from striations.

Diffuse reflection

Rough or matte surfaces neutralize the directional nature of the incident beam.

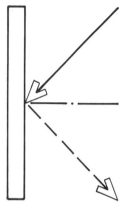

Figure 9.1 Specular reflection.

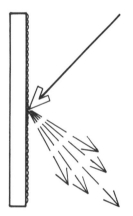

Figure 9.2 Semi-specular (spread) reflection.

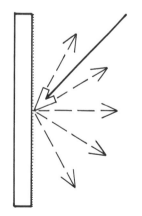

Figure 9.3 Diffuse reflection.

Light is reflected from each point in all directions, with maximum intensity perpendicular to the surface (figure 9.3).

Sand on the beach is an example of a *diffuse* reflecting surface. There are no bright spots; the surface appears the same from all angles of view. In interiors, this quality is often desirable for walls, ceilings, and work surfaces. In luminaires, diffusely reflecting materials are used to produce wide distributions of light.

Reflector Contours

Specular and semi-specular surfaces formed into geometric contours use the *law of reflection* for beam control: the angle of incidence equals the angle of reflection. This is the same law that governs the rebound of a billiard ball off a cushion.

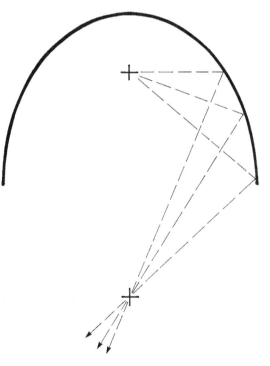

Figure 9.4 Elliptical contour.

Specular reflection is a primary technique for modifying and controlling the direction and distribution emitted by a light source. Specular reflection takes light that would otherwise be lost or wasted within a luminaire or emitted at glaring angles and conserves it by redirecting the light into a room or onto a surface at useful angles.

In addition to this more efficient use of light, the application of properly contoured reflectors produces predictable luminaire distributions and controlled room brightness patterns. Specular reflector contours commonly used in luminaires include actual or modified ellipses, parabolas, and circles.

Elliptical contour

Ellipses have two focal points; a ray of light originating at one focal point is reflected through the second focus. This produces a divergent beam; its spread depends on the distance between the two foci (figure 9.4). Most downlights use reflectors with exact or modified elliptical shapes. A special use of this contour produces a beam that passes through a small, inconspicuous opening flush with the ceiling plane.

Parabolic contour

The parabola is a special form of the ellipse, in which the two foci are far apart. A ray of light originating at the exact focal point of a perfectly shaped parabolic contour is redirected in a direction parallel to the axis of the reflector, producing a beam of parallel rays (figure 9.5). The filament or source is never an actual point; this results in a degree of beam-spread that depends on the size of the source and the diameter of the reflector.

In its pure form, the parabolic contour is used for searchlights, spotlights, and directional equipment where a concentrated beam and a limited spread of light are desired. The beam is often given additional spread by passing it through a diffusing or refracting lens, as is done with many reflector lamps.

Circular contour

The circle is also a special form of the ellipse, one where both foci are coincident; it is the opposite of the parabola. A ray of light originating at the focal point of a circular contour is reflected back through the same point (figure 9.6). It is used separately or in combination reflectors called *compound*

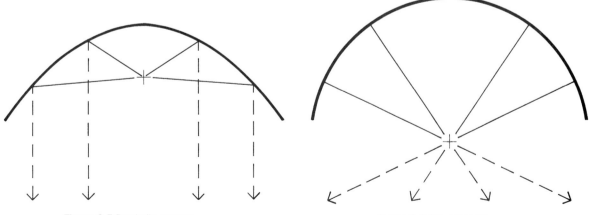

Figure 9.5 Parabolic contour.

Figure 9.6 Circular contour.

contours to redistribute light that would be otherwise misdirected or trapped.

Other reflector contours

Compound contours, which provide asymmetric distribution or maximum beamspread with a shape of minimum dimension, are useful for producing uniformity of luminance from a position close to the surface being lighted; for example, to light the ceiling in a low-height room (figure 9.7).

Innumerable other possible reflector contours can be mathematically defined and tailored for a particular function. These reflectors do not have a specific focal point.

Reflectors

Specular reflectors

Almost all reflector design presumes a compact "point" source of light or a linear source of light at the focus or other precise location. The most compact source is an incandescent filament in a clear bulb.

Large variations in beam control occur, however, with the use of lamps that emit light from a larger area, such as an arc tube or a phosphor-coated bulb or tube. In these cases the bulb or tube, rather than the filament, is the actual light source. This kind of lamp is both a large source displaced from the focus and a diffuse emitter. The result is a diffuse or less precisely defined beam and a reduced projection distance.

The first reflectors for electric luminaires were designed by trial and error or by "longhand" mathematics (figure 9.8). Today, computer-aided reflector design accounts for all of the characteristics of a light source and optimizes a reflector contour.

Semi-specular reflectors

Although clear incandescent lamps in specular reflectors produce efficient beam control, there is often a need to smooth out irregularities in the beam. These striations are reflected images of the filament coil. They are eliminated by a slight diffusion of the beam, accomplished by using (1) an inside-frosted lamp, (2) a lightly etched, faceted, or hammered reflector surface, or (3) a moderately diffusing lens in the beam path.

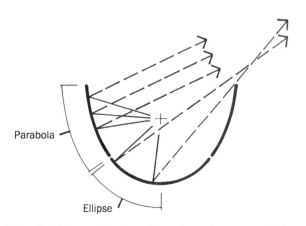

Parabola

Ellipse

Figure 9.7 Compound contour for maximum beam-spread (often used to produce asymmetric distribution).

Diffuse reflectors

The reflection of light from a perfectly diffuse, flat surface is multidirectional, giving a circular distribution curve; the angle of reflection is independent of the angle of incidence. With incident light dispersed in all directions, the beam is wide (figure 9.9); because of this lack of directional control, long projection distances are impractical.

The shape of a diffuse reflector has little influence on the resulting direction and distribution of light. Diffuse reflectors are often useful in luminaires that provide uniform, ambient brightness in a space, but they are unable to direct light toward a surface, such as the workplane.

Reflector materials

Aluminum is the material most frequently used for the fabrication of reflectors. It can be stamped, spun, hydroformed, or extruded into almost any desired shape or contour; it can be processed chemically and electrically to make it more specular; and it can be sandblasted or etched chemically to provide varying degrees of semi-specular reflection.

A hard, protective surface layer of high transparency produced by the anodizing process prevents scratching and abrasion of specular aluminum surfaces and makes cleaning practical.

TRANSMISSION

Transmission of light through a material is affected by two things: (1) the reflections at each surface of the material and (2) the absorption and redirection within the material (called refraction; see page 111). Just as a continuous degree of reflection exists from mirrored, fully specular surfaces to matte, fully diffusing ones, a similarly continuous degree of transmission exists from fully transparent, clear materials to fully diffusing, translucent ones.

Direct transmission

Transparent materials leave the light distribution unchanged (figure 9.10). They are used as protective covers for absorbing or reflecting infrared or ultraviolet radiation or where a change in the color of light is desired while maintaining the light distribution pro-

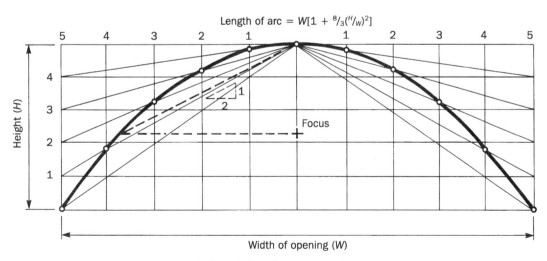

$$\text{Length of arc} = W[1 + {}^8/_3({}^H/_W)^2]$$

Figure 9.8 Parabolic reflector construction guide.

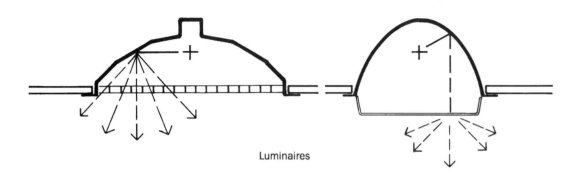

Luminaires

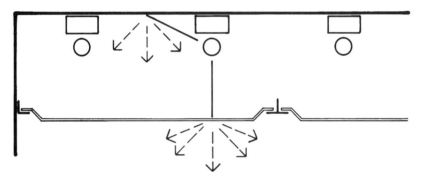

Self-luminous ceilings and walls

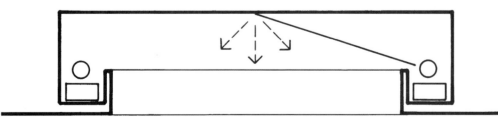

Coffers and coves

Figure 9.9 Diffuse reflector techniques.

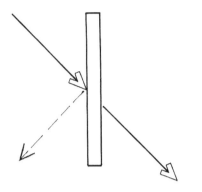

Figure 9.10 Direct transmission. Some first-surface reflection occurs with all forms of transmission.

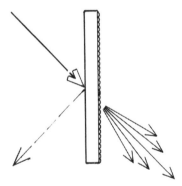

Figure 9.11 Semi-diffuse (spread) transmission.

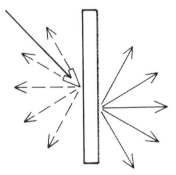

Figure 9.12 Diffuse transmission.

duced by reflecting contours. Because the light source remains visible, materials such as clear glass and plastic are ineffective for glare control.

Semi-diffuse (spread) transmission

Translucent materials emit light at wider angles because of configurations on at least one side of the material (figure 9.11). A slight redirection of the transmitted beam is achieved by minor surface irregularities, such as shallow facets or flutes, which smooth out imperfections and striations. A greater degree of diffusion is achieved by etching, sandblasting, hammering, and matte aerosol sprays applied to the outer surfaces; or the interior of the material is modified to achieve the diffusion. Semi-diffuse materials provide lamp concealment and glare control.

Diffuse transmission

Diffuse transmission disperses light in all directions and eliminates the directional quality of the beam (figure 9.12). Full diffusion is achieved by using opal glasses and plastics that incorporate microscopic particles and remove all directionality from the transmitted beam.

REFRACTION

When a straw is placed in a clear glass of water, it appears to bend at the point where it enters the water. This is because the speed of light changes when a light ray passes from air to water; the phenomenon is called *refraction*.

A similar result occurs when light passes from air to clear glass and plastics. When these transparent materials are formed into prisms or lenses, they become techniques for controlling the direction and, consequently, the distribution of light.

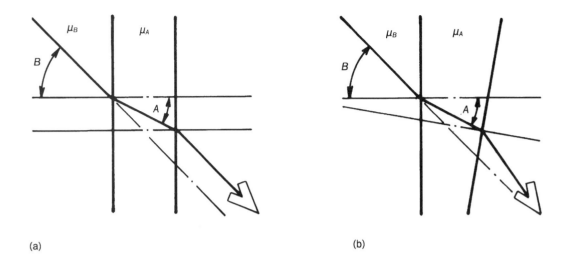

(a)   (b)

$$\mu = \text{Index of refraction}$$

$$\sin B = \left(\frac{\mu_A}{\mu_B}\right)\sin A$$

Figure 9.13a and b The index of refraction is the ratio of the sines of the angles of incidence of a ray of light passing from one medium (usually air) into another medium (such as water, glass, or plastic).

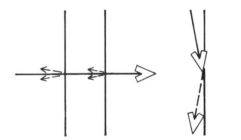

Figure 9.14 Deviation with index of refraction.

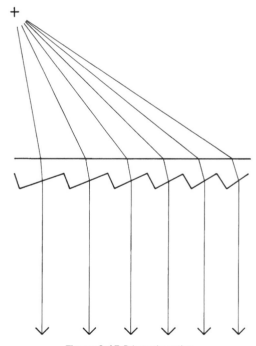

Figure 9.15 Prismatic action.

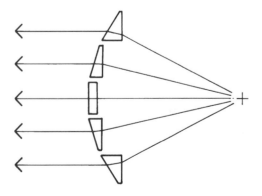

Figure 9.16 A lens is a system of prisms.

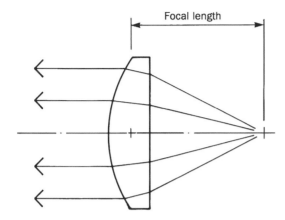
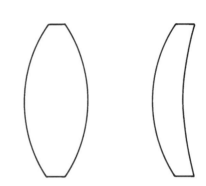

Figure 9.17 Convex lens.

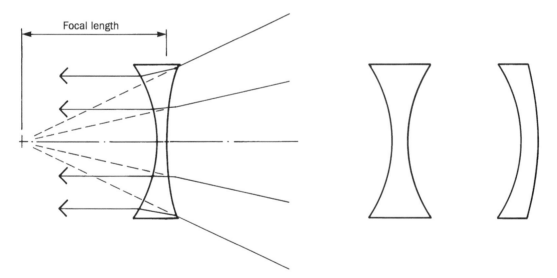

Figure 9.18 Concave lens.

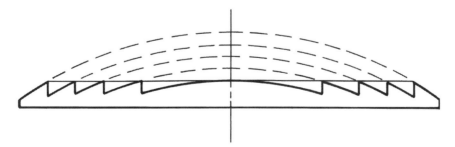

Figure 9.19 Fresnel lens.

Prisms

A beam of light is displaced at the surface of a transmitting material. If the material is formed with two parallel "faces," the displacements neutralize each other; no angular change in the direction of the beam occurs, only a slight displacement (figure 9.13a). If the opposite faces are not parallel, the unbalanced refraction permanently alters the direction of light (figure 9.13b).

Light rays deviate toward the perpendicular when entering a material with a higher index of refraction and deviate away from the perpendicular when entering material with a lower index (figure 9.14).

A *prism* is a transparent body bounded in part by two nonparallel faces. A beam of light projected through one face is emitted in a different direction through another. By providing the proper angle between prism faces, light is emitted in a desired direction (figure 9.15).

Lenses

A *lens* is formed by two opposite refracting surfaces, which have a common axis. It may be thought of as a multiple array of prisms with a continuously changing *included angle* to produce an organized distribution of light (figure 9.16). Two basic kinds of lens systems are used: convex and concave.

The *convex* (*positive* or *converging*) *lens* is thicker in the middle than it is at the edges. Its focal point lies on the axis, at the

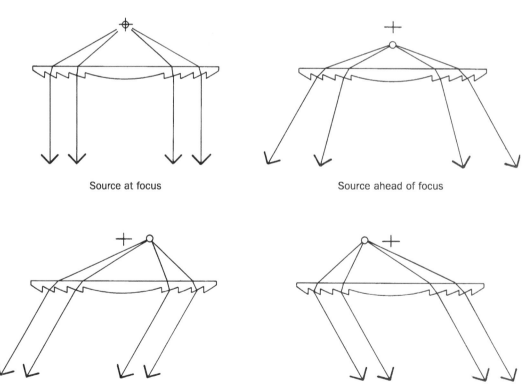

Source at focus

Source ahead of focus

Source offset from focus

Figure 9.20 Distribution of light through a Fresnel lens.

point where the diverging rays from the source are refracted to produce a parallel beam of light (figure 9.17).

The *concave* (*negative* or *diverging*) *lens* is thinner in the middle than it is at the edges. This causes a parallel beam of light to diverge. The focus is called a virtual focal point; it is the artificial point at which the diverging rays would meet if they were traced backward as straight lines through the lens (figure 9.18).

Because refraction takes place at the surface of the material, with the direction of the ray unchanged between surfaces, part of this transmitting material can be removed without affecting the optical control. A convex lens with sections of the glass removed produces a lens that is thinner and lighter in weight.

The *Fresnel* lens, which is based on this principle, consists of a series of concentric lens sections regressed into a planar array (figure 9.19). It is named for the French physicist Augustin Jean Fresnel (1788– 1827), who developed the lens for use in lighthouses. In luminaires, the Fresnel lens produces a concentrated beam of light while also reducing the brightness of the source, providing a degree of glare control.

The Fresnel lens has a short focal length. A light source located at this focus produces a single, concentrated beam of light with parallel rays. When the light source is positioned at points other than the primary focus of the optical system, the lamp-refractor combination produces either a spread or asymmetric distribution (figure 9.20).

Glasses and plastics that incorporate a regular pattern of small prisms or other refractive elements are called *prismatic lenses*. They do not concentrate the distribution of light the way Fresnel lenses do; prismatic lenses spread the distribution of the source but also reduce its luminance, providing a degree of glare control.

Total Internal Reflection

Total internal reflection occurs when light passes into a transparent medium, such as glass or plastic, at an appropriate angle and travels inside the medium repeatedly reflecting from side to side. Edge lighting and light transmission through rods are examples of this phenomenon.

Fiber optics

With *fiber optics*, light entering one side of a glass or plastic fiber of optical quality is transmitted to the other end by the process of total internal reflection. Light rays that strike the core at the acceptance angle are reflected back and forth inside the core and travel to the other end of the fiber in a zigzag path of successive reflections.

In use, a single, large-diameter fiber is impractical because it lacks flexibility. To increase flexibility, a large number of small-diameter fibers are clustered together in a *bundle*. In order to prevent light leaking from one fiber to another, each is coated with a transparent sheath that has a lower *refractive index* than the fiber (figure 9.21). The sheathing process protects the surfaces of the fiber and allows the bundle to be embed-

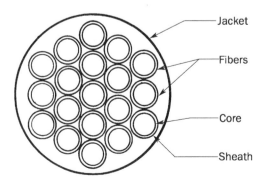

Figure 9.21 Enlarged section of optical fiber.

115

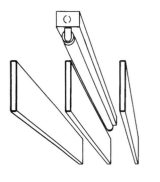
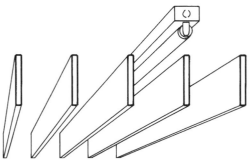

Figure 9.22 Baffles.

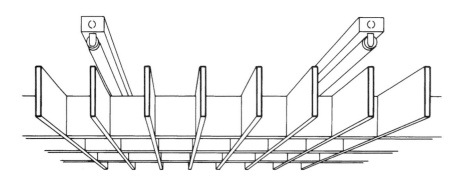

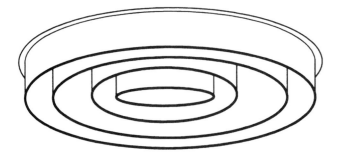

Figure 9.23 Louvers.

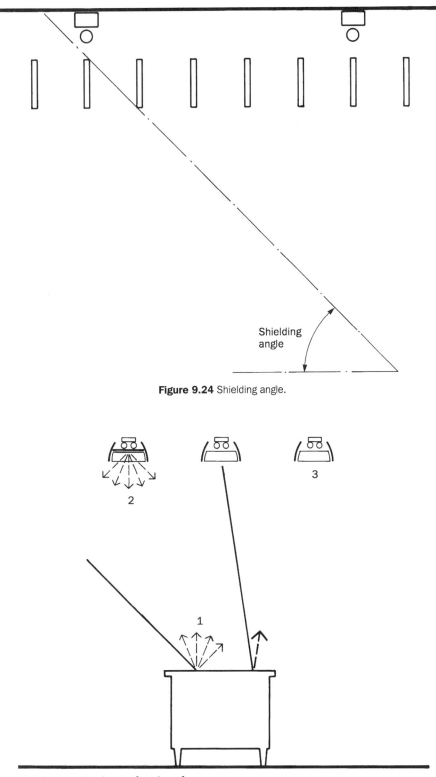

Figure 9.24 Shielding angle.

1. Reduce glossiness of work surface.
2. Add diffuse transmitting material to increase the diffusion of the light source.
3. Locate lighting equipment outside the reflected field of view.

Figure 9.25 Corrective solutions.

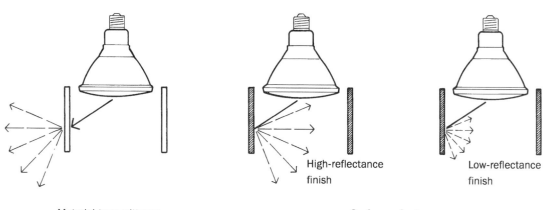

Material transmittance   Surface reflectance

Figure 9.26 Transmitting materials: translucent white and colored plastic or glass, perforated metal. High-reflectance finish: lightly etched metal, light wood, light-colored paint. Low-reflectance finish: matte black finish, dark wood finish, dark-colored paint.

ded into other materials without loss of light from the sides.

Optical fibers are combined in two kinds of bundles: coherent and incoherent. *Coherent bundles* contain fibers that are identically positioned at the point of light entrance and light exit. Because each fiber conducts a portion of the light pattern to the same point on the receiving end of a bundle, images can be transmitted through the bundle. *Incoherent bundles* contain a random arrangement of fibers that can be used to transmit light but not images.

A typical fiber-optic lighting system consists of: (1) a light projector, (2) a tungsten-halogen or metal halide light source, (3) an optical-fiber harness, (4) a fitting for each of the bundles, and (5) the bundles of optical fibers themselves. Silicone rubber sheathing gives the bundles protection without loss of flexibility.

GLARE CONTROL
Sometimes the lens or reflector that is providing the light control is also used to achieve concurrent glare control and lamp concealment. At other times separate elements are used.

Baffles and Louvers
Baffles and louvers shield glare at normal viewing angles, thereby contributing to visual comfort.

Baffles provide shielding in one direction, along a single axis (figure 9.22). For small-aperture luminaires, a baffle around

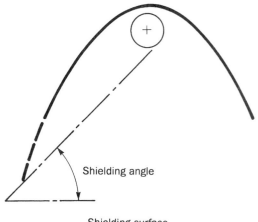

Shielding angle

Shielding surface

Figure 9.27 Shielding as an aspect of contour design.

the perimeter provides shielding from all directions.

Louvers are a series of baffles or shielding elements placed in a geometric pattern to provide shielding from many directions with minimum interference to the desired beam distribution (figure 9.23).

Shielding conceals the lamp and controls glare within a zone called the *shielding angle*. This is the maximum angle that the eye is raised above horizontal without seeing the light source beyond the shielding system (figure 9.24).

Although baffles and louvers conceal the light source from direct view within this specified zone, horizontal work surfaces are still directly exposed to the source. The mirrored image of the light source becomes a source of *reflected glare* from glossy paper, photographs, objects behind glass, and polished tabletops (figure 9.25).

Baffles and louvers may be black or made from reflective and transmitting materials. The intensity of light directed toward the eye is determined by the luminance of these surfaces. The choice of materials is based on various considerations including

visual comfort and design harmony with the space (figure 9.26).

To achieve concurrent glare control and lamp concealment with minimal change in the diffuse beam, use open louvers, or plastic or glass with a slight degree of diffusion. Whether the beam is modified by diffuse reflection or by diffuse transmission, the distribution of light is the same.

Reflectors

An opaque (light-blocking), concave reflector also functions as a baffle, which shields the light source. Additionally, the reflector's shape affects the appearance of the visible interior surface. If light is redirected toward the eye, the result is high luminance and unpleasant direct glare. If light is directed downward and away from the eye, luminance is reduced and glare is avoided.

In the most efficient reflector designs, source shielding is incorporated into the contour design. This involves extending the reflector surface to provide the necessary shielding (figure 9.27).

As reflector depth is increased, total efficiency is reduced because of absorption

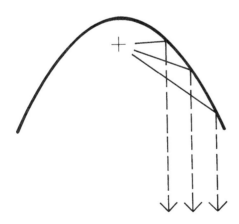

Reflector action

Figure 9.28 Parabolic reflector used for glare control.

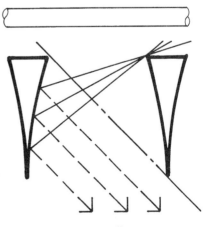

Louvers and baffles

Figure 9.29 Parabolic reflector design for louvers and baffles.

losses at the reflector surface. Because a greater portion of the emitted light is brought under control and redirected, however, candlepower and useful lumens increase.

Parabolic reflectors are often used for glare control. Little reflected luminance occurs in the cross view of these reflectors because most of the light is directed downward with minimal light directed toward the eye; this gives an impression of low brightness from normal angles of view (figure 9.28).

Diffusion of the reflector surface causes more light to be directed toward the eye. As a result, luminance is increased when reflector surfaces are etched or brushed.

Parabolic reflector design is applied to both reflectors and baffles. Figure 9.29 shows the pattern of light reflections for light rays originating above the louver. Ideally, light is reflected at an angle equal to the shielding angle.

Well-designed, specular, parabolic louvers provide equal or superior glare control to matte-black or gray louvers, with greater system efficiency because of the reduced absorption of light.

Photometrics 10

It is impossible to see a footcandle. What is seen is luminance, which is a function of the amount of light falling on a surface and the reflectance of that surface, modified by the surrounding conditions and adaptation of the eyes.

MEASUREMENT OF LIGHT

Photometry is the science that measures light. Five terms are commonly used to quantify light: intensity, flux, illuminance, exitance, and luminance.

1. **Intensity** is the light emitted in a specific direction by a source. Properly called *luminous intensity* and defined as *flux per solid angle in a given direction*, it is measured in candelas (cd). Intensity in a succession of directions is plotted on a distribution curve or polar graph (figure 10.1).

2. **Flux** is the light emitted in all directions by a source. Properly called *luminous flux* and defined as *time rate flow of light*, it is measured in lumens (lm).

3. **Illuminance** is the density of light at any given point on a surface. Properly defined as *density of flux incident on a surface measured perpendicular to the surface*, it is measured in footcandles (fc).

4. **Exitance** is the total quantity of light emitted, reflected, or transmitted in all directions from a surface. Properly defined as *density of flux leaving a surface*, it is measured in lumens per square foot (lm/ft^2).

5. **Luminance** is the accepted term for light that is reflected from a surface in a given direction (back toward the eyes). Properly defined as *intensity of flux leaving a surface in a given direction*, it is measured in candelas per square foot (cd/ft^2).

Measurement Limitations

Illuminance is frequently used to measure the quantity of light in architectural space because it is the easiest and least expensive unit to measure. Yet it is impossible to *see* a footcandle!

What is seen is *luminance*, which is a function of the amount of light falling on a surface and the reflectance of that surface (its ability to reflect light). We see an object or surface only when light is reflected from that object or surface back toward the eyes, or when it is emitting light itself (self-luminous).

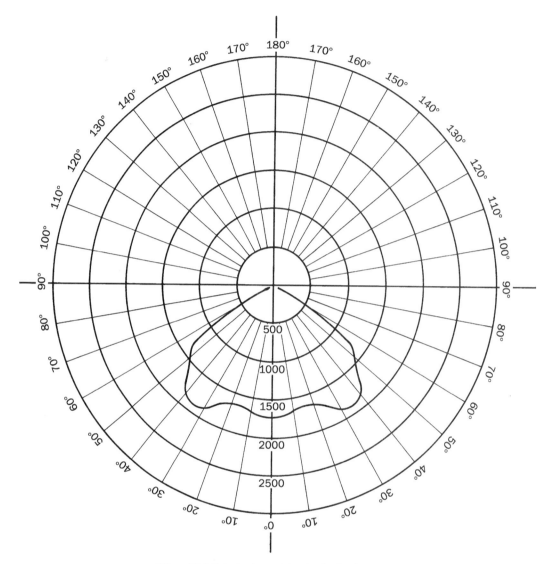

Figure 10.1 Polar luminous intensity distribution curve.

Brightness is what we perceive. It is a subjective attribute perceived in varying degrees of intensity. Reflected light was formerly measured in *footlamberts* (*fL*). Because brightness changes with viewing angle, the term footlamberts has been deprecated by the Illuminating Engineering Society of North America (IESNA). Perceived luminance is now measured by exitance.

It is only meaningful to measure exitance, however, if this quantity remains constant (or nearly so) for a wide range of viewing angles. Diffuse surfaces, called *Lambertian* for the German physicist and philosopher Johann Heinrich Lambert (1728–1777), exhibit this property; thus, it is appropriate to measure exitance only for Lambertian surfaces.

Calculations for illuminance (footcandle values) overlook the aesthetic, psychological, and physiological variables of the human visual process. When a convenient measure of perceived luminance becomes available, it will be more useful to calculate perceived surface luminance values, which account for these factors.

The perception of surface luminance is based largely on the eye's ability to *adapt*. The iris *dilates* (opens) when illuminance is low and *contracts* (closes) when illuminance is high. It takes the eye longer to adapt from light to dark than from dark to light. When you enter a dark theatre on a sunny day, it takes twenty to thirty minutes for the eyes to adapt completely to the lower illuminance. When you leave the theatre and return to daylight, it sometimes takes only seconds for the eyes to adapt to the higher luminance.

In a more subtle way, the eyes are continually adapting as you move in and through variously lighted spaces or look around at objects of varying illuminances. Even measured luminance does not indicate the *apparent* brightness because of the eye's ability to adapt. Measured luminance, then, yields a poor indication of perceived brightness, which is modified by the surrounding conditions and adaptation of the eyes.

It is the *balance* of these relative luminances, not the *quantity of illuminance* received on a surface, that determines successful lighting design. Therefore, the illuminance measurements that follow are *not* to be used as the starting point for a design. They are to be used only for lamp and luminaire selection or to evaluate a lighting design.

Luminous Intensity Distribution Curve

The intensity distribution curve represents the amount of luminous intensity (cd) generated in each direction by a light source in a plane through the center of the source. Consequently, the luminous intensity curve gives a picture of the total light pattern produced by a source.

Luminous intensity distribution curves are available from luminaire manufacturers and are often found on the back of the manufacturer's product data sheet. A *polar graph* is used to represent the distributional intensity of a luminaire, and a *rectilinear* or *Cartesian graph* to represent the distributional intensity of a directional lamp.

In the polar graph (figure 10.1), the luminaire is located at the center of the radiating lines. The radiating lines represent specific degrees of angular rotation from the 0° axis of the luminaire (*nadir*). The concentric circles represent graduating intensity expressed in candelas, with values entered along the vertical scale.

To determine the luminous intensity of this luminaire at 30°, find the appropriate angled line drawn from the center of the luminaire. Follow the line until it meets the polar curve, then follow the circular line originating at that point and read the luminous intensity (in candelas) on the vertical scale. In figure 10.1, the luminaire produces 1,850 cd at 30° from nadir.

For luminaires with symmetrical light distributions, a single curve fully describes the luminaire's distribution. Often only one side of the polar graph is shown, since the other side is an identical, mirror image.

A luminaire with an asymmetrical distribution, such as a linear fluorescent downlight, requires curves in a number of planes to adequately represent its distribution. Typically, one curve is parallel to the luminaire and another is perpendicular to

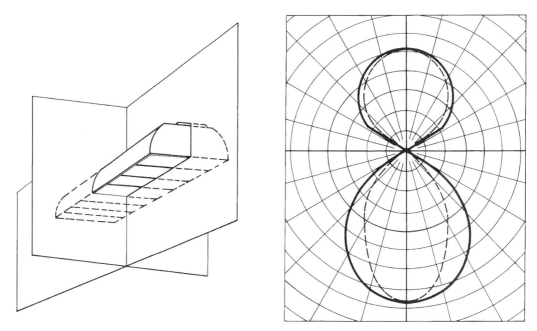

Figure 10.2 Polar graph for a fluorescent luminaire.

the luminaire; sometimes either a third plane at 45° or three planes at 22½° intervals are added (figure 10.2).

Reflector lamp sources or luminaires with directional distributions and abrupt cutoffs, where the light intensity changes rapidly within a small angular area, give values that are difficult to read on a polar graph. Consequently, a rectilinear or Cartesian graph is substituted to portray the candela distribution (figure 10.3).

On this graph, the horizontal scale represents the degrees from the beam axis and the vertical scale represents the intensity in candelas. In the graph on the right of figure 10.3, approximately 3,000 cd are produced by the light source at 10° from the beam center.

When selecting luminaires for a lighting application, be sure that the proposed luminaire *and its source* are precisely those shown in the manufacturer's photometric test data. It is inaccurate to extrapolate from

one source or reflector finish to another unless the photometric report includes multipliers for various tested sources and reflector finishes.

RECOMMENDED ILLUMINANCE VALUES

Illuminance value recommendations are published as footcandles (fc) at the *work-plane*. For almost all commercial and industrial activities, this surface is considered to be a horizontal plane 2 ft 6 in AFF (above finished floor)—standard desk height—even though the space may be a corridor or a basketball court with no desk in sight.

Remember that these values refer to illuminance on the horizontal work surface only; they have limited significance to us when we interpret the actual environment. Such factors as wall lighting, brightness accents, shadow, sparkle, and color have a greater influence on emotional reaction. These factors are particularly important in areas involving casual seeing where low

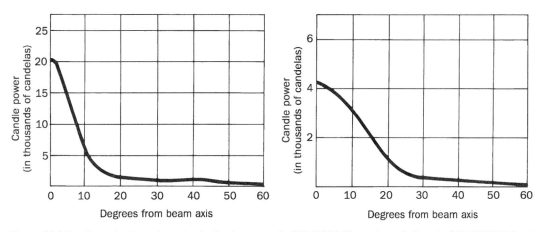

Figure 10.3 Rectilinear luminous intensity distribution curve of a 60PAR38/HIR spot lamp (left) and a 60PAR38/HIR flood lamp (right).

recommended illuminance values may be misleading because a dull or gloomy environment will be unsatisfactory.

True illuminance requirements vary with the visual difficulty of the work task, the age and eyes of the worker, and the importance of speed and accuracy in the completion of the task. Typical illuminance values are shown in table 15 in the Appendix. At best, these values provide a *guide* to the quantity of illuminance needed on the work surface for accurate and comfortable seeing.

In its *Lighting Handbook*, ninth edition, the IESNA publishes an illuminance selection procedure with horizontal illuminance recommendations for specific applications. It is supplemented by a "Design Guide" that attempts to account for other factors that influence perception: including the appearance of the interior, color appearance and color contrast, daylighting integration, glare, vertical illuminance, surface finishes and textures, brightness contrast, facial modeling, and the presence of sparkle.

A consolidated listing of the IESNA horizontal illuminance recommendations appears in table 16 in the Appendix. It covers illuminance values for seven categories and a variety of tasks.

Categories A, B, and C include casual activities that take place over the entire area of a space. For example, in a circulation space such as a hotel lobby or office building corridor, the visual task of circulation is a constant throughout the space, and an illuminance value of 5 fc is recommended.

Categories D, E, and F refer to common tasks that remain fixed at one or more particular locations; these values are to be applied only to the appropriate task area, recognizing that several different kinds of tasks may occur in the same room. The IESNA recommends a value of 20 fc as the minimum illuminance on the horizontal work surface for the "non-task" parts of the room where less demanding visual work is performed.

Category G is for special, visually difficult tasks. The lighting system for these tasks requires careful analysis. Recommended illuminance values are achieved with supplemental task lighting, and range from 300 to 1,000 fc.

Age

IESNA illuminance recommendations do not account for the age of the occupants. The visual requirements of older persons differ from those of younger persons in two ways: (1) the lens of the eye thickens, decreasing the eye's ability to change its shape to properly focus at varying distances (figure 1.6), and (2) pupil size becomes reduced, decreasing the amount of light reaching the retina.

Older persons require higher illuminance values for the same tasks (a sixty-year-old requires three times the illuminance of a twenty-year-old for equal retinal illuminance). At the same time, glare sensitivity within the field of view is significantly increased.

IESNA illuminance recommendations assume an age of forty to fifty-five. As a rule-of-thumb, for persons under age forty, illuminance values may be reduced by up to one-third; for persons over age fifty-five, illuminance values may be increased by up to two-thirds.

ILLUMINANCE CALCULATIONS

Although people see not footcandles but luminance contrast, the question of how much light is necessary for tasks must still be answered. Calculations are performed during the design process to obtain information about lamp and luminaire performance, to evaluate design alternatives, or to refine a particular design.

Following are descriptions of simple calculation methods, with examples for determining illuminance at a specific point and the average illuminance on a specific plane.

Illuminance at a Point

To find the value of incident illuminance at a specific point produced from a compact source, the *inverse-square method* is used. This method closely approximates the illumination where the distance from the source is at least five times the maximum dimension of the source.

Source aimed at a target

Illuminance is proportional to the luminous intensity of the source in the given direction, and inversely proportional to the square of the distance from the source.

To calculate illuminance (fc) from a source aimed at a surface perpendicular to the source:

$$fc = \frac{I}{D^2}$$

where I is the intensity of the source (in candelas) in the direction of the point and D is the distance from the source to the point (figure 10.4).

Example

A 60PAR/HIR/SP10 lamp is aimed at a point on a surface 12 ft away. From a luminous intensity distribution chart (figure 10.3, left), find that the 60PAR/HIR/SP10 lamp produces 20,000 cd at 0°:

$$fc = \frac{20,000}{12^2} = 139$$

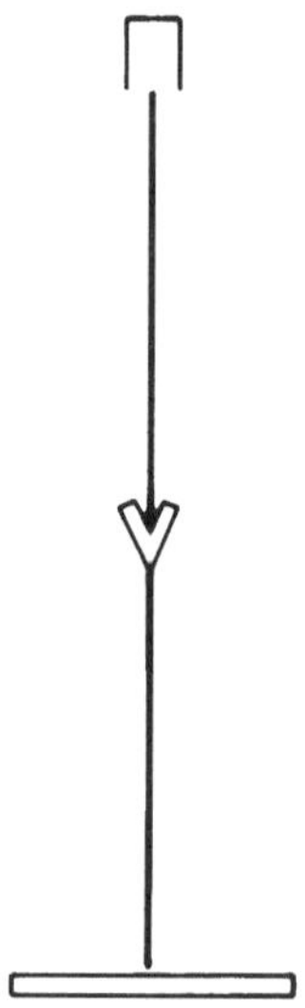

Figure 10.4 Illuminance on a surface perpendicular to the source.

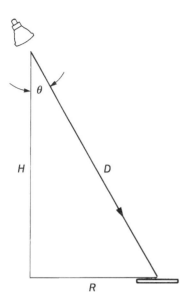

Figure 10.5 Illuminance on a horizontal surface—source at an angle.

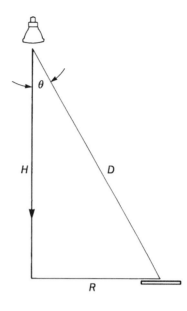

Figure 10.6 Illuminance on a horizontal surface—target located to one side of a source at nadir.

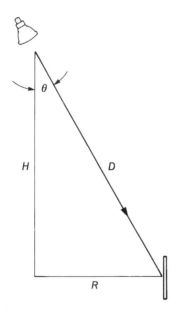

Figure 10.7 Illuminance on a vertical surface—source at an angle.

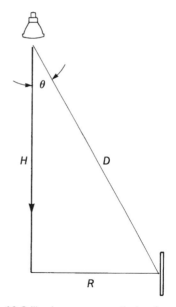

Figure 10.8 Illuminance on a vertical surface—target located to one side of a source at nadir.

Source aimed at an angle to a horizontal surface

If the source is aimed at an angle toward the target instead of being perpendicular to the target, the light will spread over a greater area, reducing the illuminance at a specific point. For a *horizontal* surface, the reduction is equal to the *cosine* of the angle of incidence or "tilt."

To calculate illuminance from a source at an angle to a horizontal surface:

$$fc = \frac{I}{D^2} \times \cos\theta$$

where *I* is the *i*ntensity of the source (in candelas) in the direction of the light ray, θ is the angle of tilt between nadir and the direction of the light ray, and *D* is the *d*istance from the source to the target surface (figure 10.5).

In figure 10.5, *H* is the vertical mounting *h*eight of the light source above the target of measurement, and *R* is the horizontal distance (*r*un) from the light source to the target.

Example

A 60PAR/HIR/SP10 lamp is tilted at 30° from nadir (straight down) to cast light on a horizontal surface 12 ft away (D). To determine illuminance on the surface, follow these steps:

1. From an intensity distribution chart (figure 10.3, left), find that the 60PAR/HIR/SP10 lamp produces 20,000 cd at 0° (the direction of the ray).

2. From the table of trigonometric functions (table 10 in the Appendix), find that the cosine of 30° is 0.866.

$$fc = \frac{20,000}{12^2} \times 0.866 = 120$$

Source at nadir, target on horizontal surface located to one side

If the source is aimed straight down but the target is located to one side of the central ray, the illuminance at the target on a horizontal surface will be the intensity of the beam at nadir reduced by the cosine of the angle from the source to the target.

To calculate illuminance from a source at nadir to a point located to one side on a horizontal surface, the same formula is used:

$$fc = \frac{I}{D^2} \times \cos\theta$$

where *I* is the *i*ntensity of the source (in candelas) in the direction of the light ray, θ is the angle between nadir and the direction of the target, and *D* is the *d*istance from the source to the target surface (figure 10.6).

Example

A 60PAR/HIR/FL30 lamp is pointed straight down. To determine the illuminance at a target that is 10° to one side of nadir on a horizontal surface 12 ft away, follow these steps:

1. From an intensity distribution chart (figure 10.3, right), find that the 60PAR/HIR/FL30 lamp produces 2,800 cd at 10° (the direction of the ray).

2. From the table of trigonometric functions (table 10), find that the cosine of 10° is 0.985

$$fc = \frac{2,800}{12^2} \times 0.985 = 19$$

Source aimed at an angle to a vertical surface

If the source is aimed at an angle toward a target on a *vertical* surface, the reduction in illuminance at the target is equal to the *sine* of the angle of incidence or tilt.

$$fc = \frac{I}{D^2} \times \sin\theta$$

where *I* is the *i*ntensity of the source (in candelas) in the direction of the light ray, θ is the angle of tilt between nadir and the direction of the target, and *D* is the *d*istance from the source to the target (figure 10.7).

In figure 10.7, *H* is the vertical mounting *height* of the light source above the target and *R* is the horizontal distance (*r*un) from the light source to the target.

Example

A 60PAR/HIR/SP10 lamp is tilted at a 30° from nadir to cast light on a vertical surface 6 ft away. To determine illuminance on the surface, follow these steps:

1. From an intensity distribution chart (figure 10.3, left), find that the 60PAR/HIR/SP10 lamp produces 20,000 cd at 0° (the direction of the ray).

2. From the table of trigonometric functions (table 10), find that the sine of 30° is 0.500

$$fc = \frac{20,000}{12^2} \times 0.500 = 69$$

Source at nadir, target on vertical surface located to one side

If the source is aimed straight down but a vertical target is located to one side of the light ray, the illuminance at the target on the vertical surface will be reduced by the sine of the angle between nadir and the target.

To calculate illuminance from a source at nadir to a target located to one side on a vertical surface, the same formula is used:

$$fc = \frac{I}{D^2} \times \sin\theta$$

where *I* is the *i*ntensity of the source (in candelas) in the direction of the light ray, θ is the angle between nadir and the direction of the target (to one side), and *D* is the *d*istance from the source to the target surface (figure 10.8).

Example

A 60PAR/HIR/FL30 lamp is pointed straight down. To determine the illuminance at a target that is 10° to one side of nadir on a vertical surface 12 ft away, follow these steps:

1. From an intensity distribution chart (figure 10.3, right), find that the 60PAR/HIR/FL30 lamp produces 2,800 cd at 10° (the direction of the ray).

2. From the table of trigonometric functions (table 10), find that the sine of 10° is 0.174.

$$fc = \frac{2,800}{12^2} \times 0.174 = 3$$

Shortcomings

The inverse-square method yields only a rough idea of what is perceived. Its chief use is for comparison, as when establishing the illuminance ratio between an object and its surround. Even here, the inverse-square method fails to account for any inter-reflections within the space. And more significantly, perceived brightness depends on the reflectance of the surface and the position of the observer.

Average Illuminance Calculations

To ensure that adequate illuminance is provided over a large area, the *lumen method*, or *zonal-cavity calculation*, is used. This calculation is performed by hand or generated by computer; it predicts the *average* illuminance incident on a horizontal work surface, usually the workplane.

For a rough estimate of the average illuminance on a horizontal surface, the abbreviated version of the lumen method described below will suffice. It considers both the interreflections of light from room surfaces and the contributions of several light sources. It corrects for maintained illuminance, accounting for typical depreciation in lamp lumens over the life of the source and for dirt accumulation on the luminaire surfaces.

This shorthand method is not a substitute for more precise illuminance calculations. It is merely a guide to be used as a quick analysis during the design process.

To calculate the average maintained illuminance falling on a horizontal surface,

$$fc = \frac{\text{Number of lamps} \times \text{Initial lamp lumens} \times \text{LLF} \times \text{CU}}{\text{Area}}$$

Number of lamps. For single-lamp luminaires, the number of lamps equals the quantity of luminaires in a given area. If the luminaires contain more than one lamp, multiply the number of luminaires by the number of lamps per luminaire.

Initial lamp lumens. The initial lamp lumens are published by the lamp manufacturers in their large-lamp catalogs.

LLF is an abbreviation for *light loss factor*. As a system ages, a natural depreciation in light output occurs. (With tungsten-halogen lamps, the loss is negligible.) Also, dust and dirt accumulate on room and luminaire surfaces. Other light loss factors such as ambient temperature, actual input voltage, ballast factor, HID lamp position, and lamp burnouts influence the illuminance in a space; for this quick method, only two are considered: LLD and LDD.

- **LLD** is an abbreviation for *lamp lumen depreciation*. This is the amount of light output that is reduced over the life of the lamp because of filament evaporation, tungsten deposits on the bulb wall, and phosphor degradation.

  A list of lamp lumen depreciation for many sources is found in table 11 in the Appendix. When mean lamp lumens (sometimes called "design lumens") are listed in the lamp catalog, this value may be used directly in the formula without the LLD factor.

- **LDD** is an abbreviation for *luminaire dirt depreciation*. This is the reduction of light output over time owing to the accumulation of dust and dirt on the reflecting and transmitting surfaces of the luminaire. This figure is dependent on the cleanliness of the space, the frequency of luminaire cleanings, and the luminaire's tendency to collect dirt (for example, open-top luminaires have a greater ability to collect dirt than closed-top luminaires; some luminaires have a ventilation pattern designed so that the flow of air slows the accumulation of dust). See tables 12 and 13 in the Appendix.

With this method, LLF = LLD × LDD. Typical light loss factors for open light-shielding systems (such as louvers) are 0.85 for very clean spaces, 0.75 for clean spaces, 0.65 for medium spaces, and 0.55 for dirty spaces.

CU stands for coefficient of *utilization*. The CU is an expression of the percentage of light output that is expected from a specific luminaire in a room. It accounts for the efficiency of the luminaire: its ability to deliver light to the work surface compared to the lumens supplied by the lamp(s). This is the amount of light that is not trapped and lost inside the luminaire.

The CU also accounts for the efficiency of the room in redirecting and inter-reflecting the incident light that strikes its surfaces. This is affected by the room's proportions as well as its reflectances. A large, low room is more efficient than a tall, narrow one. In the large, low room, little incident light is interrupted by the walls; almost all of the light is received directly by the workplane. In a high, narrow room, much of the incident light strikes the walls at least once before reaching the workplane, sometimes being reflected between several surfaces before reaching the task.

These variables produce an infinite number of CUs for each luminaire. For practical purposes, they are reduced to a group of figures for typical room proportions and reflectances.

Room Cavity Ratio. The CU is found by checking the manufacturer's coefficient-of-utilization table, which is usually published on the back of product data sheets. In order to use the CU table, it is first necessary to calculate the room cavity ratio.

The room cavity ratio provides an expression of the efficiency of room proportions. To determine this ratio:

$$\text{RCR} = \frac{5(h)(l + w)}{l \times w}$$

where h is the *height* of the ceiling above the task surface, l is the *length* of the room, and w is the *width* of the room. The task surface is usually considered to be 2 ft 6 in AFF (*above finished floor*) (figure 10.9).

A sample coefficient of utilization table for a compact fluorescent, open-reflector downlight is shown in table 14 in the Appendix.

Example

Calculate the average maintained illuminance on the workplane in a 15 ft × 30 ft

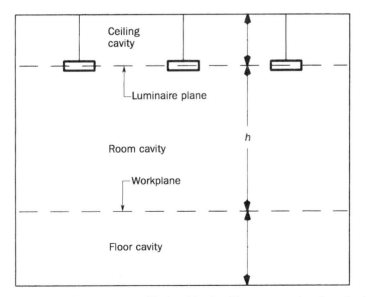

Figure 10.9 The room cavity used in the abbreviated lumen or zonal-cavity method.

office with an 8 ft ceiling and a regular arrangement of eight luminaires; each luminaire uses two 26 W compact fluorescent lamps.

$$fc = \frac{\text{Number of lamps} \times \text{Initial lamp lumens} \times \text{LLF} \times \text{CU}}{\text{Area}}$$

1. The number of lamps (2 lamps per luminaire × 8 luminaires) is 16.

2. From a large-lamp catalog, find that the initial lumens for a 26 W compact fluorescent lamp are 1,800 lm.

3. LLF = LLD × LDD.

   a. LLD: in table 11, under *fluorescent, compact*, find that the lamp lumen depreciation factor is 0.85.

   b. LDD: in table 12, find that a direct downlight with an opaque, unapertured top enclosure and without a bottom enclosure is maintenance category IV. In table 13, a very clean room that will have its luminaires cleaned every six months yields a luminaire dirt depreciation factor of 0.96.

   c. 0.85 × 0.96 = 0.82.

4. To find the coefficient of utilization, first calculate the room cavity ratio:

   a. *h* = ceiling height of 8 ft 0 in minus desk height of 2 ft 6 in = 5 ft 6 in (5.5 ft).

   $$RCR = \frac{5(h)(l + w)}{l \times w}$$
   $$= \frac{(5)(5.5)(15 + 30)}{(15)(30)} = 2.75$$

   b. In table 14, which is supplied by the manufacturer of this compact fluo-

rescent, open-reflector downlight, find that for a room with 80% ceiling reflectance, 50% wall reflectance, 20% floor reflectance, and an RCR of 3, the CU is 0.68.

$$fc = \frac{(16)(1,800)(0.82)(0.68)}{(15)(30)} = 36$$

This office, lighted by eight, two-lamp, 26 W, compact fluorescent, open-reflector downlights, will have an average maintained illuminance of 36 fc on the desk. Although the lumen method does not demonstrate it, in all spaces the illuminance value is higher in the center of the room and drops off near the walls because of the absorption of the perimeter surfaces.

Shortcomings

Whether executed by hand or calculated by computer, the lumen method fails to provide the *range* of light intensity in a room and identify *where* differences in illuminance values occur. It is, therefore, inaccurate for nonuniform and task-ambient lighting systems.

This method is also unable to provide information about lighting quality, visual comfort, and luminance patterns. The lumen method is useful mainly for predicting horizontal illuminance with general lighting systems.

Computer Assistance

The complete zonal-cavity method is found in the ninth edition of the IESNA *Lighting Handbook*, Chapter 9, and is available on disc from several software companies for use with a personal computer.

Computer-generated point calculations yield illuminance at selected points throughout a room. They also provide average, maximum, minimum, and standard deviation of illuminance values; room surface luminances; and lighting power density (watts/ft^2). Output is usually a chart of calculated values, an isofootcandle plot, or a shaded plan with gray scales representing the range of illuminance values. This software can model reflections only from perfectly diffuse surfaces, however, although this is adequate for most lighting calculations.

Computer-generated ray-tracing calculations are the most accurate method of computing illuminance. By tracing each "ray" of light, realistic depictions of illuminance patterns on room surfaces, partitions, furniture, and artwork are displayed, including reflection from specular surfaces and refraction by transparent objects. Output is in the form of renderings or video images. Hardware requirements for this kind of program are greater than for other methods; at a minimum, a personal computer with powerful graphics capabilities is necessary.

The IESNA publishes an annual survey of lighting software in its magazine *Lighting Design + Application*. Products are reviewed for analysis features, applications, outputs, user features, hardware requirements, and costs.

SURFACE REFLECTANCE

Although interior surfaces are not light control devices, their reflectance properties are fundamental to the lighting design. The quantity and direction of light reflected from these surfaces affect both the efficiency of the initial light distribution and our perception of surface brightness.

Wall, ceiling, and floor surfaces are large-area "reflectors" that redistribute light in the room. High-reflectance finishes, such as white and off-white, promote maximum use of the available light; increasingly darker finishes intercept and absorb increasingly greater proportions of the light.

Because a useful amount of light reaches the workplane after reflection from the walls and the ceiling, the efficiency of the lighting system depends in part on the reflectance of room surfaces and finishes. This is particularly true of ambient-diffuse and indirect systems, where a large portion of the light is initially directed toward the ceiling or the walls or both.

In task-oriented spaces such as offices, factories, or cafeterias (where the "task" is seeing the food and the people), the following surface reflectances are recommended for the efficient use of light:

20–50%	floor
50–70%	wall
70–90%	ceiling

The illuminance values in tables 15 and 16 in the Appendix presume that commercial reflectances are:

20%	floor
50%	wall
80%	ceiling

and presume that industrial reflectances are:

20%	floor
50%	wall
50%	ceiling

The recommended reflectances for furniture, machinery, partitions, and work surfaces are the following:

25–45%	furniture and machinery
25–50%	work surfaces

Room surface finish reflectances are obtained from the manufacturers of paints, wall coverings, ceiling tiles, floor coverings, furniture, and machinery. The following *room reflectances* are a guide:

white, off-white, gray, light tints of blue or brown	75–90%
medium green, yellow, brown, or gray	30–60%
dark gray, medium blue	10–20%
dark blue, brown, dark green, and many wood finishes	5–10%

Electricity

Knowledge of the basic principles of electricity is necessary for understanding lighting circuitry, electrical distribution, power consumption, operating costs, switch control, and dimming control.

PRINCIPLES OF ELECTRICITY

Electrically charged particles called *electrons*, which orbit the nucleus of an atom, can be made to flow from one point to another. This is observable in objects charged by friction and in natural phenomena: lightning is a huge spark of electricity.

A flow of electricity is called an *electric current*; the rate of flow of an electric current is measured in *amperes* (*amps*, A). The potential of the flow of electricity is called *voltage*; it is measured in units called *volts* (V).

Water provides a helpful analogy to these concepts. The amount of pressure that moving water exerts inside a pipe is analogous to volts; amperes are similar to the "gallons-per-second" measurement, the rate at which water passes through the pipe. The pipe is the conductor or wire, the wall of the pipe is the insulator, and the faucet is the resistance or dimmer. The larger the pipe, the greater the flow it can carry.

The path through which an electric current flows is called a *circuit*. When no gap exists in the path, it is called a *complete circuit* (figure 11.1). When a gap occurs, it is called a *break in the circuit*.

Resistance impedes the flow of current and is determined by the composition of a material. This results in the production of light or heat or both. A *resistor* is a device placed in the path of an electric current to produce a specific amount of resistance. If electricity flowing along a path is slowed by

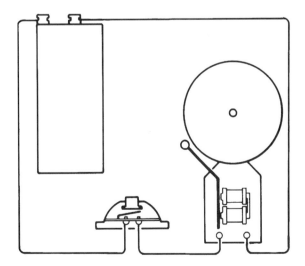

Figure 11.1 Complete circuit.

135

resistance or interrupted by an open switch, there will be little or no current (amps) even though the potential to produce it (volts) is high.

Wiring

Materials that electricity flows easily through are called *conductors*. Materials through which it does not flow easily are called *poor conductors,* or *insulators*. All metals are good conductors: silver is the best conductor, but it is too costly for most wiring purposes; copper is an excellent conductor and is used widely.

Almost all wire is encased within an insulator, which confines the current to its metallic conductor. Wire that is wrapped with a poor conductor, such as rubber or synthetic polymers, is called *insulated wire*. Before connections are made with insulated wire, the wrapping is removed from the ends of the wire.

Insulated circuit wires are sometimes covered by a mechanically protective conduit for installation in buildings. Flexible, nonmetallic sheathed cable ("romex") and flexible, metal sheathed cable ("BX") are often used in single-family homes. Commercial installations use wires inserted in flexible metal conduit ("greenfield"), or in rigid electrical metal tubing ("EMT") for long runs.

Circuits

Direct current (dc) is electric current that always flows in one direction. *Alternating current* (ac) also moves in a single direction; however, that direction is reversed at regular intervals. Alternating current is the prevailing electrical current in use today (figure 11.2).

A *cycle* includes the complete set of values through which the alternating current passes. The unit *Hertz* (Hz) is used to measure the number of times the cycle occurs each second, which is also called the *frequency* of the cycle. Power distribution sys-

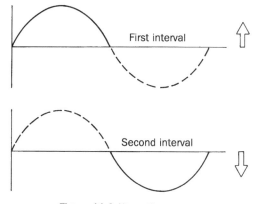

Figure 11.2 Alternating current.

tems operate at 60 Hz in the United States and 50 Hz in most other parts of the world.

Series circuit

If one lamp fails in an inexpensive strand of Christmas tree lights, the remaining lamps in the strand go out. When the tungsten wire in one lamp breaks, it causes a break in the circuit because its filament is part of the conductive path carrying current to other lamps.

Lamps connected in this way are wired in *series*. All lamps in a series circuit must be of the same wattage; if a lamp of different wattage is substituted, the remaining lamps will grow brighter or dimmer due to the substituted lamp's resistance. A series circuit is therefore said to be *load-sensitive* (figure 11.3).

Parallel circuit

If one lamp in figure 11.4 goes off, all of the others remain lighted; the current still flows to the other lamps and the circuit remains complete. These lamps are wired in *parallel*. Since the voltage of the circuit is present across all branches of the circuit, several different *loads* (for example, a 60 W lamp and a 100 W lamp) may be connected to the

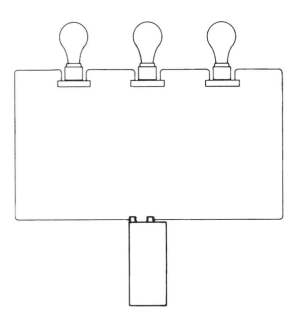

Figure 11.3 Series circuit.

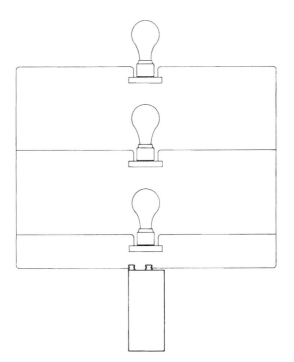

Figure 11.4 Parallel circuit.

same circuit. Parallel circuits are therefore not load-sensitive.

A current will always follow the easiest path that is available. If the wires of a circuit are uninsulated and touch each other, the current will pass from one to the other because this is a shorter and easier path than the one intended: there will be a *short circuit*.

In the drawing on the left in figure 11.5, the current will take a shortcut back to the cell without going through the push button; the bell will ring continuously whether the switch is open or closed. In the drawing on the right, the bell will not ring at all; the current will take a shortcut back to the cell without going through the bell.

A short circuit allows a stronger-than-usual flow of electricity through the wires; this excessive current causes the wires to overheat. A *fuse* or *circuit breaker* is a safety device that opens the circuit before the wire becomes a fire hazard. Because the fuse is part of the circuit, it also overheats and a metal strip in the fuse melts and breaks the circuit. If the protective device is a circuit breaker, the excess current of the short circuit causes the breaker to flip open, interrupting the path of the current.

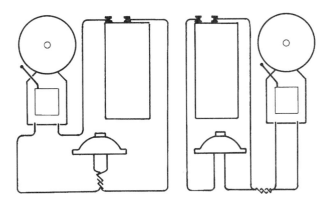

Figure 11.5 Two short circuits. The wire in these circuits is bare wire. Where the wires are twisted together, the current would flow from one to the other.

Electrical Distribution

Electric current generated and delivered by an electric utility enters a building through a *service panel*. In the United States, three kinds of systems are common:

1. 120/240 V, single-phase, three-wire.

2. 120/208 V, three-phase, four-wire.

3. 277/480 V, three-phase, four-wire.

The 120/240 V, single-phase, three-wire system is commonly used in single-family homes and small commercial buildings. Wire conductors leading from the entrance panel distribute the power throughout the building. Because the wire has resistance, the longer the distance that power is carried, the greater the voltage *losses*, causing lights to dim and appliances to operate sluggishly. This is corrected by using larger-diameter wires, which have less resistance.

Distributing current at higher voltages reduces losses occurring because of the wire's resistance. Therefore, in large commercial buildings, 120/208 V, three-phase, four-wire and 277/480 V, three-phase, four-wire systems are used to reduce resistance losses.

In commercial buildings, running each circuit from the entrance panel will create a substantial voltage loss or require the use of large-diameter, expensive wires. To avoid voltage loss, *feeder circuits* conduct power from the entrance panel to secondary distribution panels, called *panel boards*, located throughout the building. The wires that distribute power locally between the panel board and the luminaires or receptacles are called *branch circuits*.

Power Consumption

A *watt* (W) indicates the rate at which electricity is changed into another form of power—light or heat. Power consumption in watts is calculated by multiplying volts times amps ($W = V \times A$).

Theoretically, a 20-amp circuit operating at 120 V will handle a possible maximum load of 2,400 W (that is, $20 \times 120 = 2,400$). In practice, the National Electrical Code limits the possible load of a branch circuit to 80 percent of the branch circuit ampere rating: a 15 A, 120 V circuit to 1,440 W; a 20 A, 120 V circuit to 1,920 W; a 20 A, 277 V circuit to 4,432 W.

Energy is the amount of electric power consumed over a period of time; it is measured in *kilowatt-hours* (kWh). One kilowatt (kW) = 1,000 W. Hence, kWh = kW × hours used. For example, a 150 W lamp is equivalent to 0.15 kW. When operated for 40 hours it uses 6 kWh (0.15kW × 40 hrs = 6 kWh). Utility rates are based on monthly kWh usage.

In estimating the connected load for discharge and low-voltage incandescent sources, the power consumed by the ballast or transformer must be included.

To obtain lighting *watts per square foot* for an installation, divide the total luminaire watts by the area of the space in square feet.

Life Cycle Costs

The cost of lamps and luminaires plus their installation is a minor part of the total cost over the life of a lighting system. The cost of electricity (*operating costs*) is the single largest cost in lighting. Except in homes, maintenance (*labor costs*) to replace lamps and clean luminaires is the second greatest expenditure. Lighting systems, therefore, must be evaluated in terms of *life cycle costs*.

A typical *cost analysis* will include initial lamp and luminaire costs; installation costs; electricity costs based on burning hours per year; labor costs, including those incurred because of dirt conditions; and interest costs on the original capital investment.

When comparing the life cycle costs of one system with those of another, the greater initial cost of an energy-effective system will almost always be recouped after a period of time because of the saving in energy costs. This *payback period* varies with different systems.

In comparing dissimilar systems, it is impossible to place a dollar value on the quality of light. A direct system, for example, is usually less costly than an indirect one that produces the same quantity of light on a horizontal workplane, but the *quality* of light is vastly different.

Cost comparisons are made on equal illuminance values of equivalent quality. If there is a difference in the connected load, the additional air-conditioning required to handle the larger load must also be counted.

SWITCH CONTROL

An electric current is the flow of electrons between two points along a path. If the path is interrupted, the current cannot flow. A switch *breaks* the flow of electricity in a circuit when it is open ("off") and it allows unimpeded flow when closed ("on").

Manual Switches

The manually operated *toggle switch* makes contact by snapping one metal piece against another. *Mercury switches* contain a vial of mercury; contact is made between two electrodes when the vial is tripped to the "on" position. These switches operate silently. The toggle designates "on" in the up position and "off" in the down position. A *rocker switch* and a *push-button switch* operate in the same manner (figure 11.6).

A *single-pole, single-throw* switch is connected at any point between the luminaire and the power supply. It opens only one side of the circuit and is therefore called a "single-pole"; it moves only between an open and a closed position and is therefore called a "single-throw." This is the switch most frequently used to control electric luminaires and wall receptacles.

A *single-pole, double-throw* switch directs the current in either of two directions. It is used to alternately turn on two different luminaires with a single switch action, such as a safelight and the general light in a darkroom. The up position will designate "on" for one luminaire, the down position "on" for the

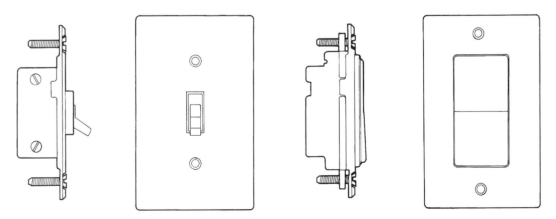

Figure 11.6 Toggle switch and rocker switch.

other; an optional center position will turn both "off."

A *double-pole, single-throw* switch is able to direct the current to two paths at once. It is used to control two devices simultaneously, such as a luminaire and an exhaust fan; it functions as if two separate toggle switches were operated by the same handle.

A *three-way* switch controls an electrical load from two locations. This allows the circuit to use one of two alternate paths to complete itself. (Several explanations exist for why a switch that provides control from *two* locations is called "three-way." Although these explanations are hypothetical and flawed, the term is still customary.)

A *four-way* switch controls a circuit from three locations, a *five-way* switch controls a circuit from four locations, and so forth. For control from many different locations, a low-voltage switching system is used.

Timers

A *timer* automatically turns on electric lighting when it is needed and turns it off when it is not needed. Timers range in complexity from simple integral (spring-wound) timers to microprocessors that can program a sequence of events for years at a time. With a simple integral timer, the load is switched on and held energized for a preset period of time, usually within a range between a few minutes and twelve hours.

An *electromechanical time clock* is driven by an electric motor, with contacts actuated by mechanical stops or arms affixed to the clock face. *Electronic time clocks* provide programmable selection of many switching operations and typically provide control over a seven-day period. Electromechanical and electronic time clocks have periods from twenty-four hours to seven days and often include astronomical correction to compensate for seasonal changes.

Occupancy Sensors

Occupancy sensors (also called *motion sensors*) automatically switch luminaires on and off to reduce energy use. They operate in response to the presence or absence of occupants in a space. Electrical consumption is reduced by limiting the number of hours that luminaires remain in use.

Occupancy is sensed by one of four methods: audio, ultrasonic, passive infrared, or optical. Occupancy sensors can be mounted in several ways: they can be recessed or surface-mounted on ceilings, corners, or walls; they can replace wall switches; and they can plug into receptacles. The floor area covered by individual sensors can range from 150 sq ft in individual rooms, offices, or workstations to 2,000 sq ft in large spaces. Larger areas are controlled by adding more sensors.

Occupancy sensors can be used in combination with manual switches, timers, daylight sensors, dimmers, and central lighting control systems. Careful product selection and proper sensor location are critical to avoid the annoying inconvenience of false responses to movement by inanimate objects inside the room or people outside the entrance to the room.

Photosensors

Photosensors (also called *daylight sensors*) use electronic components that transform visible radiation from daylight into an electrical signal, which is then used to control electric lighting. The photosensor comprises different elements that form a complete system. The word "photocell" (short for "photoelectric cell") refers only to the light-sensitive component inside the photosensor. The term "photosensor" is used to describe the entire product, including the housing, optics, electronics, and photocell.

The photosensor output is a control signal that is sent to a device that controls the quantity of electric light. The control signal can activate two modes of operation: (1) a simple on-off switch or relay, or (2) a variable-output signal sent to a controller that continuously adjusts the output of the electric lighting.

Different photosensors are manufactured for indoor or outdoor use. In the northern hemisphere, photosensors used in outdoor applications are usually oriented to the north. This orientation ensures more constant illumination on the sensor because it avoids the direct sunlight contribution.

Wireless Remote Control

Radio-controlled systems

Some systems allow wireless remote control and can interface to audiovisual and other systems in both commercial and residential applications. *Radio-controlled* systems eliminate the need for wiring between the sensor, processor, and controller. Radio transmitters communicate with controllers via *radio frequency* (RF) signals. Controllers, in turn, regulate and adjust electric lighting. These systems can employ multiple transmitters for multiple-location control and multiple controllers for multiple areas.

Radio frequencies from many sources can interfere with proper operation of this equipment, however. These systems are also relatively expensive, but they are useful where the controlled luminaires are difficult to access. They are also suited to retrofit applications where control wiring would be difficult or expensive to install.

Infrared preset controls

Infrared preset controls allow you to create and recall settings for electric lighting the same way you set and recall AM and FM stations on a stereo tuner/receiver. The hand-held remote control sends an infrared (IR) signal to wall-mounted switches and dimmers that have a receiving IR window. An unlimited number of dimmers may be connected in the same room.

Typically, infrared preset controls have an IR range of up to 50 ft along the line of sight. They use standard wiring and can be retrofitted to replace switches or dimmers, using the existing wires for installation. Good-quality infrared controls will minimize chances of interference from radio, audio, and video equipment.

DIMMING CONTROL

A *dimmer* provides variation in the intensity of an electric light source. *Full-range dimming* is the continuous variation of lighting intensity from maximum to zero without visible steps.

All dimming systems operate on one of two principles for restricting the flow of electricity to the light source: (1) varying the voltage or (2) varying the length of time that the current flows during each alternating current cycle.

Resistance Dimmers

Historically, *resistance* dimmers were the first dimming method; they were used mainly in theatres in the early part of the twentieth century. A resistance dimmer, or "rheostat," controls voltage by introducing into the circuit a variable length of high-resistance wire. The longer the length of the wire, the greater the resistance, the lower the voltage, and the lower the intensity of the lamp.

In order to absorb a sufficient amount of energy, the resistance wire must be quite long; for this reason it is often coiled. Current flows into one end of the coil and an arm slides along the resistance wire in increments. Dimming is thus achieved in a series of steps, often a minimum of 110 to appear "flicker-less."

A large drawback to this kind of dimmer is that the portion of the current that would otherwise produce light is instead converted to heat. Also, no savings in energy is realized: although light output is reduced, connected wattage remains unchanged. In addition, these dimmers are bulky; consequently, they are no longer used.

Autotransformer Dimmers

Autotransformer dimmers avoid these problems by using an improved method of dimming. Instead of converting the unused portion of the current into heat, the autotransformer *changes* the standard-voltage current into low-voltage current, with only a 5 percent power loss.

A transformer has two coils of wire; the ratio of the number of turns in one coil to the other produces the ratio of the voltage change induced by the transformer. An autotransformer is simply a variable transformer: the primary coil remains fixed, while the number of turns in the secondary coil is varied by a rotating arm that controls successive turns of the coil. Because electrical power can be drawn from different points along the secondary coil, different voltages are achieved from the same transformer.

Because autotransformers do not convert energy to heat as light intensity is reduced, they are therefore cooler and more compact than resistance dimmers. Autotransformer dimmers are widely available in sizes up to many thousands of watts.

Solid-State Dimmers

Solid-state dimmers are predominant today; they use the second of the two methods of limiting current flow. A power control device—such as a silicon-controlled switch (SCS) under 6 kW, or a silicon-controlled rectifier (SCR) over 6 kW—allows electric current to flow at full voltage, but only for a portion of the time. This causes the lamp to dim just as if less voltage were being delivered (figure 11.7).

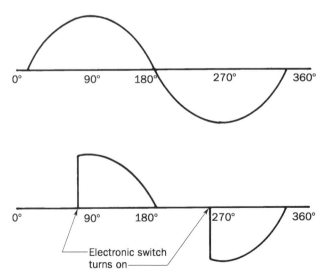

Figure 11.7 Solid state dimming control.

Square Law Dimming Curve

The manner in which light output responds to changes in the control setting is called the *dimming curve*. If a change in the setting of the dimming control, from full bright to full dim, approximates the change in the amount of electricity allowed to reach the light source, the dimmer is said to have a linear curve.

The eye is more sensitive to changes in low intensities of light than to changes in high intensities. This relationship between light perceived and light measured is called the "square law" curve (figure 11.8).

Electric lamps also respond in a nonlinear way: at 81 percent of the voltage, the light output is 50 percent. If the electrical output of a dimmer changes in a linear manner, then a light source will appear to dim faster at low intensities and slower at high intensities.

To correct this, good-quality dimmers feature a "square law" dimming curve. Here the dimmer control moves at constant speed, but causes the light to dim faster at high intensities and slower at low intensities. To the eye, the result is a consistent rate of change in the light intensity.

Incandescent Lamps

Dimming incandescent sources increases the life of the lamp. Yet both incandescent

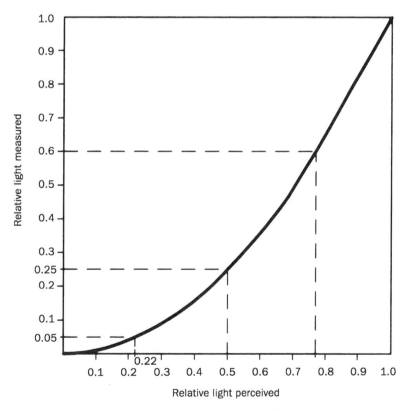

Figure 11.8 "Square law" curve: the relationship between perceived illuminance and measured illuminance.

and tungsten-halogen lamps undergo considerable shifts toward the orange-red end of the spectrum when they are dimmed. Although this increases the warm appearance of the lamps at lower light intensities, it is a positive result because people prefer warmer colors of light at lower intensities (figure 11.9).

The efficiency of an incandescent lamp is reduced when the source is operated at less than its designed voltage because the temperature of the filament is reduced. Even though the lamps are less efficient at producing light, much energy is still being saved (figure 11.10).

In some applications, normal operation of dimmers causes lamp filaments to "buzz." Lower-wattage lamps, physically smaller

lamps, rough service (RS) lamps, low-noise stage lamps, and lamp debuzzing coils help to decrease this noise.

The lamp *debuzzing coil* is a separate component. It, too, will hum during operation, so it is remotely located in an area where this noise will be acceptable (for example, a closet or adjacent room).

Low-voltage lamps

Dimmers for incandescent low-voltage luminaires are installed on the 120 V side of the low-voltage transformer. Two kinds of transformers are manufactured for low-voltage lighting: magnetic (core-and-coil) and electronic (solid-state).

Before selecting a dimmer control, it is necessary to determine which kind of trans-

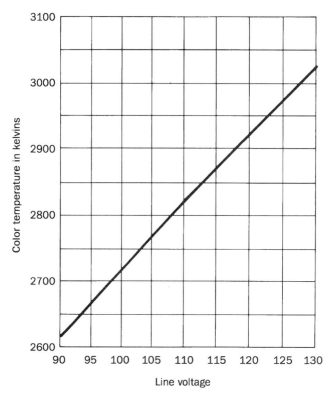

Figure 11.9 Dimming incandescent and tungsten-halogen lamps moves light toward the warmer end of the color spectrum.

former is connected to the luminaire. Each kind of transformer requires a compatible dimmer.

Magnetic-transformer low-voltage dimmers are used for dimming luminaires equipped with magnetic transformers. These dimmers protect the lighting system from the dc voltages and current surges to which magnetic transformers are sensitive. Magnetic low-voltage dimmers are specially designed to prevent dc voltage from being applied to the transformer and to withstand voltage "spikes" and current "surges."

Equipment supplied with electronic transformers requires the use of *electronic-transformer* low-voltage dimmers. Electronic low-voltage dimmers are designed specifically for electronic transformers. They eliminate the problems that occur in the interaction between the transformer and the dimmer when a magnetic low-voltage dimmer is used with electronic transformers: dimmer buzz, transformer buzz, lamp flickering, and radio frequency interference.

Electronic low-voltage dimmers combined with electronic transformers have the virtue of silent operation, although these dimmers have a smaller capacity (up to 150 W) than magnetic low-voltage ones (up to 10,000 W).

Fluorescent Lamps

Dimming fluorescent lamps requires the use of special dimming ballasts, which replace the standard ballast and must be compatible with the dimming control device. Only rapid-

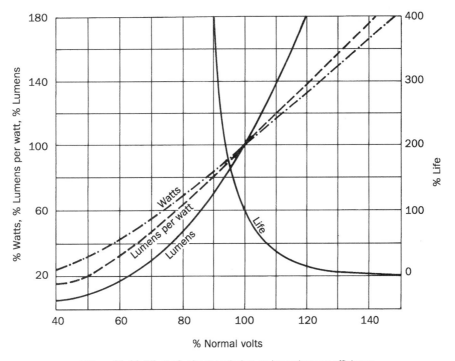

Figure 11.10 Effect of voltage variation on incandescent efficiency.

start fluorescent lamps can be dimmed because voltage is supplied continuously to the cathodes. When dimmed, the special ballast maintains the cathode voltage so that the cathodes remain heated to ensure proper lamp operation. Because instant-start and preheat lamp electrodes are turned off after the lamps are started, they cannot be dimmed.

Fluorescent lamps cannot be dimmed all the way to "off." If they are allowed to dim too far, a flicker or spiraling light pattern becomes visible inside the tube.

Many systems dim only 3- and 4-ft lamps. For optimal performance, different kinds of lamps (T4, T5, T8, or T12) are not mixed on the same circuit. It is also advisable for all lamps that are controlled by a single dimmer to be of the same length; different lengths dim at different rates.

Dimming fluorescent lamps that operate either in a cold atmosphere or in an air-handling luminaire sometimes results in variations in light output and color, which are caused by the changes in bulb wall temperature. The color shift is slight; dimmed lamps usually appear cooler in color.

Fluorescent lamp life is reduced by dimming systems. Considering that a fluorescent lamp consumes up to one hundred times its cost in energy, a slight loss in lamp life is offset greatly by the savings achieved through dimming.

HID Lamps

It is technically possible to dim high-intensity discharge lamps over a wide range of light output, but HID dimming ballasts are uncommon: the long warm-up, restrike delay, and color shift associated with HID lamps limit their applications. *Multilevel* ballasts are more frequently used, allowing the light output to be changed in steps.

A discernible color shift occurs with dimmed HID lamps. In mercury lamps, however, this slight change will be negligible; the color is already inadequate. Clear metal halide lamps shift rapidly toward a blue-green color similar to that of a mercury lamp. Phosphor-coated metal halide lamps exhibit the same trend, but less distinctly. HPS lamps slowly shift toward the yellow-orange color that is characteristic of LPS lamps.

HID lamps have a shorter life as a result of dimming. As with fluorescent lamps, the shorter life is offset by energy savings achieved through dimming.

CENTRAL LIGHTING CONTROL SYSTEMS

Local, single-room systems typically consist of one *control station* with switches or manual sliders that control large amounts of power. The dimmable wattage is limited only by the capacity of the system. These local systems are easily expanded to multiple rooms and customized to offer many combinations of manual, preset, assigned, and time-clock control. They can incorporate energy-reduction controls such as occupancy sensors and photosensors, and can handle emergency power functions.

Whole-building systems use local or small modular dimmers, a central computer, and master control stations to control all of the luminaires in a home or commercial building. Many of these systems also operate other electrical systems, such as motorized shades, fans, air-conditioning, heating, and audio systems, and they interface easily with burglar alarms, "smart" building systems, and other electrical control systems.

In centralized systems, a microprocessor assimilates the data, determines the required change, and initiates action to complete the change. More sophisticated processors can respond to a number of complex lighting conditions in the space, collect power and energy-use data, and supply summary reports for building management and tenant billing. Processors range in complexity from a microchip in a controller to a large computer.

Three kinds of processors are used: local, central, and distributed. With the local kind, the processor is located in or adjacent to the device it controls; sensor inputs go to a signal conditioner and are then fed to the processor. The central processor receives all inputs, analyzes the data, and then sends instructions to controllers located throughout a facility, allowing coördinated control of all system elements. In distributed processing, the ongoing decision making is left to local processors, but a central processor orchestrates the entire system, with the advantage that the entire system does not fail if any one processor does, and only the local processor has to be reprogrammed to accommodate changes.

Low-Voltage Control Systems

Low-voltage switching and dimming control is achieved with low-voltage wires that operate a relay installed in the luminaire wiring circuit. The relay is either mounted near the luminaire or installed in a remote location. Since the low-voltage wires are small and consume little electric power, it is possible to use many of them; they can be placed where needed without being enclosed in metal conduit, except where required by local codes.

With low-voltage switching systems, the branch circuit wiring goes directly to the luminaires; this eliminates costly runs of conduit to wall switch locations. Where switching occurs from three or more locations, the savings are considerable. Many switches can control a single luminaire, or one switch (a "master") can control many circuits of luminaires.

Power Line Carrier Systems

Power line carrier systems (also called *carrier current* systems) are low-cost, simple-to-install control systems that operate by sending a signal through the building wiring ("power line"). The switch functions as a transmitter that generates the signal. A receiver located at the luminaire or electric appliance turns a circuit on or off when it senses the appropriate signal.

As long as the transmitter and the receiver are connected to the same electric service in the building, no control wiring is required. Any number of luminaires can be attached to one receiver or to any number of receivers; any number of transmitters can control any one receiver. Great flexibility is inherent in this kind of system.

Power line carrier systems are subject to malfunction, however. Automatic garage door openers and communication systems in airplanes flying overhead may operate on the same frequency as the power line carrier system, causing luminaires and appliances to turn on and off when unintended.

Existing wiring systems in older buildings can significantly reduce the effective range of communication between the sensor, processor, and controller. Additionally, the overall capacity and speed of this kind of system is limited.

Energy Management Controls

In offices of the past, lighting controls were used to provide lighting flexibility. Today, their major application is energy management. Simple controls, such as photocells, time clocks, and occupancy sensors will automatically turn lights on when needed and off when unnecessary. For larger facilities, *energy management control* systems are designed to integrate the lighting with other building energy systems such as those used for heating and cooling.

The key to proper application of these controls is not only the selection of the proper control device, but also the careful planning of where and when the control is needed. Two basic control strategies are available: (1) control in space by electrically positioning (switching) the light *where* it is needed and (2) control in time or supplying lighting *when* it is needed.

Daylighting controls have photosensors that automatically adjust the electric lighting to preset values. When daylight is available and suitable (reaching task areas without causing glare, for example), luminaires are dimmed or turned off.

Lumen-maintenance controls compensate for the natural deterioration of the lighting system and the room surfaces over time. They automatically increase the power to the system so that the light output is kept at a constant value.

It is advisable to use control systems for daylighting, worker area individualization, and window energy management. Individual controls in office spaces go a long way toward conserving energy and, equally important, toward giving occupants a sense of control over their immediate environment.

Luminaires

12

Almost all lamps require a method to curtail glare; in addition, many need a method to modify distribution.

A *luminaire* provides physical support, electrical connection, and light control for an electric lamp. Ideally, the luminaire directs light to where it is needed while shielding the lamp from the eyes at normal angles of view.

Luminaires are composed of several parts that provide these different functions: the housing, the light-controlling element, and the glare-controlling element. Depending on the design requirements and optical control desired, some of these functions may be combined.

HOUSINGS

The electrical connection and physical support for the light source are provided by the luminaire *housing*. Often its electrical auxiliary equipment, when required, is also incorporated. Housings are divided into five categories based on how they are supported: recessed, semi-recessed, surface-mounted, pendant-mounted, and track-mounted.

Recessed housings are mounted above the finished ceiling, are entirely hidden from view, and have an *aperture* (opening) at the ceiling plane to allow light to pass through. Some recessed housings are designed to be mounted into the wall, the floor, or the ground.

The electrical connection between the building wiring and the luminaire is made at the *junction box*, which is often attached to the housing (figure 12.1). UL standards require that the connection ("splices") of luminaire wires to branch circuit wires be accessible for field inspection after the lighting fixture is installed. This access is usually accomplished through the aperture of the luminaire.

Semi-recessed housings are mounted partially above the ceiling with the remainder visible from below (figure 12.2). Sometimes the semi-recessed housing is mounted partially in the wall with the remainder projecting, and in rare cases it is mounted partially below the floor with the remainder visible from above.

Surface-mounted housings are mounted to the surface of a ceiling, a wall, or, in rare cases, a floor. If the ceiling or wall construction permits, the junction box is recessed into the mounting surface, giving a cleaner appearance (figure 12.3); otherwise, the junction box is mounted against the surface of the ceiling or wall (figure 12.4).

In both cases, the housing serves to partially or entirely conceal the junction box.

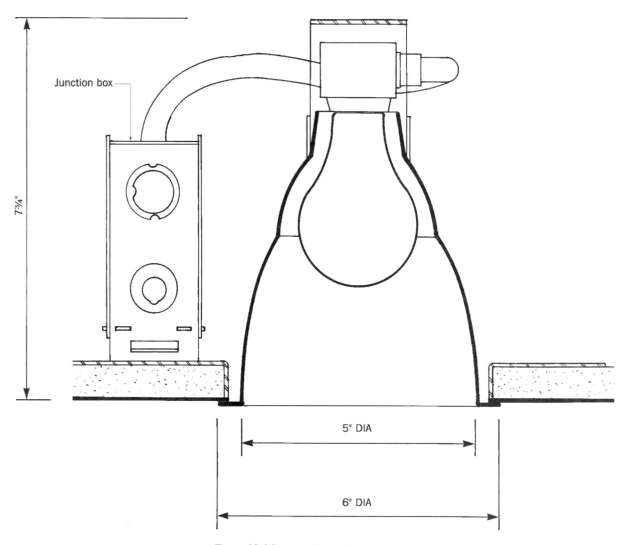

Junction box

7³/₄"

5" DIA

6" DIA

Figure 12.1 Recessed incandescent downlight with junction box.

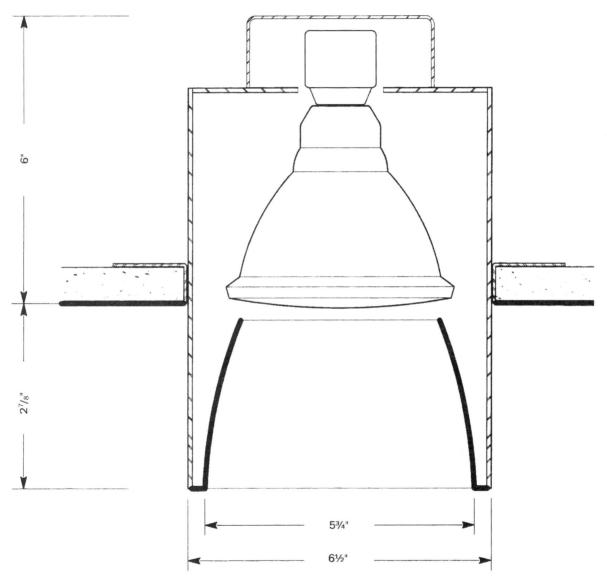

Figure 12.2 Semi-recessed incandescent downlight with junction box.

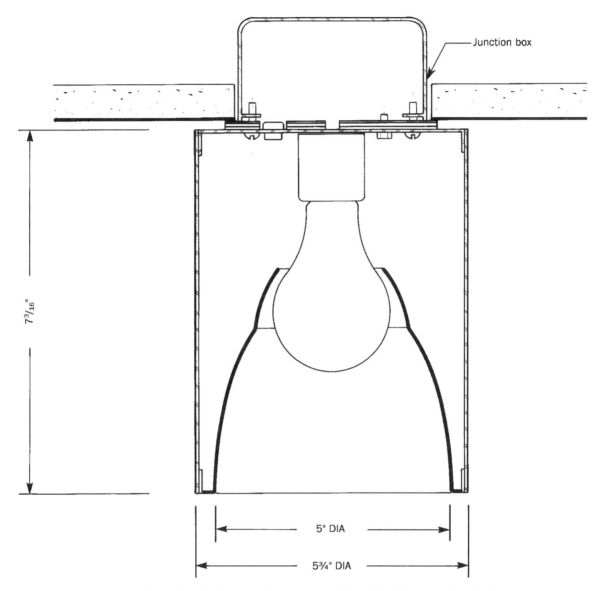

Figure 12.3 Surface-mounted incandescent downlight with recessed junction box.

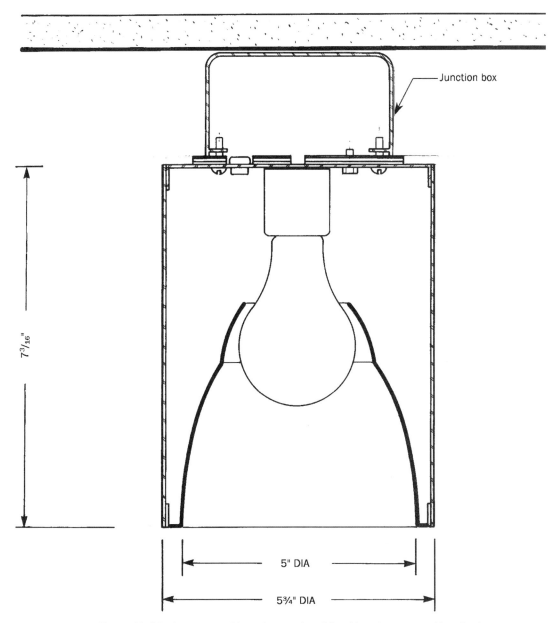

Junction box

7³/₁₆"

5" DIA

5¾" DIA

Figure 12.4 Surface-mounted incandescent downlight with surface-mounted junction box.

Because the housing of a surface-mounted luminaire is visible, it becomes a design element in the space.

Pendant-mounted housings also make use of a recessed or surface-mounted junction box located at the ceiling for electrical supply connection, but the luminaire is separated from the ceiling surface by a pendant such as a stem, chain, or cord. The junction box is concealed by a *canopy* (figure 12.5).

Pendant-mounted luminaires are used to provide uplight on the ceiling plane or to bring the light source closer to the task or activity in the space. At other times pendant-mounted luminaires are selected for decorative impact, as with a chandelier.

In high-ceiling spaces, bringing the light source down closer to the floor is often unnecessary. Instead of suspending the lighting element down into the space, where it becomes visually dominant, a more concentrated source at the ceiling plane is less conspicuous.

With *track-mounted* luminaires, a recessed, surface-mounted, or pendant-mounted lighting track provides both physical support and electrical connection through an adapter on the luminaire.

The main advantage of track is its flexibility. Track is often used where surfaces and objects to be lighted will be frequently or occasionally changed, or added or deleted, as in a museum or gallery. It also serves as an inexpensive way to bring electrical power to where it is needed in renovation and remodeling projects.

LIGHT AND GLARE CONTROL

Luminaires can be divided into five categories that describe their lighting function: downlights, wash lights, object lights, task lights, and multidirectional lights.

Downlights

Downlights, also called direct luminaires, produce a downward light distribution that is usually symmetrical. They are used in multiples to provide ambient light in a large space or for providing focal glow on a horizontal surface such as the floor or workplane (figure 12.6).

Point source downlights

A nondirectional, concentrated light source is often mounted in a reflector to control its distribution and brightness because the source would otherwise emit light in all directions. In an *open-reflector downlight*, a reflector made from spun or hydroformed aluminum accomplishes both purposes. A-lamp downlights allow for efficient use of inexpensive and readily available A-lamps (figure 12.7).

Tungsten-halogen (figure 12.8), compact fluorescent (figure 12.9), and HID open-reflector downlights (figure 12.10) operate under the same principle as the A-lamp downlight. Fluorescent and HID apertures are larger because the source is larger. For a given source, the larger the aperture, the greater is the efficiency of the luminaire.

Economy versions of the open-reflector downlight, often called "high hats" or "cans," use an imprecise reflector to direct light downward and either a black multigroove baffle or a white splay ring for brightness control. These luminaires usually provide too much glare for visual comfort and are inefficient at directing light down to horizontal surfaces. Although they are less expensive initially, they provide only short-term value: more watts are used to achieve an equivalent quantity of light.

Ellipsoidal downlights were early attempts at controlling the luminance of the source and providing a wide, soft distribution. They sometimes used silver-bowl lamps and were excellent at reducing the brightness of the aperture; they were, however, inefficient at directing light downward. These luminaires were large because the elliptical

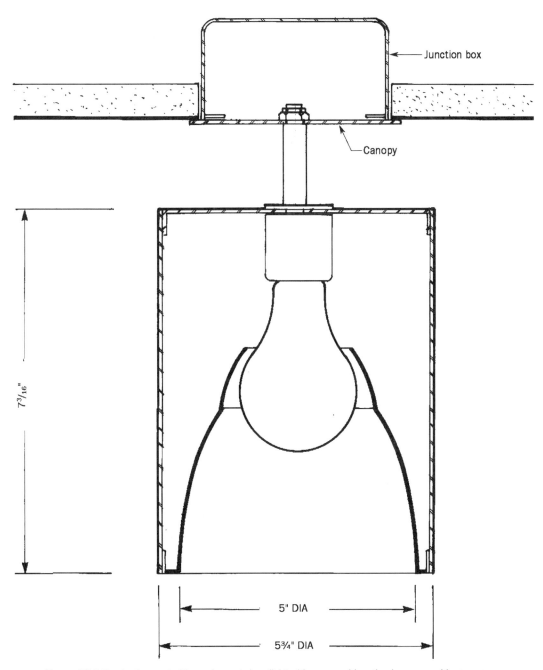

Figure 12.5 Pendant-mounted incandescent downlight with recessed junction box covered by a canopy.

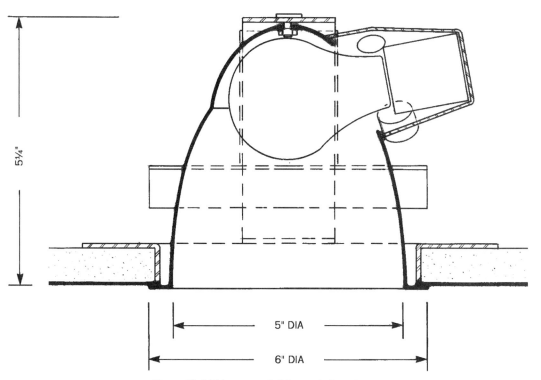

Figure 12.6 Side-mounted, A-lamp, shallow-depth downlight.

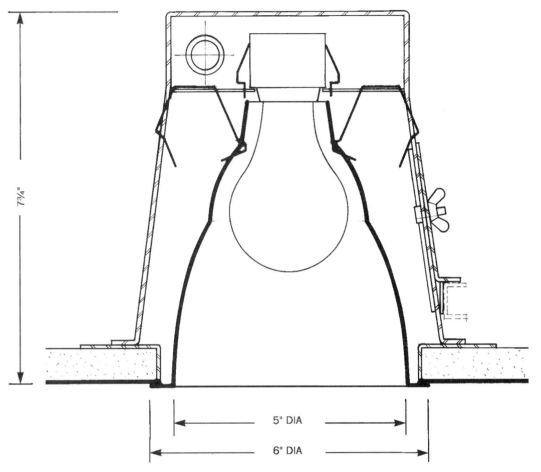

7³/₄"

5" DIA

6" DIA

Figure 12.7 Incandescent, parabolic, open-reflector downlight with 5-in aperture.

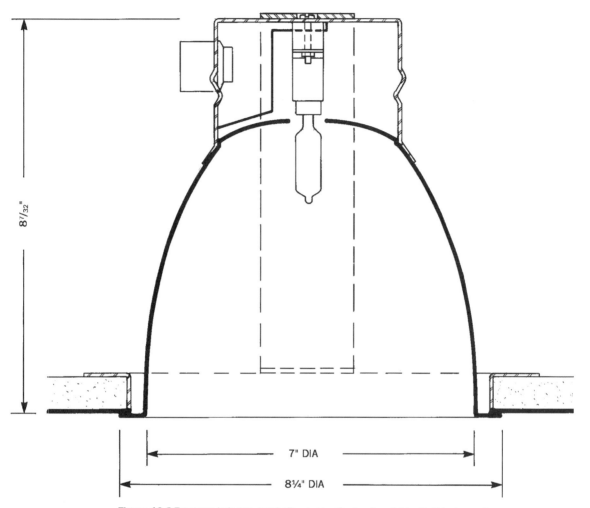

Figure 12.8 Tungsten-halogen, parabolic, open-reflector downlight with 7-inch aperture.

reflector is larger than the parabolic contour; they are used infrequently today (figure 12.11).

Shallow-contour, silver-bowl, open-reflector downlights are used for a general diffusion of light combined with sparkle at the ceiling plane, which is provided by the luminaire's "pebbled"-surface aluminum reflector. The reflecting bowl of the lamp throws light up into the luminaire reflector, which in turn redirects the light in a controlled downward beam (figure 12.12). The silver-bowl lamp provides built-in glare control.

Directional-source downlights do not require a light-controlling element because the AR, MR, PAR, or R lamp provides that

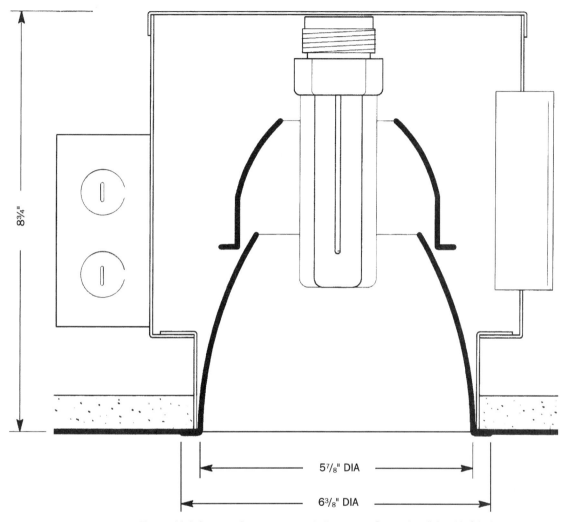

Figure 12.9 Compact fluorescent, parabolic, open-reflector downlight with 6-inch aperture.

function. Luminaires for these sources require only a brightness-controlling element; the most efficient is the open parabolic reflector. These luminaires are relatively easy to maintain: very little dirt collects on the underside of the lamp, and every time the lamp is changed, the entire optical system is replaced (figure 12.13).

R14 or R20 downlights are sometimes used with spot lamps when a narrow beam of light is desired from a small aperture (figure 12.14), but PAR16 and PAR20 lamps are more efficient. R30 and R40 downlights are infrequently used; the wide spread of the R flood lamp is available from an A-lamp downlight, which is more efficient

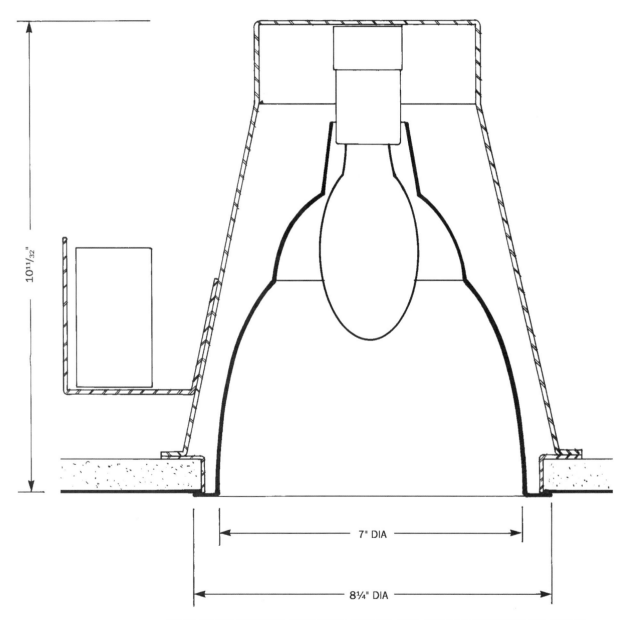

10¹¹/₃₂"

7" DIA

8¼" DIA

Figure 12.10 Low-wattage, metal halide, parabolic, open-reflector downlight with 7-in aperture.

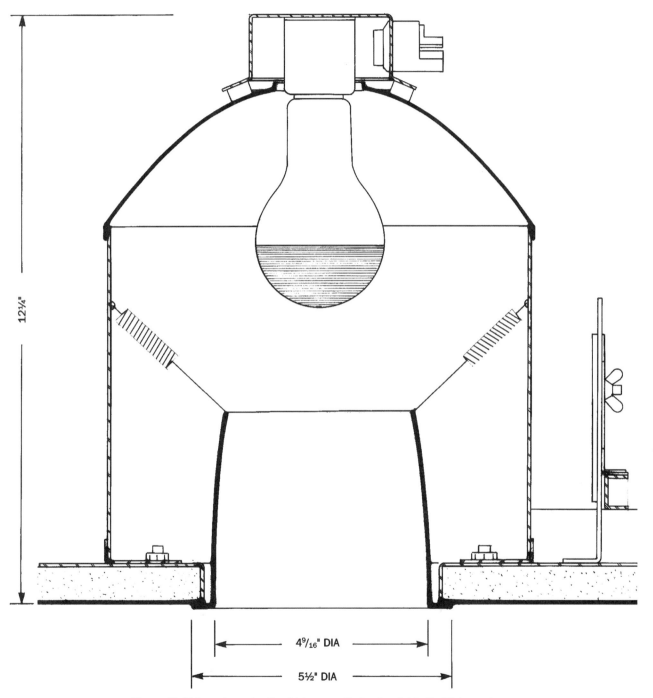

Figure 12.11 Incandescent, ellipsoidal, open-reflector downlight with 4½-in aperture.

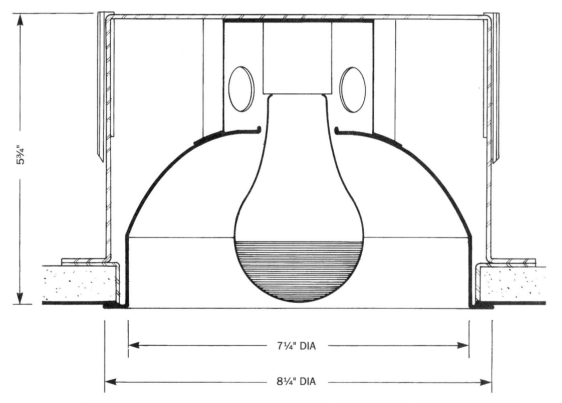

5³⁄₄"

7¼" DIA

8¼" DIA

Figure 12.12 Incandescent, shallow-contour, silver-bowl, open-reflector downlight with 7¼-in aperture.

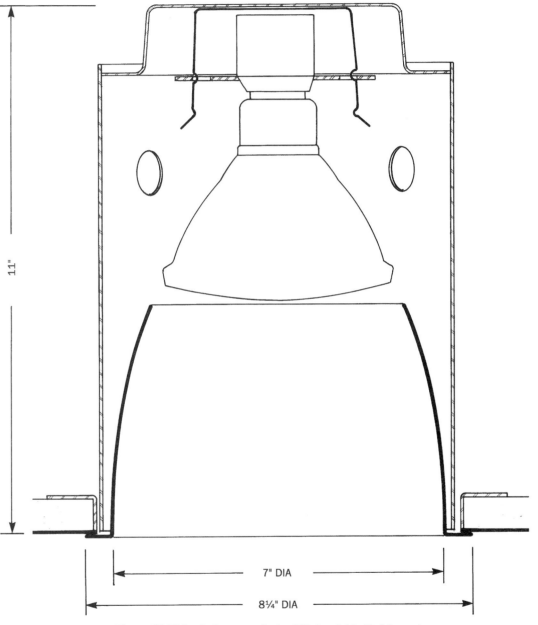

11"

7" DIA

8¼" DIA

Figure 12.13 Parabolic, open-reflector PAR downlight with 7-in aperture.

and uses a source that costs approximately one-fifth as much (figure 12.15).

When a more concentrated beam is desired, PAR lamps are more efficient, delivering more light at a given wattage for the same cost. PAR lamp downlights are used for greater emphasis on the horizontal plane than is usually produced by other downlights (figure 12.13). This greater intensity of light is called "punch."

Almost all open-reflector downlights have round apertures. Reflectors are available with either an overlap flange or a flush ceiling detail. The overlap flange is used in gypsum board and acoustical tile ceilings to conceal the uneven edge at the ceiling opening. Flush details are used in plaster ceilings to create a neat, finished appearance; the ceiling is plastered directly to the edge of a plaster ring or frame (figure 12.16).

Reflectors. Specular aluminum reflectors produce the most efficient beam control. Semi-specular reflectors are slightly less efficient, but they eliminate irregularities in the lamp beam or reflected images of the fila-

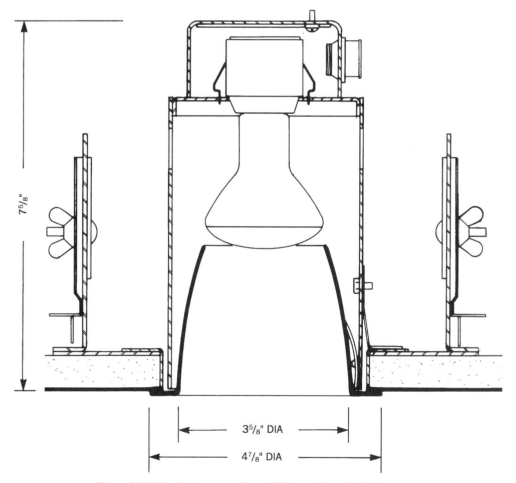

Figure 12.14 Parabolic, open-reflector R20 downlight with 3½-in aperture.

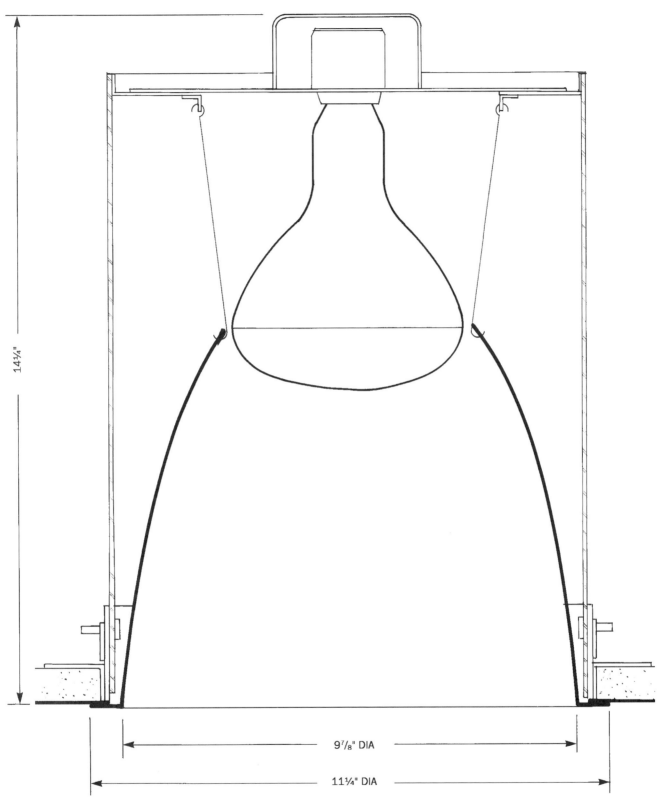

14¼"

9⅞" DIA

11¼" DIA

Figure 12.15 Parabolic, open-reflector R40 downlight with 10-in aperture.

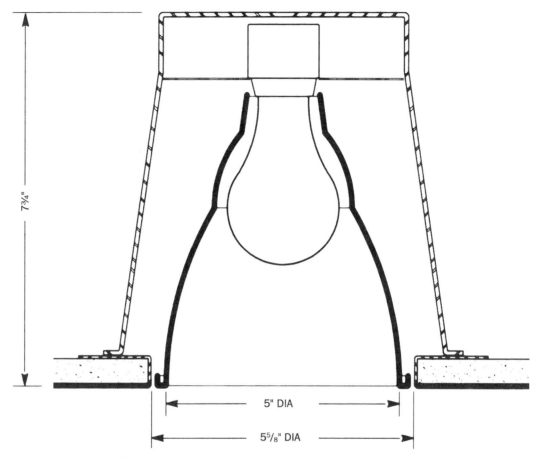

Figure 12.16 Parabolic, open-reflector downlight with flush-flange reflector.

ment coil or lamp phosphors. Although this slight diffusion of the reflector surface yields a reflector of greater luminance than a specular one, the semi-specular reflector still appears to be of low brightness when viewed in the ceiling plane.

Specular and semi-specular aluminum reflectors should be treated like fine glassware. Dirt, fingerprints, and scratches spoil the appearance and diminish the performance of reflectors. It is advisable to handle reflectors carefully during construction; once

installed they may be cleaned with a soft cloth and glass cleaner or removed and cleaned in a dishwasher or industrial washing machine.

Rectilinear fluorescent downlights

Fluorescent downlights are based on the same principles as the incandescent downlight. They typically use either rapid-start T8, T12, or long compact fluorescent sources.

Common sizes for rapid-start fluorescent downlights, also called "troffers," are 1

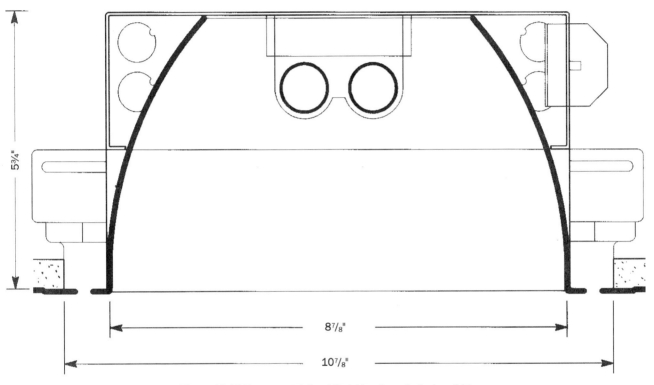

Figure 12.17 Fluorescent 1 ft ×4 ft eight-cell parabolic downlight.

ft × 4 ft, 2 ft × 4 ft, and 2 ft × 2 ft; the last of these is used when a nondirectional (square) ceiling element is desired. Because these luminaires take up such a large portion of the ceiling surface (as compared to a round-aperture downlight), they are significant factors in the design and appearance of the ceiling plane (figure 12.17).

Suspended ceiling systems frequently use 2 ft × 4 ft fluorescent downlights because they integrate easily. Square 1 ft × 1 ft and 1.5 ft × 1.5 ft luminaires with com-pact fluorescent sources take up a smaller portion of the ceiling surface, providing energy-effective luminaires in compact sizes.

Shielding. With all fluorescent downlights, the shielding material is the critical component, because this element is most prominent in the direct field of view. The purpose of diffusers, lenses, louvers, reflectors, and other shielding materials used in fluorescent downlight luminaires is to redirect light from the glare zone down toward work surfaces.

Prismatic lenses incorporate a pattern of small prisms or other refractive elements to reduce the brightness of the luminaire and inhibit direct glare. But almost all fluorescent luminaire lenses fail to reduce their luminance sufficiently to provide visual comfort and prevent bright images in VDT screens. The excessive contrast between the lens and the ceiling plane also creates distracting reflections.

Egg-crate louvers are made of intersecting straight-sided blades that reduce luminance by blocking light rays that otherwise would emerge at glare angles. They are made of translucent or opaque plastic or painted metal. Egg-crate louvers are inefficient in transmitting light, controlling glare, and preventing VDT screen reflections.

Parabolic louvers control luminance precisely; they consist of multiple cells with parabolic reflectors and a specular or semi-specular finish. The cells range in size from ½ in × ½ in to 1 ft × 1 ft.

Small-cell parabolic louvers reduce luminance, but are inefficient in light output. To maximize efficiency, they often have a highly specular finish, which may cause such a low luminance at the ceiling plane that the room seems dim and depressing.

Deep-cell open parabolic louvers offer the best combination of shielding and efficiency.

To avoid reflected glare in VDT screens, IESNA recommends that average luminaire luminance be less than

850 cd/m^2 at 55° from nadir

350 cd/m^2 at 65° from nadir

175 cd/m^2 at 75° from nadir

A manufacturer's luminaire photometric report should include a luminance summary that tabulates brightness values at angles above 45° from nadir. This summary may be used to evaluate the suitability of direct luminaires in offices with VDTs.

Although use of the footlambert (fL) is discouraged, some manufacturers still provide average luminance data in fL instead of cd/m^2. To check compliance with these limits, multiply the fL values by 3.42 to determine cd/m^2.

Spacing criterion

Manufacturers will sometimes publish the luminaire *spacing criterion* (SC) for their downlight equipment. This is an estimated maximum ratio of spacing to mounting-height above the workplane in order to produce uniform, horizontal illuminance. SC is a low-precision indicator; its purpose is to aid the designer in quickly assessing the potential of a downlight luminaire to provide uniform illumination of the horizontal plane.

SC values are sometimes assigned for uplights, but they are rarely assigned to wall-washers, object lights, task lights, or multidirectional lights because these luminaires are not intended to provide uniform, horizontal illuminance.

Luminous ceilings

A *luminous ceiling* also provides direct, downward distribution. It consists of a plane of translucent glass or plastic—often the size of the entire room—suspended below a regular grid of fluorescent lamps. The suspended element becomes the finished ceiling. This technique, popular in the 1950s and 1960s, provides uniform, diffuse, ambient light (figure 12.18).

The cavity above the luminous plane must be free of obstructions and all surfaces are to be finished with a high-reflectance (80 to 90 percent), matte-white paint. Luminous ceilings share the same drawback as indirect lighting—they light everything from all directions, with no shadows or modeling, giving the gloomy effect of an overcast sky.

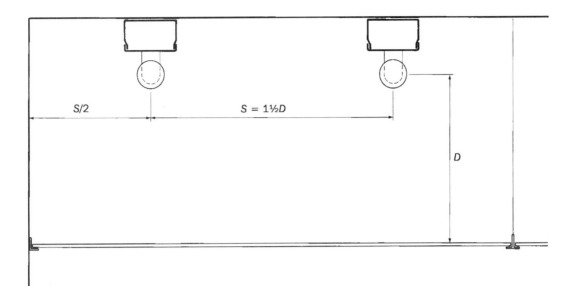

Figure 12.18 Typical luminous ceiling.

Wash Lights

Wash lights are luminaires that provide an even "wash" of relatively uniform brightness, usually on a wall but occasionally on a ceiling. In rooms of moderate size, walls are often the major element in the field of view; washing walls with light has properly become a major technique in the practice of creative illumination.

To minimize specular reflections near the top of lighted vertical surfaces, a matte (diffuse) finish is essential. Specular surfaces, such as mirrors and highly polished marble, cannot be lighted because the light received on the surface is reflected down to the floor and no impression of brightness is created.

Walls are lighted in two ways: (1) by using a row of individual, asymmetric-distribution luminaires placed parallel to the wall at a distance of about one-third the height of the wall, and with the individual units spaced about the same distance apart from each other as they are away from the wall; or (2)

by using a system of linear sources or, ideally, closely spaced directional sources mounted in a continuous "slot" adjacent to the wall.

Asymmetric wall-washers

Asymmetric *wall-washers* are used for lighting walls, sometimes to light artwork, and occasionally to create ambient light in a space.

All asymmetric wall-washers use reflectors or directional lamps or both, frequently combined with lenses to spread the light sideways and smooth the beam. They fall into two categories: downlight/wall-washers and reflector wall-washers.

Downlight/wall-washers. The combination *downlight/wall-washer* is a special kind of wall-washer. It consists of a parabolic, open-reflector downlight with an added elliptical reflector, sometimes called a "kicker" reflector (figure 12.19). This additional reflector "kicks" light up toward the top of the wall,

169

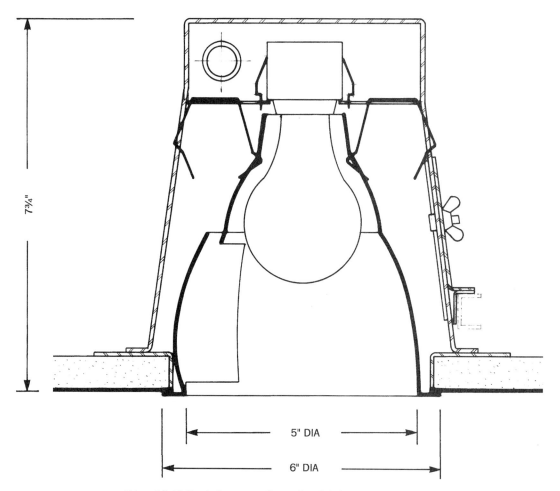

Figure 12.19 Parabolic, open-reflector downlight/wall-washer with 5-in aperture.

eliminating the parabolic scallop that is created by the normal, conical light pattern when it intersects a wall.

The downlight/wall-washer looks identical to the same-size aperture open-reflector downlight. This makes it possible to use downlights (without kickers) for general room illumination and to then add downlight/wall-washers adjacent to the walls, usually on closer centers for uniformity of illumination.

Downlight/wall-wash luminaires are available for incandescent A, tungsten-halogen, compact fluorescent, mercury vapor, metal halide, and HPS lamps. Variations of the downlight/wall-washer have been developed to light adjacent walls forming a corner (*downlight/corner wall-washer*), to light opposite sides of a corridor (*downlight/ double wall-washer*), and to light the wall next to a door without spilling through the

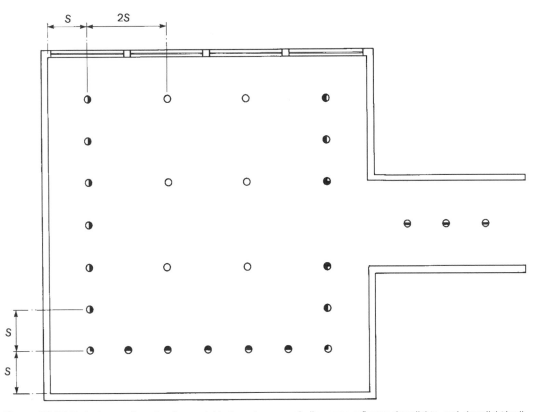

Figure 12.20 Typical room layout using matching-aperture, parabolic, open-reflector downlights and downlight/wall-washer variations.

doorway and causing glare (*downlight/half wall-washer*) (figure 12.20).

Downlight/wall-wash luminaires have downlight distributions in three directions virtually unchanged by the kicker reflector. They work well in small rooms, such as a 10-ft-wide office where opposite walls are lighted; the downlight component provides good modeling of faces throughout the room. The lighted vertical surface is moderately lighted; the horizontal and vertical planes appear to have relatively equal emphasis.

Reflector wall-washers. A greater emphasis on the vertical surface is provided by luminaires that light only the walls without any significant downward distribution. *Reflec-*

tor wall-washers make use of sophisticated optical systems to provide distribution and luminance control. There are two kinds of reflector wall-washers: lensed wall-washers and open-reflector wall-washers.

Lensed wall-washers contain a lamp, preferably a directional source; an internal kicker reflector; a spread lens; and a brightness-controlling reflector to shield glare (figures 12.21 through 12.24). Lensed wall-washers are available for tungsten-halogen MR and PAR, compact fluorescent, metal halide, and HPS lamps.

Reflectors that are not circular, parabolic, elliptical, or hyperbolic are called nonfocal reflectors. *Open-reflector wall-washers* have a compound-contour reflector shape

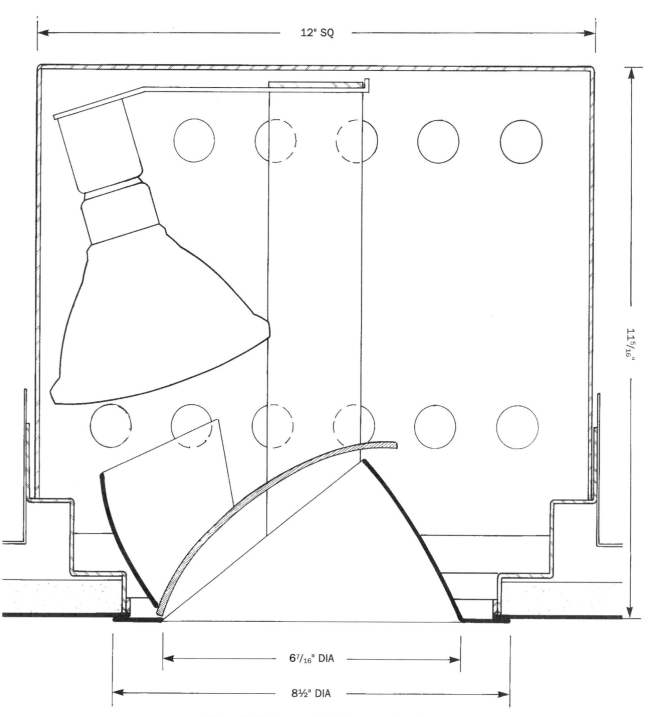

12" SQ

11⁵/₁₆"

6⁷/₁₆" DIA

8½" DIA

Figure 12.21 Recessed PAR38 lensed wall-washer.

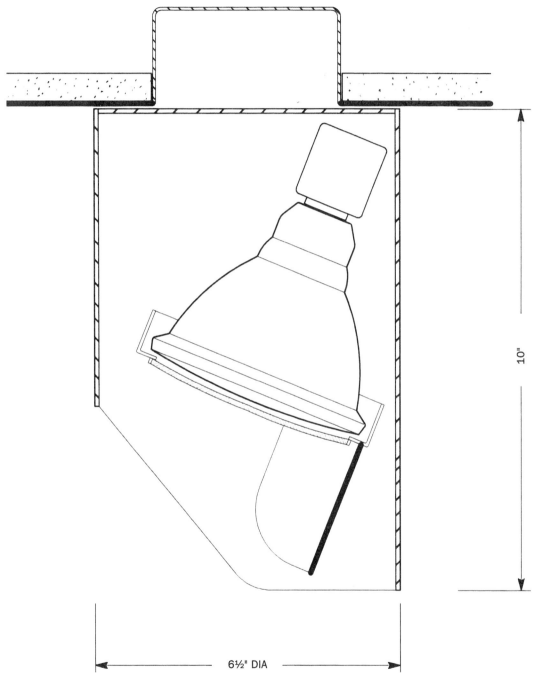

10"

6½" DIA

Figure 12.22 Surface-mounted PAR38 lensed wall-washer.

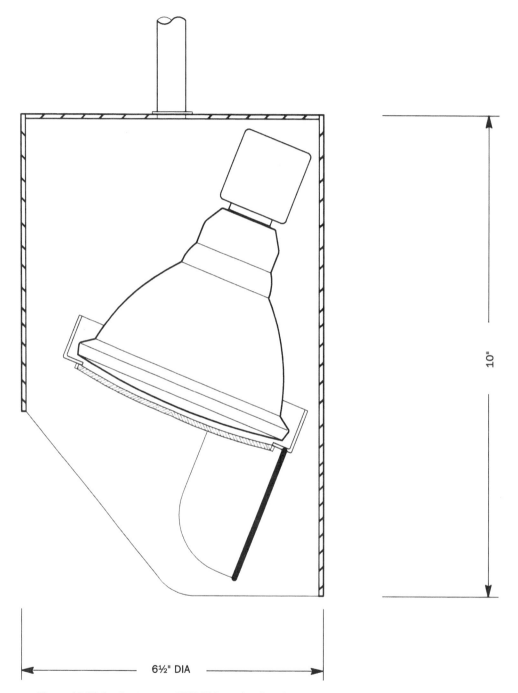

10"

6½" DIA

Figure 12.23 Pendant-mounted PAR38 lensed wall-washer.

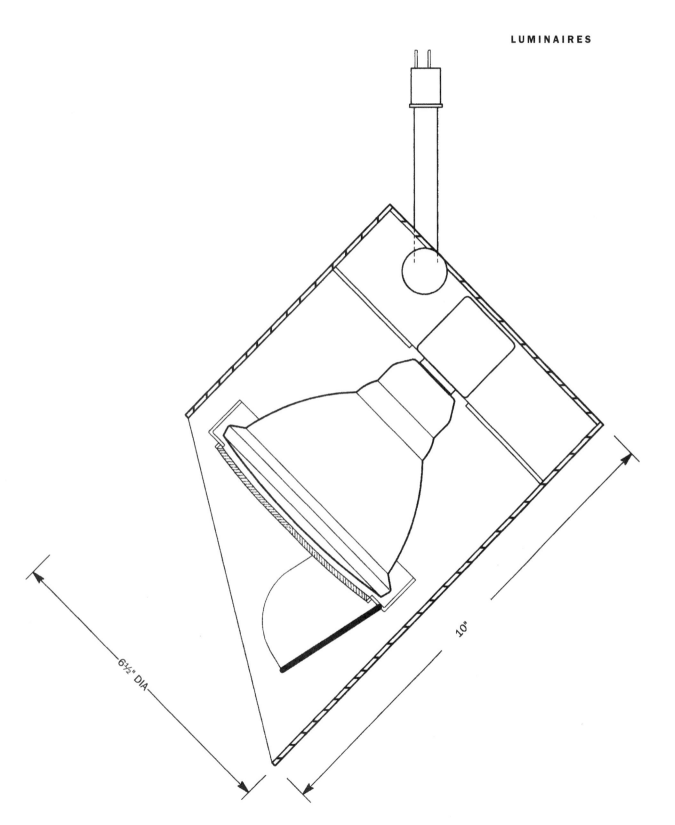

Figure 12.24 Track-mounted PAR38 lensed wall-washer.

that combines an ellipse with a parabola (figures 12.25 through 12.27) or they use non-focal shapes. Open-reflector wall-washers require a point source with a compact filament; they are available for tungsten-halogen T3 and T4 and ceramic metal halide T6 lamps.

Lensed and open-reflector wall-washers used without downlights provide a shadowless, low-contrast setting. When people are distant from the lighted wall they are seen as flat-featured; people next to the lighted wall are seen as silhouettes. These problems are avoided by adding downlights.

Wall-washing is also produced by diffuse-source, fluorescent-lamp wall-wash systems. The inability of a diffuse source to project a high intensity toward the bottom of a wall usually results in a bright area at the top of the wall and a rapid falloff of luminance thereafter. Sophisticated reflector systems with a wide aperture help to solve this problem (figure 12.28). Fluorescent wall-wash systems, sometimes called "perimeter" wall-wash systems, are more energy-effective than their incandescent counterparts.

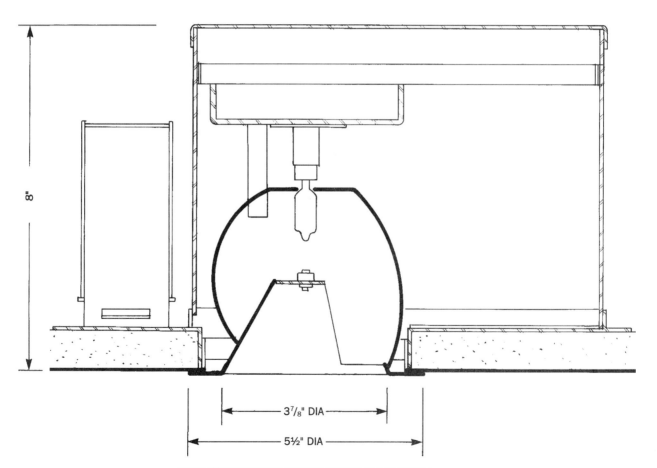

Figure 12.25 Recessed tungsten-halogen T4 wall-washer.

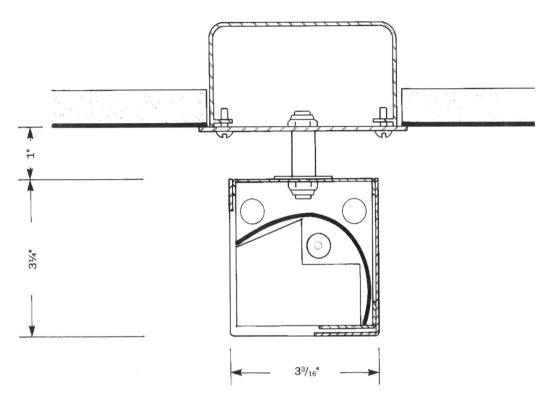

Figure 12.26 Surface-mounted tungsten-halogen T4 wall-washer.

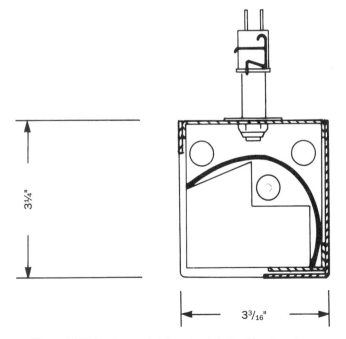

Figure 12.27 Track-mounted tungsten-halogen T4 wall-washer.

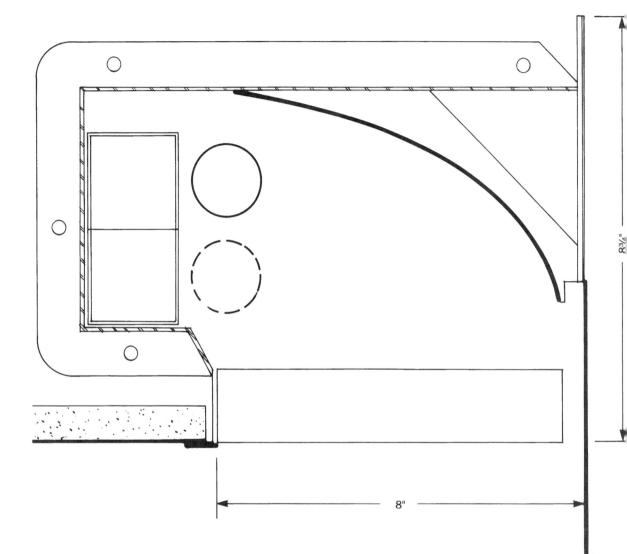

Figure 12.28 Fluorescent reflector wall-wash luminaire.

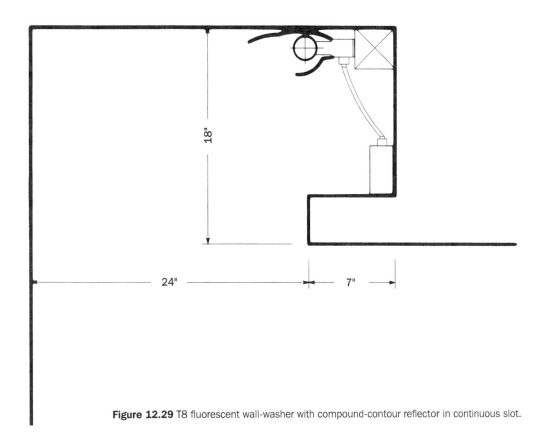

18"

24" 7"

Figure 12.29 T8 fluorescent wall-washer with compound-contour reflector in continuous slot.

Linear wall-washers

Continuous slots are located in the ceiling next to the wall and can enclose other kinds of wall-wash luminaires (figure 12.29). The ceiling is de-emphasized, while vertical surfaces such as walls, murals, and draperies are given prominence.

Incandescent systems. Wall-washing may also be provided by individual directional lamps mounted on a repetitive spacing in a continuous, linear raceway. These systems require the use of a directional point source that is able to project its light over the height of the wall (figures 12.30 and 12.31). The multiple beams of the repetitive lamps overlap, producing uniform brightness along the breadth of the wall.

Lamps are typically mounted close to the surface being lighted. The distance from the lamps to the wall and the distance between the lamps are determined by a full-size mock-up. Excessive lamp spacing will cause scallops. To minimize scallops, the following maximum lamp spacing serves as a guide:

> *For PAR flood lamps:*
> maximum spacing is 0.8 × the distance to the wall

> *For R flood lamps:*
> maximum spacing is 1.0 × the distance to the wall

Fluorescent lamps. The minimum discernible variation in luminance is approximately 2:1. Even with the aid of precisely formed

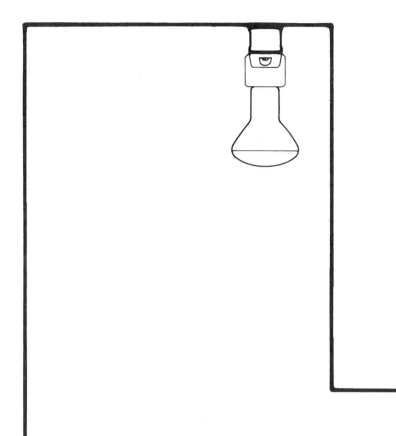

Figure 12.30 Typical incandescent raceway wall-washer system.

compound-contour reflectors, fluorescent lamps have difficulty projecting a high intensity toward the bottom of a wall. The following guide will be helpful in providing approximate visual uniformity with linear T5, T8, and T12 fluorescent lamps.

When using fluorescent lamps in standard reflector channels to light walls, display boards, or draperies, place the channels at a 1:4 ratio of distance away from the lighted surface to the height of the wall (figure 12.32). Luminance at the bottom will be about one-tenth of the luminance at the top. For many applications, the resulting perception of near uniformity is adequate.

Luminaires placed closer than the 1:4 ratio, called *grazing light*, emphasize surface texture and low sculptural relief. But this may also increase the awareness of irregularities and lack of flatness of the lighted surface. Additional frontal light, direct or indirect, reduces this problem by filling in the minute shadows cast by the irregularities.

When lighting from two opposite sides, or from four sides, place the channels at a 1:6 ratio of distance away from the lighted surface to the height of the wall. The 1:4 and 1:6 placement ratios are also applicable when fluorescent channels are mounted vertically (figure 12.33).

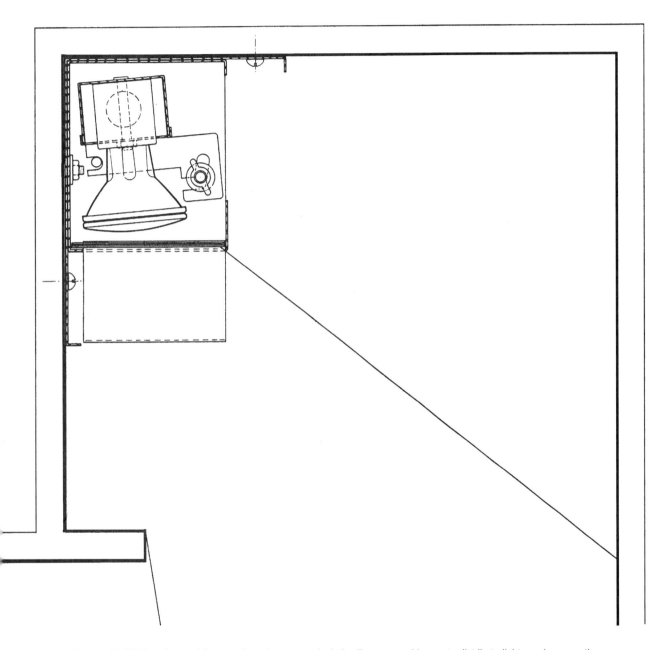

Figure 12.31 Manufactured linear wall-washer system includes linear spread lenses to distribute light evenly across the wall and baffles to shield the view of the lamps along the length of the slot.

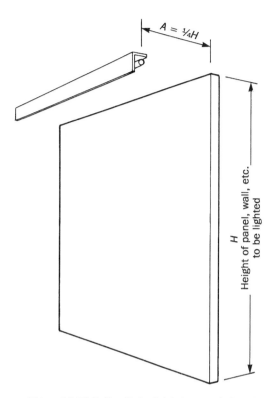

Figure 12.32 Uniformity is slightly improved when the floor has a high reflectance or has a high-reflectance border at the wall.

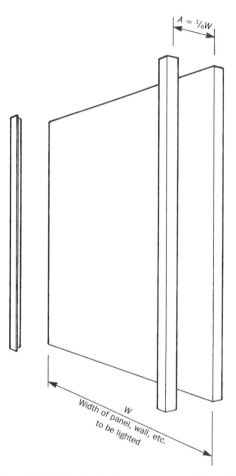

Figure 12.33 Illumination from two opposite sides with vertically mounted fluorescent channels. When fluorescent lamps are used, the cross-section dimension of the luminaire can be made smaller by locating the ballasts remotely.

Vertically mounted fluorescent channels are used for wash light when the ceiling height is low and the placement of overhead equipment is difficult (figure 12.33), but great care must be taken to avoid glare. The shielding angle for blocking the view of the vertical light source is even more critical than it is for horizontal slots and valances.

The close placement of the light source to the wall makes the luminance on the wall much higher near the source. Fluorescent continuous slots and vertically mounted channels are useful techniques when this nonuniformity of luminance is acceptable.

Lighting the ceiling plane

"Washing" with light has come to mean the use of a continuous row of lighting devices located at the edge of the "washed" surface. Ceilings are usually not "washed"; they are lighted by devices known as *uplights* or *indirect luminaires* (figure 12.34). These are

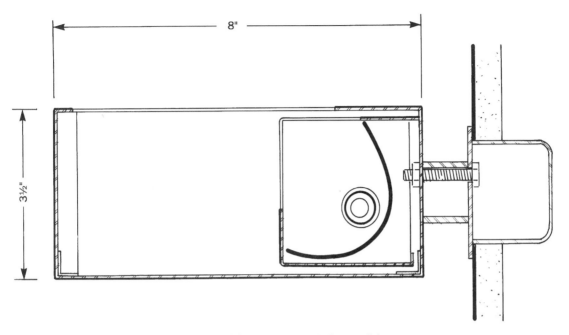

8"

3½"

Figure 12.34 Typical tungsten-halogen uplight.

suspended from the ceiling by stems or cables; mounted on top of furniture above eye level; or attached to walls, columns, or the tops of floor stands. Some provide indirect light only; others, usually stem-mounted, also have a downlight component.

Uplights. Point-source indirect luminaires often use linear sources, such as T2½, T3, and T4 tungsten-halogen lamps; ED18, T6, T7, and T15 metal halide lamps; and ED18 and T15 HPS lamps. Diffuse-source indirect luminaires use compact, T5, T8, and T12 fluorescent lamps.

Fluorescent uplights (figure 12.35) were developed primarily to provide an evenly illuminated ceiling similar to the recessed luminous ceiling (figure 12.18). The intent is the same: to create an evenly illuminated ceiling plane without variations in luminance on the ceiling surface.

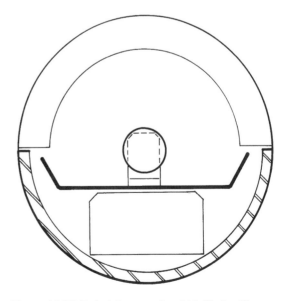

Figure 12.35 Typical fluorescent uplight ("indirect") luminaire.

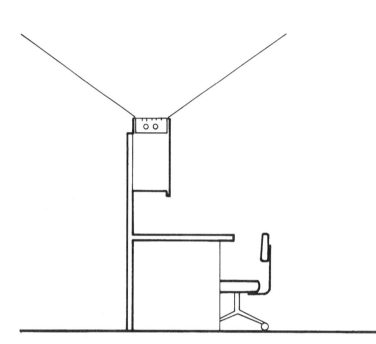

Figure 12.36 Furniture-mounted indirect luminaire.

Uplights are especially suitable for high-ceilinged rooms, which permit the luminaires to be positioned far enough below the ceiling to avoid "hot spots." If they are mounted too close to the ceiling surface, the variations in light and dark will often be unpleasant and disturbing; the ceiling surface will become a series of hot spots and dark shadows instead of an evenly illuminated plane.

Researchers have demonstrated that people perceive a greater quantity of light in a given area when they can see the source of illumination. Pendant-mounted fluorescent uprights that provide a source of brightness from below give an impression of increased illuminance. Uplights that are completely opaque (dark) from below yield an impression of lower illuminance.

Furniture-mounted uplight luminaires incorporate an indirect lighting element onto the top of furniture or freestanding partitions (figure 12.36). They are usually mounted with their apertures slightly above average eye height at 5 ft 6 in AFF in order to avoid glare. Furniture and partition layouts must accommodate the luminaire's spacing criterion to achieve uniform ceiling luminance.

Wall- or ceiling-mounted uplight luminaires are mounted to walls and columns (figure 12.37). Like wall-washers, they have an asymmetric light distribution that produces a sweep of light across the ceiling and avoids hot spots and "spill light" on adjacent surfaces.

Architectural coves. *Coves* are another method of providing general ambient light in high-ceilinged rooms (figure 12.38). Their luminaires direct light toward the ceiling plane, which—like a washed wall—becomes

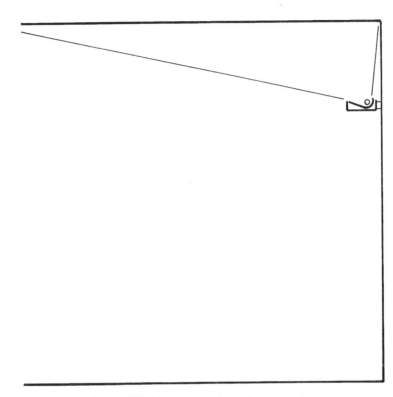

Figure 12.37 Column-mounted indirect luminaire.

a large-area diffusing source. Coves are useful to supplement more energy-effective lighting methods, such as recessed down-lighting systems.

The placement ratios in figure 12.38 are intended to produce approximate visual uniformity. Specular reflections are minimized if the ceiling surface is a high-reflectance matte or satin finish. Typical cove dimensions are shown in figure 12.39.

Custom-built coves are constructed of wood, plastic, or metal. A glass or plastic bottom is sometimes used to introduce a downward component of light for sparkle.

Fluorescent lamps or cold-cathode tubes are commonly used in coves because they are energy-efficient, linear sources. All

lamps must be of the same color, and it is best that they are of the same tube diameter and have the same manufacturer to prevent color variations on the lighted surfaces. Lamps of similar light output per foot of length are also desirable to avoid noticeable variations in luminance on the illuminated surfaces.

When the lamp mounting channels are placed end-to-end, a noticeable gap in light occurs because the lampholders take up space and the lamps emit less light near their ends. The shadows caused by this gap may be avoided by staggering the mounting channels so that they overlap by at least three inches. Prefabricated single-lamp and two-lamp staggered channels with overlap-

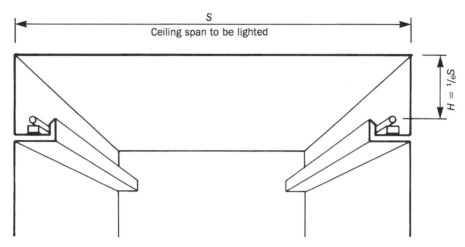

Figure 12.38 A 1:4 placement ratio is applicable when light is emitted from one side only. A 1:6 ratio is applicable when light is emitted from two or four sides.

ping lamps achieve the same result (figure 12.40).

When space constraints limit the cove design so that the source is located too close to the adjacent wall and ceiling, these surfaces will appear excessively bright. Shields can be incorporated into the cove design to intercept some of the light and prevent it from reaching the upper wall. The upper wall will be lighted by reflection from the cove lip and ceiling, reducing the light gradients (figure 12.41).

To ensure uniformity on the ceiling plane, the distance from the center line of the lamp to the ceiling must be a minimum of 12 in for rapid-start lamps and 18 in for HO and VHO lamps. Curved transitions between adjacent surfaces will produce more gradual, softer gradients (figure 12.42).

The height of the vertical shield or "lip" of the cove is determined by a *sight line* analysis. On a section drawing through the cove, draw a line between a viewer's eye, located at the farthest viewing point, and the edge of the cove lip (figure 12.43). The lip of the cove is designed to shield the lamp at normal viewing angles but must not interfere

with the distribution of light across the ceiling (figures 12.44).

When incandescent directional sources are used in a linear array, the beam axis is aimed at a point two-thirds of the way across the lighted surface. This provides relative uniformity of illumination (figure 12.45).

Object Lights

Adjustable *object lights*, sometimes imprecisely called "accent lights," provide a symmetric distribution of light aimed at one or several objects. They use a directional source such as an AR, MR, PAR, or R lamp. Also called "spot lights," they are used to provide focal glow and add contrast to a setting.

Recessed, adjustable, object lights may have a horizontal rotation stop to prevent wires from tangling as the lamp is rotated. Vertical adjustment is from 0° to between 35° and 45° (figure 12.46). Surface-, pendant-, and track-mounted luminaires have a greater range of vertical adjustment than recessed equipment (figures 12.47 and 12.48). The best track-mounted adjustable object lights are designed to rotate slightly more than 360°; inferior luminaires have a

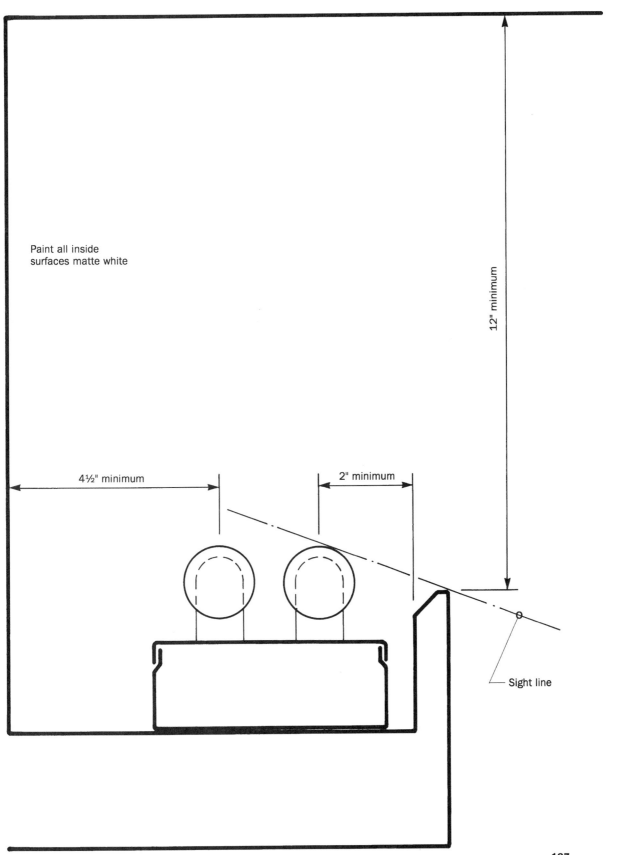

Paint all inside
surfaces matte white

4½" minimum

2" minimum

12" minimum

Sight line

Figure 12.39 Typical cove dimensions for two-lamp fluorescent cove.

187

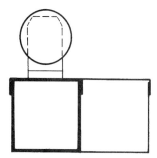

Section view

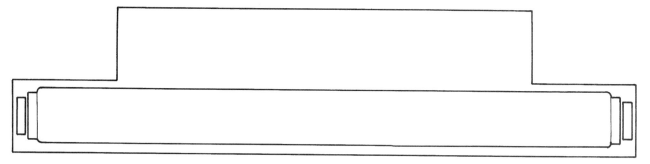

Plan view

Figure 12.40 Single-lamp fluorescent staggered channel.

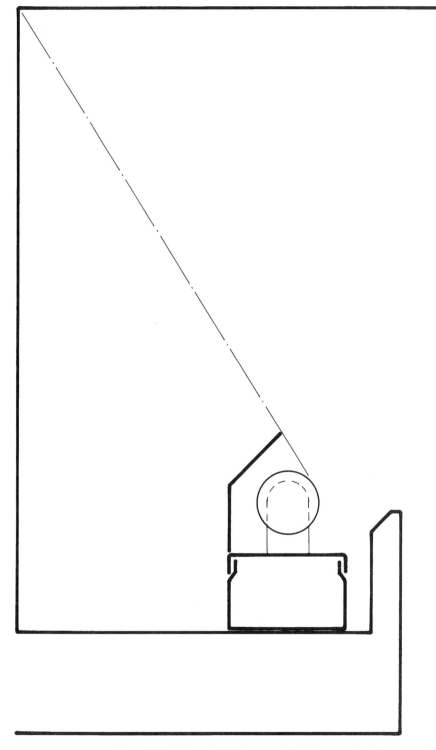

Figure 12.41 External shield to prevent light from reaching the upper wall.

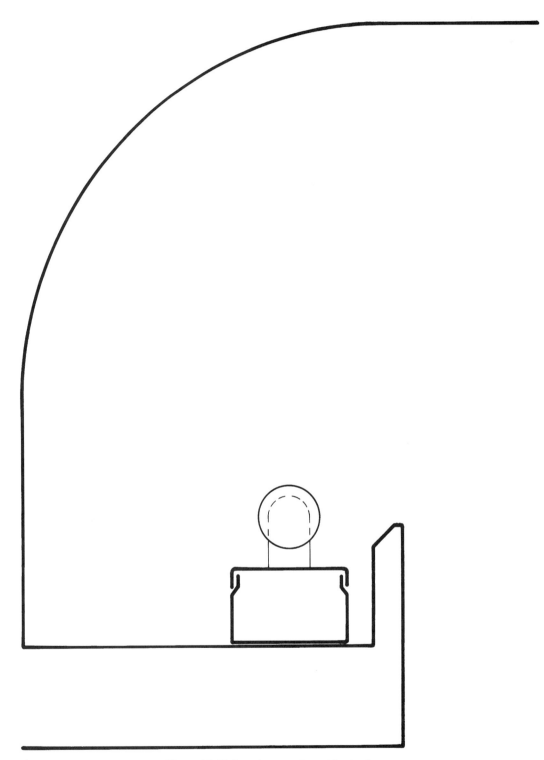

Figure 12.42 Curved contour for architectural cove.

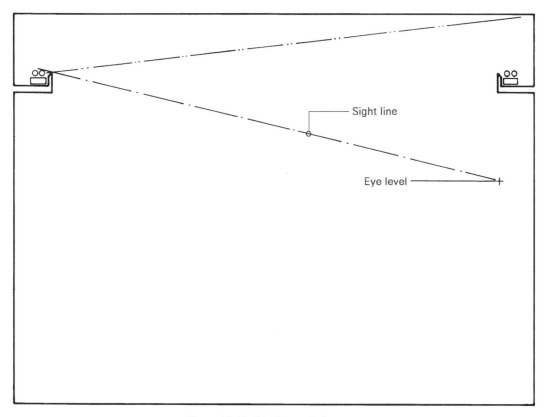

Figure 12.43 Shielding angle for coves.

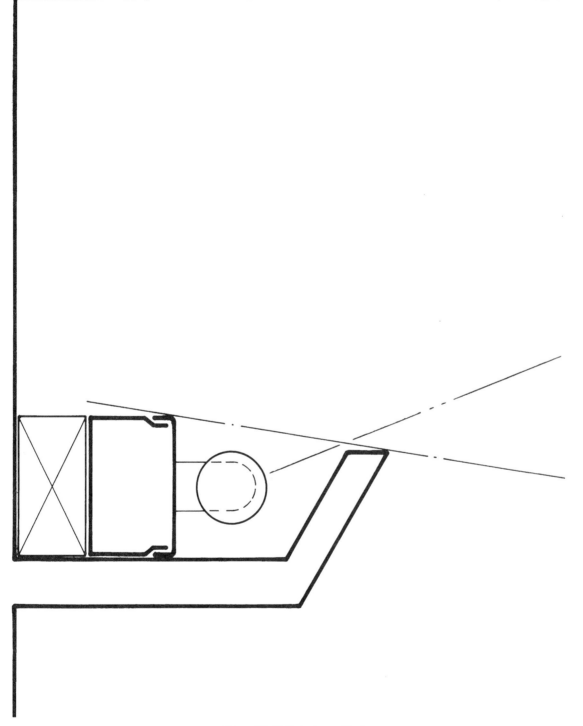

Figure 12.44 Typical cove "lip."

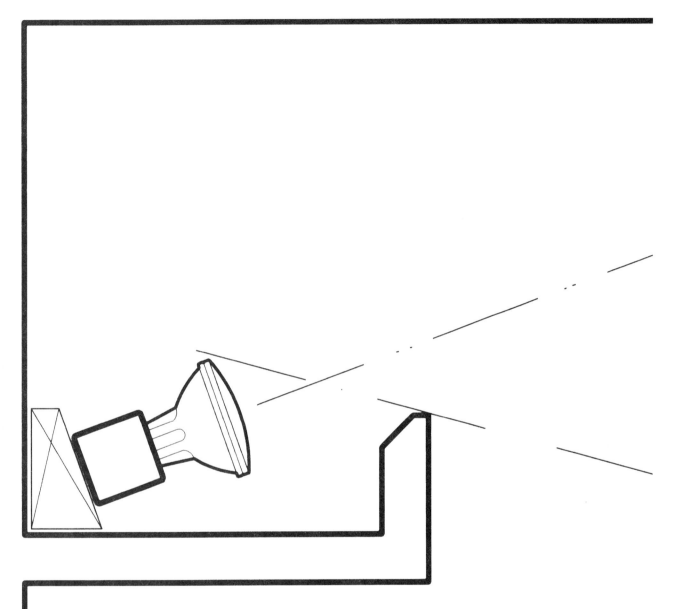

Figure 12.45 Typical incandescent lamp raceway in an architectural cove.

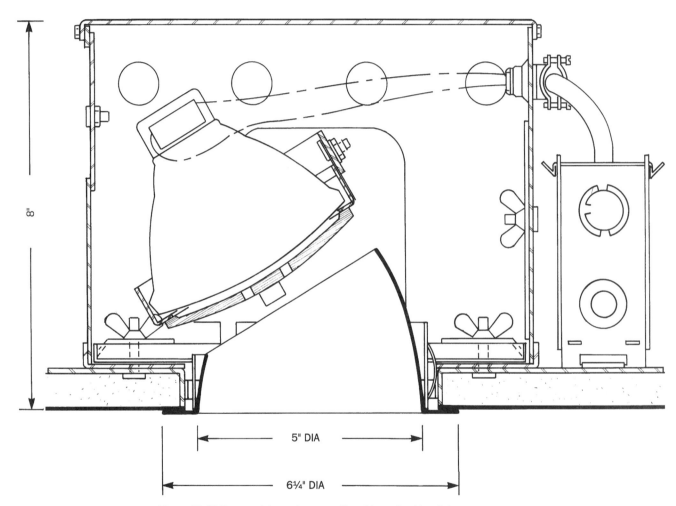

Figure 12.46 Recessed, incandescent, adjustable-angle object light.

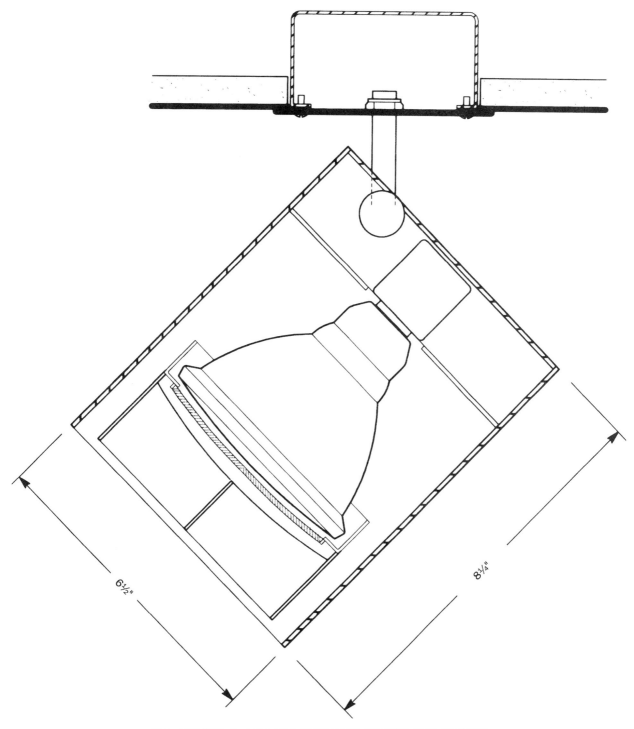

Figure 12.47 Surface-mounted, incandescent, adjustable-angle object light.

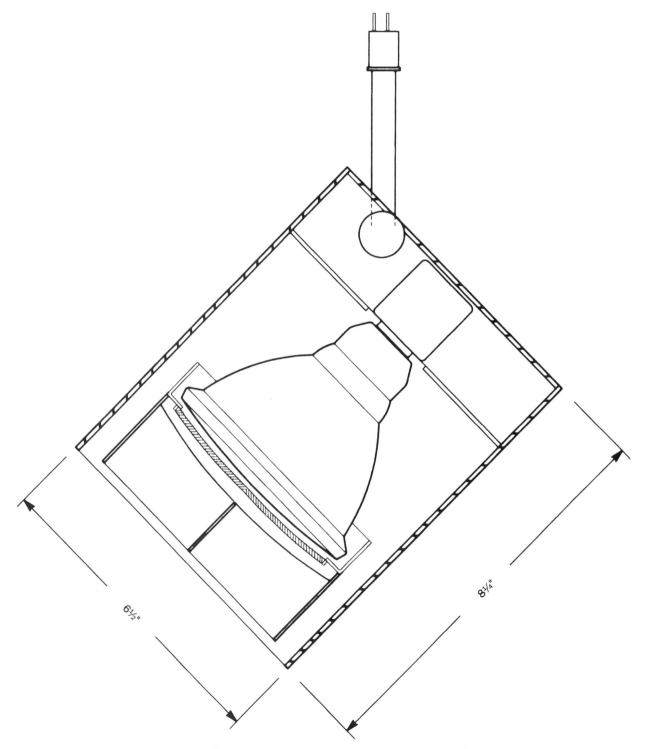

Figure 12.48 Track-mounted, incandescent, adjustable-angle object light.

"blind spot" with horizontal rotation limited to between 300° and 350°.

Whether surface-, pendant-, track-mounted, or recessed, adjustable object light housings are usually designed to shield direct view of the lamp while avoiding undue interference with the beam pattern of directional lamp sources.

The least expensive luminaires may lack any brightness control, and the source glare can be uncomfortable. Better-quality lighting fixtures provide greater degrees of brightness control, typically using an open reflector in recessed equipment and cube-cell louvers or baffles in surface-, pendant-, and track-mounted luminaires.

Louvers intercept some of the light in the beam. *Cube-cell louvers* reduce light output as much as 50 percent. *Cross-baffles* are a more efficient method of shielding lamps from the eyes because the light loss is minimized.

When used to illuminate artwork and larger objects, object lights are also supplied with a linear *spread lens* to modify the distribution and soften the edge of the beam. Linear spread lenses are typically made of borosilicate glass with a fluted pattern; they are usually designed to spread the beam in one direction only and are rotated as required during luminaire focusing. Without the spread lens, the same object light source provides a symmetrical, concentrated beam-spread suited to smaller objects and those that require a greater intensity of illumination or "punch."

Object lights contribute to a moderate-to high-contrast setting because they introduce nonuniform illumination. Medium- to wide-beam lamps give moderate contrast; narrow-beam lamps give high contrast.

Task Lights

Task luminaires bring the light source close to the surface being lighted. They are useful for work surfaces of systems furniture, which may receive insufficient light from an overhead lighting system because of shadows from vertical partitions and furniture-mounted high shelves and cabinets.

Local task luminaires are often energy-effective and useful for reducing reflections in VDTs. Task lighting uses less power because the source is closer to the surface being lighted. Task luminaires can provide the illuminance required for paper-based visual tasks while allowing the ambient light to be of a lower illuminance and decreasing the chances of distracting VDT screen reflections.

Task luminaires are often mounted under a cabinet or shelf that is directly over the work station (figure 12.49). This location is in the reflected glare zone, however; the luminaire may produce *veiling reflections* on the work surface. This is eliminated by using optical lenses for the luminaire that block the perpendicular light rays and convert them to rays that fall on the task from the side and thus do not cause veiling reflections.

Adjustable task luminaires are usually mounted at one side of the task. An adjustable arm permits positioning the luminaire to suit the task, maximizing task visibility. An asymmetric light distribution is sometimes incorporated to direct light more uniformly over the task area.

Soffits

A lighting *soffit* is used for task light (focal glow) rather than ambient light. It is located adjacent to a wall or similar vertical surface and is sometimes used to light niches. The top is often closed and all light is directed downward (figure 12.50).

Over work areas, reflectors increase the useful light (figure 12.51); open louvers or lightly etched plastic or glass perform best. Matte finishes for work surfaces minimize specular reflections (figure 12.52).

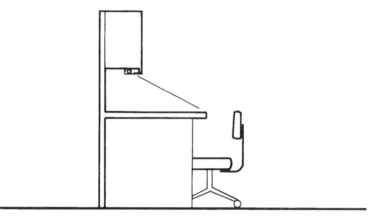

Figure 12.49 Sometimes under-cabinet or under-shelf task luminaires cause veiling reflections. This is eliminated by using a luminaire equipped with a lateral lens.

For make-up and grooming areas, a translucent diffusing panel lights faces from many directions, minimizing harsh shadows. A light-colored countertop is of further help, as it reflects light back toward the face (figure 12.53).

Low brackets. *Low brackets* are used for lighting special task areas such as countertops and writing or reading surfaces (figure 12.54).

Multidirectional Luminaires

Direct-indirect luminaires
Direct-indirect luminaires provide a combination of downlight (direct lighting) and uplight (indirect lighting), with all of the attributes of both systems. The sharper shadows created by direct systems are softened by the diffuse, indirect light. The increased ceiling luminance creates a greater diffusion of light in the space. Interreflections reduce ceiling plane luminance variations and the resulting VDT screen reflections.

Valances. A lighting *valance* is used over windows, usually combined with draperies, or special features, such as artwork. It provides both indirect uplight that reflects back from the ceiling for ambient illumination and downward wash-light for the drapery or artwork (figure 12.55).

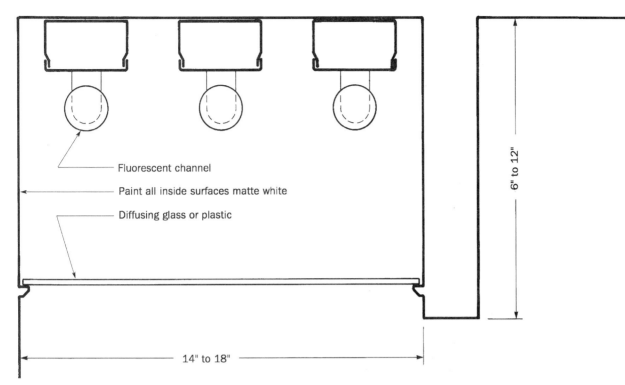

Figure 12.50 Typical lighting soffit. Electronic ballasts will eliminate noise.

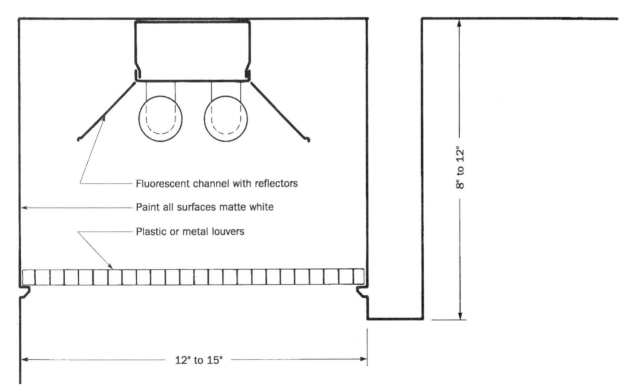

Figure 12.51 Typical lighting soffit over work area with fluorescent reflector channel.

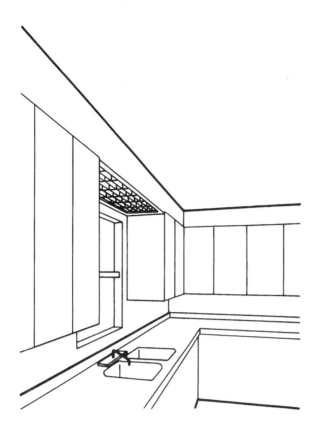

Figure 12.52 Typical lighting soffit over work area with open louver.

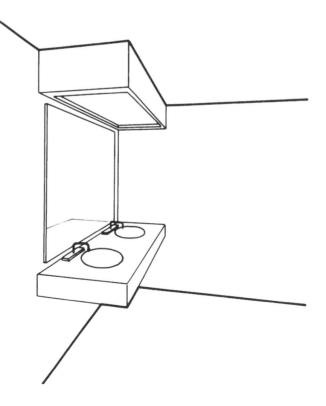

Figure 12.53 Typical lighting soffit for make-up and grooming areas.

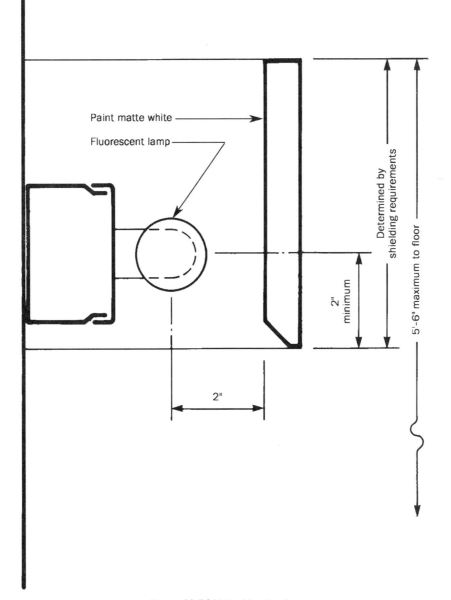

Figure 12.54 Lighted low bracket.

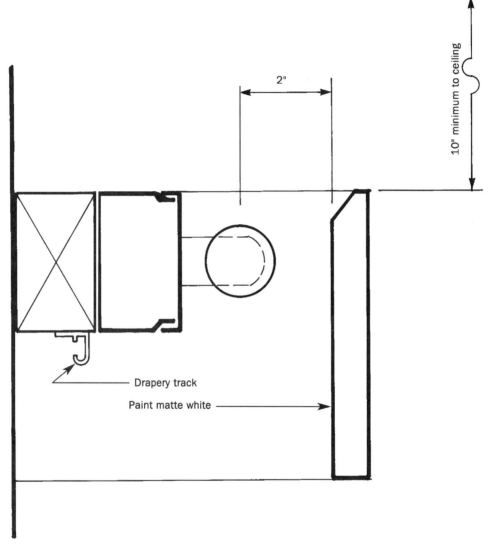

2"

10" minimum to ceiling

Drapery track

Paint matte white

Figure 12.55 Lighted valance.

High brackets. *High brackets* are used on interior windowless walls. They provide both uplight and downlight for ambient illuminance or specific emphasis on surfaces and artwork (figure 12.56).

Decorative Luminaires
Decorative luminaires are used to provide ambient lighting in areas where their appearance contributes to the design harmony of the space (figure 12.57). They are available

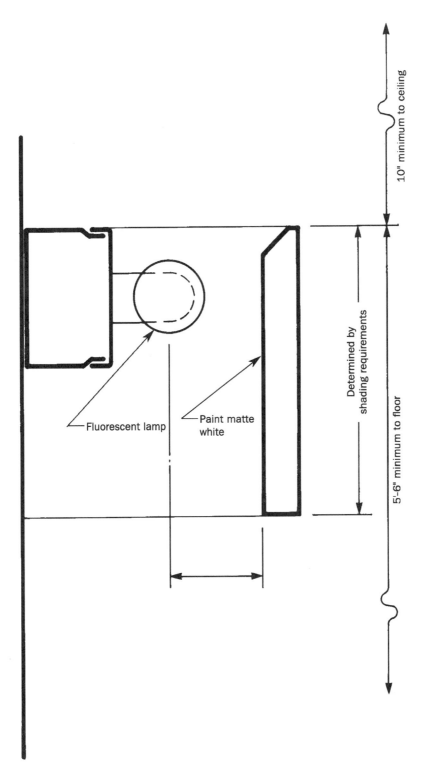

10" minimum to ceiling

Determined by shading requirements

5'-6" minimum to floor

Fluorescent lamp

Paint matte white

Figure 12.56 Lighted high bracket.

Figure 12.57 Decorative luminaires provide ambient light while contributing to the design harmony of the space.

as ceiling-mounted globes and diffusers (figure 12.58), pendant-mounted and suspended *chandeliers* (figure 12.59), wall-mounted lanterns and *sconces* (figure 12.60), floor- and ceiling-mounted corner lights, and floor-mounted *torchères* (figure 12.61).

Almost all decorative luminaires produce multidirectional distribution. Some have optical control hidden inside their decorative exteriors to provide a specific distribution of light.

Figure 12.58 Ceiling-mounted diffuser luminaires.

Figure 12.59 Pendant-mounted luminaires

Figure 12.60 Wall-mounted sconces.

Figure 12.61 Floor-mounted torchère.

Design

13

Lighting design is a process. Specifically, it is the process of integrating light into the fabric of architecture.

Successful lighting is integrated into both the architectural concept and the physical structure.

The lighting concept is integrated into the architectural concept in three ways: (1) by enhancing the original designer's conception of the space, (2) by reinforcing the activity in the space, and (3) by highlighting areas to be prominent, while de-emphasizing areas to be subdued.

Lighting equipment is integrated into the physical structure of the building in three ways: (1) by selecting visible elements that harmonize with the design motif, (2) by incorporating hidden elements within the architectural forms and surfaces, and (3) by coördinating electrical systems with the other mechanical systems of the building.

VISUAL CLARITY

People search for simplification of their visual fields when faced with demanding tasks and activities. In an environment that is used for complex activities, too many visual stimuli or too many patterns will result in an overload condition. We become tense and frustrated and have a diminished ability to perform a complex task.

When we are reading with music playing nearby, the sound competes with the written material yet allows comprehension of simpler passages. At a complex portion of the material, where the reading task becomes more absorbing, we instinctively turn the volume down or off. In doing so, the amount of information that is competing for attention is reduced.

Meaningless or confusing luminances in a space are similarly distracting. The brain becomes overstimulated, spending additional time and energy sorting out conflicting information. This is called *visual clutter*; it is analogous to noise or static in acoustical design.

As the activity or task becomes more complex (more loaded), visual clutter becomes more distracting. It affects worker performance, particularly when the worker is faced with demanding (more stimulating) tasks. Visual clutter undermines long-term performance of all complex tasks.

Visual clarity reduces the number of stimuli in the field of view. It allows us to move through space and complete tasks without any attention being drawn to the lighting system. This leaves our concentration available for the task at hand (figure 13.1).

Figure 13.1 Low-brightness louvers minimize clutter on the ceiling and establish the primary focus in the activity portions of the visual field.

It is the designer's role to simplify the visual process and the environmental background so that distortions and irrelevant clutter are minimized. The goal is to reduce distractions so that the environment assists concentration and conserves our energy for the demands of more productive tasks and activities.

Luminaire Patterns

An irregular luminaire pattern on the ceiling confuses orientation and spatial understanding. We react negatively not because tasks are poorly illuminated or because glare produces discomfort, but because of the distractions produced by the luminaire place-

ment. When the irregular luminaire pattern directs attention to the ceiling, we must overcome the distraction and consciously focus attention on the activities and more meaningful visual stimuli in the room.

An organized pattern on the ceiling minimizes the effort required to discover or impose regularity on the environment (figure 13.2). Carefully organized brightness patterns and repetitive luminaire layouts are useful techniques for simplifying the processes of orientation and activity comprehension. In addition to establishing organized luminaire patterns, matching luminaire apertures of the same dimension and finish further reduce confusion (figure 13.3). Because greater cer-

Figure 13.2 An organized ceiling pattern simplifies orientation and activity comprehension.

Figure 13.3 Matching luminaire apertures of the same dimension and finish.

tainty is felt in an organized environment, less attention is paid to it.

Lighting designers are ceiling designers. Lighting layout drawings include locations of luminaires, sprinkler heads, air diffusers, return grilles, smoke detectors, loudspeakers, and so forth. To prevent visual clutter, these ceiling elements are organized in an invisible grid (figure 13.4).

Whether providing uniform or nonuniform lighting, organize luminaires in a pattern based upon an invisible grid that is related to the architecture. For example, figure 13.5 shows a 78-ft-long room and luminaires with a maximum spacing of 10 ft. The solution presented is eight equal spaces measured to the *center line* of each luminaire. A half-space at either end ensures adequate illuminance near the walls. In the other direction, which is 36 ft, four equal spaces to the center line of each luminaire are shown.

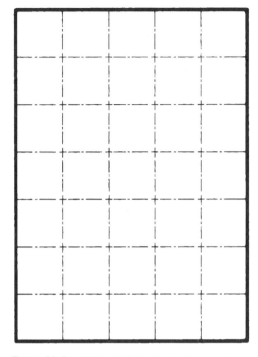

Figure 13.4 Invisible grid for luminaire placement.

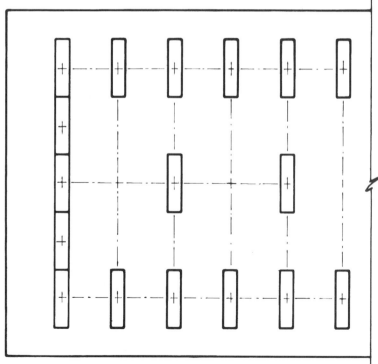

Figure 13.5 1 ft × 4 ft luminaire pattern.

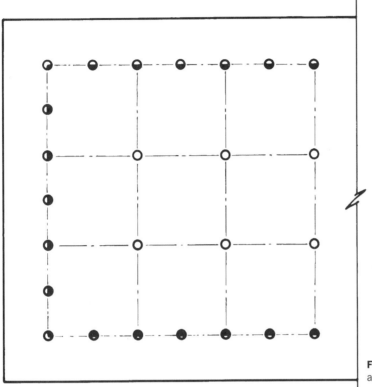

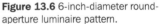

Figure 13.6 6-inch-diameter round-aperture luminaire pattern.

It is unnecessary to fill each cross-point of the invisible grid to maintain the order supplied by that pattern. With the round-aperture luminaires in figure 13.6, spacing at the perimeter is half the spacing of the room to provide uniform wall lighting with open-reflector downlight/wall-wash luminaires.

ARCHITECTURAL SURFACES

When the primary emphasis of lighted space is within the visual field, the resulting patterns of brightness reinforce our priorities for defining space (orientation) and defining activities (participation).

People define their environment through a process of additive perception. Information is gathered by scanning the boundaries of a space, thereby forming a concept of direction and limits. When the lighting system is designed to establish the physical boundaries of a space, it helps people to maintain a sense of direction and an understanding of spatial form with minimal distraction from the environment.

Lighting helps to define and separate the major surfaces of a space if the shape of the light distribution relates to the form of the surface. For example, a wall or ceiling lighted with a uniform wash of light will approximate the form and dimension of that surface.

A linear wash of light facilitates clear visual separation between the vertical and horizontal planes (the wall and ceiling sur-

Figure 13.7 A linear wash of light facilitates spatial clarity.

faces and the wall and floor), the borders of interior space (figure 13.7). The evenly lighted wall is perceived as an integrated visual form (figure 13.8). The same is true of the evenly lighted ceiling plane.

Lighting Vertical Surfaces

Vertical surfaces require special attention: they are the first surfaces that we see upon entering a space. Vertical surfaces define the boundaries of the space; they are used for displaying works of art and communicating a message. Clear perception of vertical surfaces significantly impacts our perception of the overall design.

Reliance upon formulas to provide a specific illuminance value on the horizontal plane disregards the importance of vertical surfaces. Consequently, luminaires used for ambient illumination often cast unanticipated

or undesired light patterns on the vertical surfaces, or leave them in relative darkness. If not distracting, the resulting environment is unintentionally dull and monotonous.

It is critical to anticipate where downlight distributions will intersect vertical surfaces. *Scallop* patterns and similar irregularities are to be minimized. Except for special situations, a lighted surface is not intended to be perceived as a form or surface that is intersected by arbitrary patterns of light; it is intended to be perceived as a unified form.

Scallops of light are incompatible with the plane form of the wall. Because the eye is involuntarily attracted to areas that contrast with the ambient brightness, scallops result in a disorienting pattern of superimposed light that confuses perception of the visual form of the wall (figure 13.9).

Figure 13.8 An evenly lighted wall is perceived as an integrated visual form.

Figure 13.9 Scallops distort the plane form of the wall.

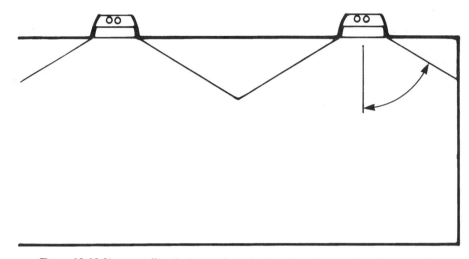

Figure 13.10 Sharp-cutoff luminaires produce shadows along the top of an adjacent wall.

To alleviate scallops when using open-reflector point-source downlights, use downlight/wall-wash reflectors at the perimeter, as indicated in figure 12.20, if the wall surface is matte. If the wall surface is specular, no adjustment is necessary; the intersecting light pattern is unnoticeable on a mirror-like surface.

Rectilinear fluorescent downlights with sharp luminance *cutoff* show an abrupt fall-off of light at the upper part of adjacent walls. This results in a shadow line along the top of the wall, which often causes a space to be perceived as dimly lighted (figure 13.10). Wall-washers or a continuous perimeter system will fill in this shadow. A similar result is achieved by using a specular wall finish in the shadow area with a matte finish below it.

Irregular patterns of light are sometimes desirable. A shaft of sunlight has intrinsic value, as do some electric light patterns that avoid a relationship to the physical form of a space. The value of these irregular patterns of light is that they serve as a temporary visual stimulant.

Irregular light patterns are also successful when they relate to an appealing attribute of the physical space, such as a painting, sculpture, plant, or architectural detail. Unless specifically intended, however, avoid irregular light patterns.

Matte vertical surfaces

Three kinds of lighting systems are available for *uniform* vertical surface illumination of matte surfaces: (1) individual unit, point-source wall-wash; (2) continuous, linear, point-source wall-wash; and (3) continuous, linear, diffuse-source wall-wash.

Individual unit, point-source wall-wash. To provide uniform illumination from top to bottom, luminaires are placed parallel to the wall at a distance of about one-third the height of the wall. For uniform lighting from side to side, the "square rule" applies: luminaires are located on centers closer than or equal to their distance from the wall. The center-to-center spacing varies with the ceiling height and the light intensity desired on the surface.

Continuous, linear, point-source wall-wash. Uniform lighting is also provided by a grazing light from luminaires located close to the surface being illuminated (figure 13.11). The same square rule applies: the lamps are spaced on centers closer than or equal to their distance from the wall. Again, the center-to-center spacing varies with the ceiling height and the light intensity desired

on the wall surface. The goal is also the same: to provide the perception of uniform brightness both horizontally across the wall and vertically from top to bottom.

A full-scale mock-up tests for the following:

1. Beam-spread overlap (spot beam-spreads usually require a spread lens).

Figure 13.11 Continuous, linear, point-source wall wash.

2. The optimum distance away from the wall and on-center spacing.

3. The mounting cavity height, depth, and finishes required.

4. The necessity of baffles to shield the lamps from view along the length of the cavity.

A full-size mock-up is the only way to ensure that the finished installation will achieve the desired illuminance value and avoid scallops and striations at the top of the wall. No miniature light sources exist to test the performance of architectural lamps in a scale model.

Continuous, linear, diffuse-source wall-wash. The diffuse fluorescent source is good at providing even lighting across the wall in the horizontal direction but is inadequate at providing even illuminance vertically from top to bottom. Reflectors help to mitigate the problem but fail to solve it for walls exceeding 10 ft in height. The use of a fluorescent wall-wash system is reserved for low ceiling areas with wall heights from 8 to 10 ft.

Specular vertical surfaces

When providing light for glossy surfaces, such as glass, marble, high-gloss enamels, and varnishes, specular reflections complicate the placement of lighting equipment. Careful location and shielding of the source prevents distracting reflections and veiling images.

Think of the glossy surface as a mirror; eliminate glare by minimizing high luminance in the reflected field of view. To reduce reflected images, remove bright elements in the reflected field of view or shield them with properly located baffles or screens.

People, objects, and other surfaces in the room become secondary light sources. If they are located in the reflected field of view, they will cause distracting or veiling reflections in glossy surfaces. In some cases, the perception of varnished or glass-covered paintings, or of marble and other specular materials, is partially or completely obscured by such reflected images.

TASK LIGHTING

Lighting systems in the workplace provide for accurate perception at a specific task area (a desk, counter, machine, or workbench). This is achieved by using one of two lighting methods: a general-ambient approach or a task-ambient approach.

General-ambient systems provide a uniform quantity of light throughout a space. This approach is often used when the task location is apt to vary widely or when the space will be reconfigured frequently.

Task-ambient systems are more energy-effective. Higher values of task illuminance are provided for the workplane while lower values of ambient illuminance are provided for surrounding areas.

Task-ambient systems are appropriate in rooms where task areas are permanently located, such as private offices, factories, laboratories, and stores. Task lighting is provided for task areas, with the remaining space lighted for more casual activities (figure 13.12).

When designing a task-ambient system, first light the task (focal glow), then supplement the task lighting with ambient room lighting. In typical task-ambient systems, task-oriented luminaires are mounted on or near the furniture and supplemented by an ambient (uniform) lighting system that provides lower illuminance.

Ambient lighting provides overall illumination for circulation, provides balance between the VDT task luminance and its surround, and provides part of the illuminance for paper-based tasks. Areas surrounding visual tasks need less illuminance than the

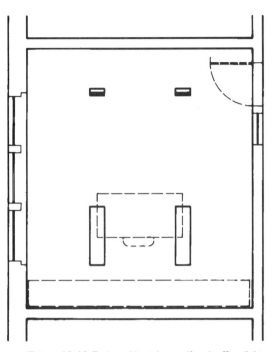

Figure 13.12 Task-ambient (nonuniform) office lighting layout.

visual tasks. For comfort and ease of adaptation, make the ambient illuminance at least 33 percent of the task illuminance.

VDTs

VDT screens present a particular challenge for designers. Almost all VDT screens have a dark, glossy, or satin surface that reflects images of the surrounding space; the operator will see luminaires, ceilings, walls, or windows as elements of excessive brightness reflected in the screen (figure 13.13). The designer must carefully select and locate luminaires to minimize reflected images.

VDT tasks often require an almost horizontal line of sight when viewing the screen. Because of this, a large area of the ceiling will be in the field of view in large open offices. It is critical to minimize variation in luminance on the ceiling plane in order to prevent discomfort glare (figure 13.14).

With well-designed direct luminaires, the luminance of the aperture will be equivalent to the luminance of the ceiling. This results in minimal brightness contrast

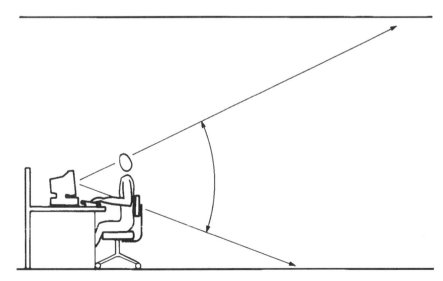

Figure 13.13 Normal range for reflected line-of-sight angles in a VDT (65° to 110° from vertical).

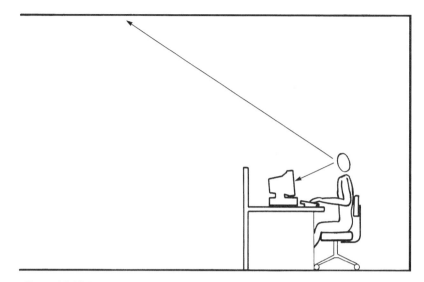

Figure 13.14 A large area of the ceiling is within the field of view when viewing a VDT.

between the reflected screen images of the luminaire and ceiling.

With a well-designed indirect system, the light received on the ceiling plane exhibits an even luminance, yielding minimal brightness contrast in the VDT screen. The underside of the indirect luminaires must be approximately the same luminance as the ceiling plane. When the luminance seen across the VDT screen is uniform, minimal interference occurs.

Paper-based tasks

Almost all office work involves paper-based tasks. Paper documents are referenced for word processing, order entry, information retrieval, and computer-aided design. In addition to the lighting requirements for VDT tasks, lighting for paper-based visual tasks must also be considered.

AMBIENT LIGHTING

Ambient lighting is provided by two basic methods: (1) downlighting (direct), where overhead luminaires provide a downward light distribution, and (2) uplighting (indirect), where pendant luminaires provide upward light that is then reflected from the ceiling.

Downlighting (Direct)

With downlighting (direct lighting), luminaires are arranged according to the ambient lighting requirements for either uniform or nonuniform distribution over the horizontal workplane.

For direct ambient lighting, the spacing criterion (*SC*), or spacing-to-*m*ounting-*h*eight (*S/MH*) ratio, provided by the luminaire manufacturer, gives the maximum recommended spacing between luminaires to achieve uniform, ambient lighting.

To quickly assess the potential of a downlight luminaire to provide uniform illumination of the horizontal plane, *SC* is the center-to-center distance between luminaires (spacing) based on their mounting height above the workplane.

$$S = MH \times SC$$

For example, if the $SC = 1.5$, then for an 8-ft ceiling height,

MH = 8 ft 0 in – 2 ft 6 in to the workplane
     = 5 ft 6 in AFF

$S = 5.5$ ft $\times$ 1.5 $= 8.25$ ft

The center-to-center maximum spacing from the center of one luminaire to the center of the next is thus 8.25 ft (figure 13.15).

For rectilinear luminaires, SC is expressed as parallel or perpendicular, indicating the spacing-to-mounting-height ratio in either the direction parallel to or perpendicular to the orientation of the lamps within the luminaire.

To maintain uniformity of light intensity over a large work area, avoid exceeding the manufacturer's recommended maximum SC. Because of wall surface absorption, maximum distance from the last row of luminaires to the wall is usually one-half to one-third the spacing in the room to prevent a falloff in illuminance near the walls (figures 13.16 to 13.18).

Even with this reduced spacing, work surface illuminance near the walls is often only half that measured in the center of the room. In critical seeing areas, supplementary luminaires are added near the wall (figure 13.19).

Office partitions block some overhead light from a direct system, preventing it from reaching work surfaces. Depending on the location of the downlights, some areas will be left in shadow (figure 13.20). Well-designed uplighting, because it produces even illuminance overhead, softens and reduces this shadowing.

Uplighting (Indirect)

The primary use of uplighting (indirect lighting) is to create evenly luminous ceilings that reduce VDT screen reflections. For uplighting to be successful, luminance differences on the ceiling plane must be minimal. If bright patches of higher luminance occur, they are reflected in the VDT screen, causing a distracting background.

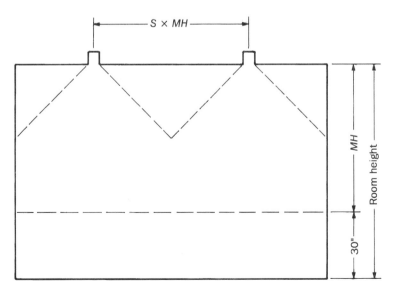

Figure 13.15 Spacing-to-mounting-height ratio.

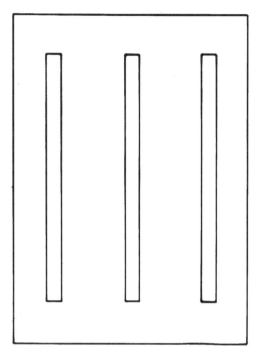

Figure 13.16 Linear pattern, continuous 1 ft × 4 ft rectilinear luminaires.

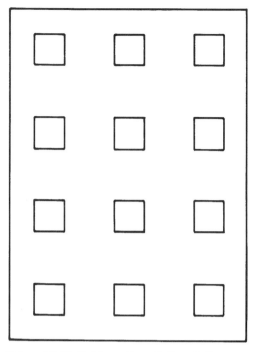

Figure 13.17 Regular pattern, 2 ft × 2 ft square luminaires.

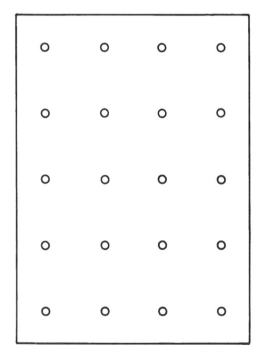

Figure 13.18 Regular pattern, 6-inch-diameter round-aperture luminaires.

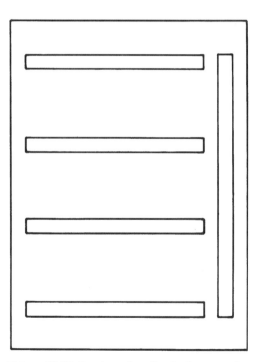

Figure 13.19 Supplementary illumination near the wall.

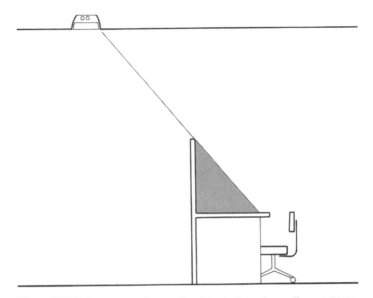

Figure 13.20 Some areas have noticeable shadows from office partitions, especially when partitions are located on three sides of the work surface.

Uplighting systems also increase the vertical illumination in a space. While this is desirable for many surfaces, it reduces image contrast on VDT screens. Although indirect lighting systems eliminate the most offensive image glare common with direct lighting on VDTs, they may introduce less-problematic veiling reflection and contrast reductions on the surface of the screen.

A well-designed indirect luminaire has a wide distribution. Multiple luminaires are located so that their light output will be evenly distributed across the ceiling without hot spots or areas of high luminance (figure 13.21). The goal is uniform ceiling brightness, where luminances and luminance ratios are consistent throughout the space.

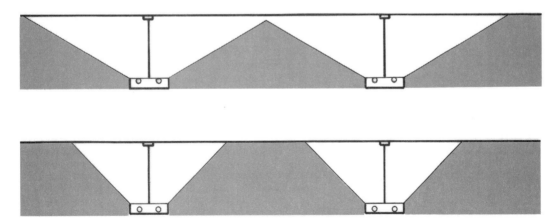

Figure 13.21 Above, properly located indirect luminaires with wide distributions produce even luminance; below, improperly located indirect luminaires with narrow distributions produce areas of uneven luminance.

To avoid distracting brightness variation in VDT screens, keep the variation in ceiling luminance to a ratio of less than 4 : 1. In addition, limit the average luminance of any 2 ft × 2 ft area of the ceiling to less than 850 cd/m^2, measured at any angle. Apply this same limit to windows, walls, and partitions that will be reflected in the VDT screen.

The diffuse light from indirect systems, however, reduces our sense of visual clarity, depth perception, and sense of orientation. This lack of highlight and shadow is mitigated by a greater use of surface color, wall lighting, or object lighting; these techniques add visual interest, thus enhancing perception of the environment.

Some indirect luminaires incorporate a luminous element that is visible from below. This is psychologically beneficial because people feel more comfortable when they can identify the source of light. This visible luminous element also increases the perception of brightness in a space and introduces visual highlight into a shadowless environment.

In a small office, only part of the ceiling will be reflected in the VDT screen. Here, it is the walls that are of concern. The walls of a small office must have sufficient luminance to avoid noticeable contrast between these walls and the ceiling, a condition that causes distracting contrast in VDT screens.

Downlighting Versus Uplighting

The appearance of a low-brightness direct lighting system differs considerably from an indirect lighting system. The direct system produces negligible luminance on the ceiling plane and provides great emphasis on the horizontal work surface, furniture, and floor coverings. The indirect system places luminance emphasis on the ceiling plane and de-emphasizes the surfaces in the lower half of the room. A direct-indirect system accomplishes both.

LIGHTING ART

Lighting Three-Dimensional Objects

Three-dimensional objects are perceived as a result of the relationship between highlight and shadow. Concentrated beams create higher contrast and deeper shadows, emphasizing form and texture. Frontal lighting, located 30° to 45° from the center of an object in the horizontal plane and 30° to 45° from nadir in the vertical plane, models objects in a manner that replicates sunlight.

Lighting a vertical surface behind an object provides a luminous backdrop to separate the object visually from its background (figure 13.22), much the way an actor is separated from the scenery on a stage. Lighting an object from the side as well as from above provides added dimension to the piece.

Perception is disturbed when the expected relationship of highlight and shadow is reversed or when an object is lighted from a less conventional angle. Uplighting creates an ominous, ghoulish impression (see figures 3.27 and 3.28). Backlighting leaves an object in silhouette.

Paintings and Flat Works of Art

For lighting paintings and flat works of art, two principal methods exist: uniform illumination and nonuniform illumination.

Providing *uniform* lighting for all vertical surfaces that will receive art gives prominence to the architecture; no hierarchy is established among the individual works of art, allowing viewers to select their own focus. Objects can be changed without readjusting the lighting equipment (figure 13.23).

Providing *nonuniform* lighting focuses light on individual works while leaving the surround in comparative darkness. This gives prominence to the art over the architecture, creating a more dramatic environment. Every time the art changes, the

Figure 13.22 Lighting the vertical surface behind an object.

lighting equipment must also be adjusted (figure 13.24).

The placement of the light source depends upon the medium, surface texture, kind of frame, and enclosure (glass or plastic) of the object. For flat works mounted on a vertical surface, the optimum location for a light source is usually at an angle of 30° from nadir (straight down) to average eye level (5 ft 3 in AFF) (figure 13.25).

An aiming angle of less than 30° (more nearly vertical) creates disturbing shadows from the frame and distorts the object because it exaggerates its texture. An aiming angle greater than 30° (more nearly horizontal) results in reflected glare from the surface of the object, washing out detail. This greater angle also casts a shadow of the viewer on

the artwork and causes the luminaire to be a source of glare to others moving through the space.

For nonuniform wall lighting, point-source object lights are ideal. When more than one luminaire is required because of the size of the work to be lighted, the square rule applies once again: the luminaires are spaced on centers closer than or equal to the distance away from the wall. The distance from the wall varies with the ceiling height (figure 13.26).

When a space with nonuniform vertical-surface illumination has frequently changing exhibits, a flexible lighting system is appropriate. Track systems are often selected because the track luminaires are easy to locate and aim (*focus*) as needed. The track

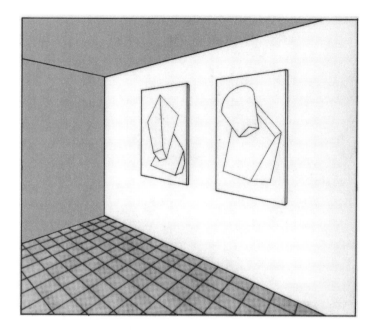

Figure 13.23 Uniform illumination for art.

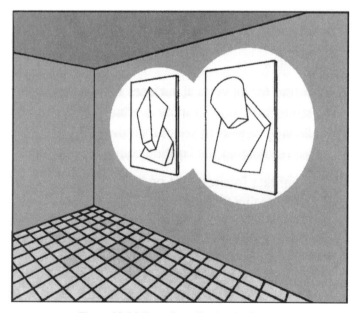

Figure 13.24 Nonuniform illumination for art.

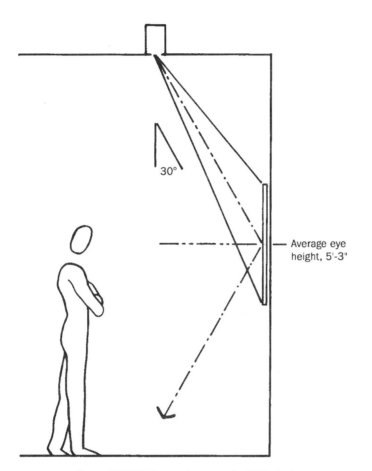

Figure 13.25 Optimum placement for lighting art.

itself also serves as the wireway, providing a simple method of power distribution.

With either method for lighting art, excellent color rendering is essential for the proper appreciation of objects. Continuous-spectrum, high-color-rendering sources allow the art to be viewed under spectral distribution conditions similar to those under which it was created.

Conservation of Materials

Conservation of materials is a fundamental concern in the lighting of art. All organic material is susceptible to pigment change and weakening from exposure to light and its accompanying heat. In the museum environment, these materials include paper, cotton, linen, parchment, leather, silk, wool, feathers, hair, dyes, oils, glues, gums, resins, and—because of similarities in chemical structure—almost all synthetic dyes and plastics.

Damage is related to wavelength. Ultraviolet (UV) radiation causes more damage, but much less UV than visible radiation is present in all light sources, including day-

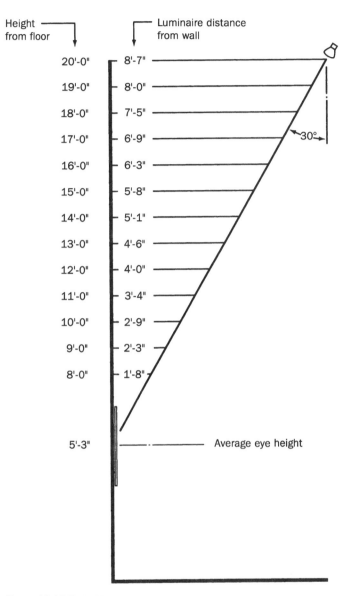

Figure 13.26 Typical luminaire mounting locations with 30° aiming angle.

light. A material that is fairly *fast* (more stable) but nevertheless susceptible to damage, such as the oil in paintings, will be changed mainly by UV radiation. But more sensitive dyes and pigments, which are damaged by either UV or visible radiation, will be changed mainly by the visible radiation, since it is more plentiful. In the museum environment, it is necessary to limit both UV and visible radiation.

Three steps will help to protect fugitive materials from the potential damage caused by light and heat: (1) evaluate daylight exposure, (2) evaluate electric light exposure, and (3) evaluate duration of exposure.

Evaluate the daylight first, because it contains a much higher proportion of UV than do electric sources. The highest-quality UV filters for daylight are made of acrylic and other plastics formulated to eliminate the transmission of UV but allow the passage of visible light. They are available as self-supporting sheets used in place of glass, thin acetate applied to glass, and varnish.

White paint is also a good UV absorber. If all light entering a room is reflected at least once from a white surface, the UV problem will be solved. Titanium dioxide pigment is best for this purpose, but zinc white is also a good absorber.

Second, evaluate the fluorescent and HID lamps. Although they emit UV radiation less strongly than daylight, all discharge lamps require UV filters. Fluorescent and HID lamps with correlated color temperatures above 3100 K need careful attention, because both UV radiation and short-wavelength visible radiation increases with color temperature. Plastic sheets of UV-absorbing material are available from manufacturers of color filters.

Incandescent lamps emit too little UV to require a filter. UV radiation from almost all incandescent lamps is less than 0.1 percent of the input wattage. Tungsten-halogen lamps emit slightly more UV below 300 nm, owing to their higher filament temperature. This is still a small amount; fortunately, ordinary glass, transparent to longer-wavelength UV, completely blocks this extra-short emission. (Tungsten-halogen lamps in U.S. luminaires will already have a lens or cover glass that provides safety protection in case of lamp breakage.)

It is more difficult to limit visible radiation than to limit UV radiation because the artwork will then be left in darkness.

Museum practice suggests that for oil and tempera paintings, oriental lacquer, undyed leather, horn, bone, and ivory, maximum maintained illuminance is 15 fc on the surface. For objects especially sensitive to light, such as drawings, prints, watercolors, tapestries, textiles, costumes, manuscripts, and almost all natural history exhibits, maximum maintained illuminance is 5 fc.

With the quantity of light maintained at 5 to 15 fc, radiant heat is also controlled to reasonable limits. Lamps should be located outside exhibition cases and ventilated with air that avoids traveling directly past the exhibits. Dichroic cool-beam lamps are useful. Their color appearance is somewhat cooler than standard sources; the color rendering, however, is undisturbed.

Third, evaluate the time of exposure. *Exposure* is the simple product of illuminance and time. The same amount of damage will be produced by a large quantity of illuminance for a short time or a small quantity of illuminance for a long time. If the illuminance is halved, the rate of damage is halved. The optimal strategy is to reduce both illuminance and time of exposure.

With low illuminance values, warm versus cool colors of light are preferred. The low quantity of light is less important to the viewer than the balance of brightness between the works of art and the surround (the remaining space). Adaptation plays an important role in the enjoyment of art: the viewer's eyes must be adapted to the lower illuminance before entering the exhibit room.

BALANCE OF BRIGHTNESS

In chapter 2 we learned that lighting design involves the balance of three elements of light: ambient light, focal glow, and sparkle. The balance of these three elements causes a worker's task to be easily distinguished from the background, an artwork to stand out from its surround, and a conference or

Figure 13.27 Lighting opposite walls establishes a balance of brightness.

restaurant table to be the focus of its participants' attention. The result is known as the *balance of brightness*.

It is often desirable to light opposite walls in a space, thereby establishing a balance of brightness (figure 13.27). *Balance* is different from *symmetry*: lighting the opposing walls in the same manner is unnecessary, although one may choose to do so. Instead, one wall may be uniformly illuminated with a wall-wash system and the other will be nonuniformly illuminated with object lights (figure 13.28).

It is also desirable to balance the perimeter illumination of a space with its center. If a room's breadth is greater than its height, it

is impossible to light it successfully solely from the walls. When diffusely lighted walls are distant from each other in a low-ceilinged space and they are the only source of illumination, the resulting environment is bland and gloomy. Downlighting is added to the center; otherwise all persons and objects in the center of the space will appear in silhouette (figure 13.29).

Remember that people interpret the overall environment chiefly through brightness relationships. Their subjective impressions of visual space are primarily a function of brightness patterns and pattern organization—the relationship of surfaces that are lighted or left in relative darkness.

Figure 13.28 Lighting opposite walls in different ways also provides a balance of brightness.

Figure 13.29 When lighted walls are distant from each other in a low-ceilinged space, downlighting addded to the center provides balance of brightness.

Some lighting patterns affect personal orientation and understanding of a room's surfaces and objects. Object-lighting and shelf-lighting influence attention and consciousness (figure 13.29); wall-lighting and corner-lighting enhance understanding of room size and shape (figure 13.30). Together, the resulting balance of brightness establishes or modifies our sense of enclosure.

Other lighting patterns involve the communication of ideas and impressions of activity setting or mood. Because the eye is involuntarily drawn to bright objects or to areas that contrast with the background, high-contrast settings are effective at direct-ing attention and interest to selected detail while de-emphasizing other objects, areas, or surfaces (figure 13.31).

When the balance of brightness is purposefully established, designers provide an appropriate background for the intended activity or more: the purposeful manipulation of light can delight, enchant, and command attention (figure 13.32).

An Example

In a restaurant, if the lighting system is designed to illuminate horizontal surfaces, such as tabletops, while de-emphasizing the architecture, people and activities become

Figure 13.30 Wall-lighting and corner-lighting enhance understanding of room size and shape.

Figure 13.31 High contrast lighting is effective at directing attention and interest.

Figure 13.32 The purposeful manipulation of light can enchant and command attention.

the dominant feature. This lighting condition increases awareness of nearby detail, people, and movement, and encourages conviviality among patrons. The architecture will appear as a neutral or subordinate visual influence (figure 13.33).

The architectural environment, however, is interpreted by illuminating vertical and overhead surfaces. When lighting focuses the visual emphasis on these peripheral surfaces, the intensity of illumination on the tabletops is reduced; objects and people in the center fall into silhouette. Activity is then visually subordinate to the general space, inducing a more intimate atmosphere in which individuals feel a sense of privacy or anonymity (figure 13.34).

Successful restaurant design is the balance of the two: a convivial atmosphere in which one feels a sense of intimacy and privacy, where other guests at other tables become the background, and where your table is the most important one in the room (figure 13.35).

Luminance Ratios

In offices, controlling the luminance variations within limits ensures good visibility. Within these limits, variation is desirable and will make the office environment more pleasing. Luminance differences are specified in terms of the ratio between one luminance and the other (figure 13.36).

It is undesirable to maintain these ratios throughout the entire environment, however. For visual interest and distant eye focus (required for eye muscle relaxation periodically throughout the day), small areas that

Figure 13.33 When the lighting system illuminates horizontal surfaces, people and activities become dominant.

Figure 13.34 When the lighting system illuminates vertical and overhead surfaces, the architecture becomes dominant.

Figure 13.35 When the lighting system illuminates both horizontal and vertical surfaces, the brightness is balanced.

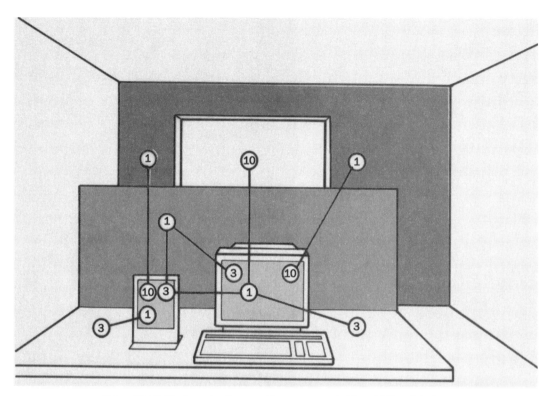

Figure 13.36 Maximum luminance ratios recommended for a VDT workstation.

exceed the luminance ratio recommendations are advantageous. These include artwork, accent finishes on walls or floors, accent finishes on chairs and accessories, and focal lighting.

The perception of brightness depends on surface reflectance as much as it does on illuminance. Consideration of surface finish reflectances is just as important as the lighting design.

Shadows

Lighting design includes shadows as well as light. Just as musicians make sounds to capture silence and architects develop complex shapes to envelop empty space, lighting designers illuminate with shadows (figure 13.37).

Light and dark are not antagonistic to each other. They are counterparts, like the yin and yang of Chinese cosmology that combine to produce all that comes to be. Without shade or darkness, light loses much of its meaning; patterns of light and shade render the prominences of surfaces and objects in the visual field (figure 13.38).

Again, three-dimensional form is perceived as a relationship of light and shadow. If a projecting corner formed by the meeting of two white planes is lighted so that the two sides look equally bright, the eye can no longer discern the edge of the corner. You may still recognize it because of the binocular function of your eyes or because you can see where the two planes intersect other planes. But you have lost an essential means of seeing that there is a corner.

It will not help to increase the light equally on both sides. If the light on one side is reduced to produce a marked difference in

Figure 13.37 Lighting design includes shadows as well as light.

the two planes, however, the corner becomes evident, even if the total intensity of light has decreased.

Only with shadows, then, can much of light be appreciated. Just as a good listener appreciates conversation by its pauses, we can appreciate light by its shadows.

ENERGY-EFFECTIVE DESIGN

Successful lighting design is *energy-effective* design. It uses the available watts to supply light where it is needed, when it is needed, and limits light from where it is unwanted (figure 13.39). Energy-effective design includes both careful control of light and

careful control of brightness. It means making every watt count (figure 13.40).

Energy efficiency and lighting quality have sometimes been considered conflicting design objectives. Energy limits are just one of the many design constraints that designers face. Design means working within project parameters, whether they are space limitations, fixed budgets, time constraints, color palettes, or connected lighting power limits (figure 13.41).

Within a given power budget, the designer has unlimited freedom. Distributing light on room surfaces and objects in a way that facilitates orientation, aids perception,

Figure 13.38 Patterns of light and shade render the prominences of surfaces and objects in the visual field.

Figure 13.39 Energy-effective design uses the available watts to supply light where it is needed.

Figure 13.40 Energy-effective design includes careful control of light and brightness.

Figure 13.41 Design means working within the project parameters

and supports activities, is another way of saying that limited lighting watts are being distributed in the most effective way (figure 13.42). Stringent energy codes simply require more careful design to establish visually satisfying environments that also meet regulatory requirements.

INTEGRATING LIGHT AND ARCHITECTURE

To be successful, lighting design is integrated into the fabric of the architecture. It integrates the lighting concept with the architectural one (figure 13.43); it integrates the technology that produces light with the mechanical and structural systems that erect the building (figure 13.44). The objective is to use modern lighting techniques in a manner sympathetic to, and expressive of, the spirit of the architectural concept (figure 13.45).

When light and architecture are integrated, we are not aware of the mechanics of light production—only of a comfortable environment that encourages productivity and enhances well-being. Because light influences our sense of well-being, we are ultimately concerned with not only the quality of light, but the quality of life.

Figure 13.42 Limited lighting watts distributed in an effective way.

Figure 13.43 Integrating the lighting concept with the architectural concept.

Figure 13.44 Integrating the lighting technology with the mechanical and structural systems.

Figure 13.45 Modern lighting techniques used in a manner sympathetic to and expressive of the spirit of the architectural concept

Appendix

TABLE 1

TYPICAL COLOR RENDERING INDICES

Lamp Description	Color Rendering Index (CRI)	Color Temperature in Kelvin (K)
Incandescent and Tungsten-Halogen		
Incandescent	100	2800
Light blue incandescent	100	4000
Daylight incandescent	100	5000
Tungsten-halogen	100	3100
Tungsten-halogen with light blue filter	100	4000
Tungsten-halogen with blue filter	100	5000
Fluorescent		
Cool white	62	4100
Cool white deluxe	89	4100
Warm white	53	3000
Warm white deluxe	85	3000
Natural	90	3700
Lite white	51	4200
Daylight	79	6500
Daylight Deluxe	84	6500
Cool green	70	6450
RE–730	70–79	3000
RE–735	70–79	3500
RE–741	70–79	4100
RE–750	70–79	5000
RE–830	80–89	3000
RE–835	80–89	3500
RE–841	80–89	4100
RE–850	80–89	5000
RE–930	95	3000
RE–950	98	5000
Chroma 50	92	5000
Chroma 75	95	7500
T8/ADV/830	80–89	3000
T8/ADV/835	80–89	3500

Lamp Description	Color Rendering Index (CRI)	Color Temperature in Kelvin (K)
T8/ADV/841	80–89	4100
T8/ADV/850	80–89	5000
T12/ADV/830	82	3000
T12/ADV/835	82	3500
T12/ADV/841	82	4100
T12/ADV/850	82	5000
High-Intensity Discharge		
Standard mercury	20	5900
Mercury deluxe white	45	3900
Standard metal halide	65	4000
Standard coated metal halide	70	3800
Cool ceramic metal halide (39-70 W)	92	4000
Cool ceramic metal halide (100-400 W)	93	4000
Warm ceramic metal halide (39-70 W)	82	3000
Warm ceramic metal halide (100 W)	85	3000
Combined metal halide/HPS	90	4000
Standard high-pressure sodium	22	2000
Deluxe high-pressure sodium	65	2200
White high-pressure sodium	85	2700
Low-pressure sodium	0	1700

TABLE 2

INCANDESCENT LAMP DESIGNATIONS AND PROPERTIES

ANSI Lamp Designation	Design Volts	Watts	Design Life (Hrs.)	Initial Candle-power	Beam-Spread 50%	10%	Notes
Aluminum reflector (AR) lamps							
15ALR18/NSP6 (GBA)	6	15	2,000	5,200	6°	—	
15ALR18/SP14 (GBC)	6	15	2,000	1,900	14°	—	
20ALR12/NSP6 (GBD)	12	20	2,000	6,400	6°	—	
20ALR12/SP18 (GBE)	12	20	2,000	1,000	18°	—	
20ALR12/FL34 (GBF)	12	20	2,000	350	34°	—	
						—	
50ALR18/SP10 (GBJ)	12	50	2,000	12,000	10°	—	
50ALR18/NFL22 (GBK)	12	50	2,000	2,000	22°	—	
						—	
20AR70/SP8	12	20	3,000	7,700	8°	—	Filament shield
20AR70/FL25	12	20	3,000	900	25°	—	Filament shield
50AR70/SP8	12	50	3,000	12,500	8°	—	Filament shield
50AR70/FL25	12	50	3,000	2,600	25°	—	Filament shield
35AR111/SSP4/6V	6	35	3,000	30,000	4°	—	Filament shield
35AR111/SSP4	12	35	3,000	45,000	4°	—	Filament shield
35AR111/SP8	12	35	3,000	14,000	8°	—	Filament shield
35AR111/FL25	12	35	3,000	2,500	25°	—	Filament shield
50AR111/SSP4	12	50	3,000	50,000	4°	—	Filament shield
50AR111/SP8	12	50	3,000	20,000	8°	—	Filament shield
50AR111/FL25	12	50	3,000	3,500	25°	—	Filament shield
75AR111/SP8	12	75	3,000	30,000	8°	—	Filament shield
75AR111/FL25	12	75	3,000	5,300	25°	—	Filament shield
75AR111/WFL45	12	75	3,000	1,700	45°	—	Filament shield
100AR111/SP8	12	100	3,000	48,000	8°	—	Filament shield
100AR111/FL25	12	100	3,000	8,500	25°	—	Filament shield
100AR111/WFL45	12	100	3,000	2,800	45°	—	Filament shield
Mirror-reflector (MR) lamps							
20MR11/SP10 (FTB)	12	20	4,000	5,500	10°	—	

ANSI Lamp Designation	Design Volts	Watts	Design Life (Hrs.)	Initial Candle-power	Beam-Spread 50%	Beam-Spread 10%	Notes
20MR11/SP15 (FTC)	12	20	3,500	1,760	15°	—	
20MR11/FL35 (FTD)	12	20	4,000	700	35°	—	
35MR11/SP10 (FTE)	12	35	4,000	8,500	10°	—	
35MR11/SP15 (FTF)	12	35	3,500	3,000	15°	—	
35MR11/FL40 (FTH)	12	35	4,000	1,500	40°	—	
20MR16/NSP8 (ESX)	12	20	4,000	6,000	8°	—	
20MR16/FL40 (BAB)	12	20	4,000	700	40°	59°	
20MR16/VWFL60	12	20	4,000	350	60°	—	
20MR16/IR/SP8	12	20	5,000	6,500	8°	—	IR-reflecting
20MR16/IR/FL36	12	20	5,000	1,000	36°	—	IR-reflecting
35MR16/NSP8 (FRB)	12	35	4,000	11,000	10°	—	
35MR16/SP20 (FRA)	12	35	4,000	2,800	20°	—	
35MR16/FL40 (FMW)	12	35	4,000	1,400	40°	—	
35MR16/VWFL60	12	20	4,000	650	60°	—	
35MR16/IR/SP8	12	35	5,000	14,000	8°	—	IR-reflecting
35MR16/IR/NFL24	12	35	5,000	4,400	24°	—	IR-reflecting
35MR16/IR/FL36	12	35	5,000	2,200	36°	—	IR-reflecting
35MR16/IR/WFL60	12	35	5,000	1,050	60°	—	IR-reflecting
37MR16/IR/SP10	12	37	4,000	13,100	10°	—	IR-reflecting
37MR16/IR/NFL25	12	37	4,000	4,600	25°	—	IR-reflecting
37MR16/IR/FL40	12	37	4,000	2,500	40°	—	IR-reflecting
45MR16/IR/SP8	12	45	5,000	16,000	8°	—	IR-reflecting
45MR16/IR/NFL24	12	45	5,000	5,450	24°	—	IR-reflecting
45MR16/IR/FL36	12	45	5,000	2,850	36°	—	IR-reflecting
45MR16/IR/WFL60	12	45	5,000	1,300	60°	—	IR-reflecting
50MR16/NSP10 (EXT)	12	50	4,000	11,500	10°	24°	
50MR16/NFL25 (EXZ)	12	50	4,000	3,200	27°	49°	
50MR16/NFL30 (EXK)	12	50	4,000	2,500	32°	52°	
50MR16/FL40 (EXN)	12	50	4,000	2,000	40°	64°	
50MR16/WFL60 (FNV)	12	50	4,000	1,000	60°	—	
50MR16/IR/SP10	12	50	4,000	15,700	10°	—	IR-reflecting
50MR16/IR/NFL25	12	50	4,000	6,000	25°	—	IR-reflecting
50MR16/IR/FL40	12	50	4,000	3,000	40°	—	IR-reflecting
65MR16/NSP10 (FPA)	12	65	4,000	14,000	10°	—	

ANSI Lamp Designation	Design Volts	Watts	Design Life (Hrs.)	Initial Candle-power	Beam-Spread		Notes
					50%	10%	
65MR16/NFL25	12	65	4,000	4,000	25°	—	
65MR16/FL40 (FPB)	12	65	4,000	2,100	40°	—	
65MR16/VWFL60	12	65	4,000	1,050	60°	—	
71MR16/NSP15 (EYF)	12	71	4,000	11,500	15°	—	
71MR16/NFL25 (EYJ)	12	71	4,000	5,500	25°	—	
71MR16/FL40 (EYC)	12	71	4,000	2,200	40°	—	
75MR16/SP10 (EYF)	12	75	4,000	14,000	10°	—	
75MR16/FL36 (EYC)	12	75	4,000	2,500	36°	—	
Parabolic aluminum reflector (PAR) lamps							
35PAR14/H/FL	120	35	2,000	85	50°	—	
45PAR16/H/NSP10	120	45	2,000	5,000	10°	—	
45PAR16/H/NFL27	120	45	2,000	1,400	27°	—	
50PAR16/H/FL40	120	50	2,000	800	40°	—	
60PAR16/H/NSP10	120	60	2,000	5,700	10°	—	
60PAR16/H/NFL27	120	60	2,000	2,000	27°	—	
75PAR16/H/NSP10	120	75	2,000	7,500	10°	—	
75PAR16/H/NFL30	120	75	2,000	1,900	30°	—	
35PAR20/H/NSP10	120	35	2,500	3,000	10°	—	
35PAR20/H/NFL30	120	35	2,500	800	30°	—	
35PAR20/H/WFL40	120	35	2,500	500	40°	—	
50PAR20/H/NSP9	120	50	2,000	6,200	9°	—	
50PAR20/H/SP16	120	50	2,000	3,200	16°	—	
50PAR20/H/NFL30	120	50	2,000	1,400	30°	—	
50PAR20/H/WFL40	120	50	2,500	900	40°	—	
35PAR30L/H/NSP9	120	35	2,500	5,700	9°	—	
35PAR30L/H/WFL50	120	35	2,500	450	50°	—	
45PAR30/HIR/SP9XL	120	45	6,000	9,750	9°	—	IR-reflecting
45PAR30/HIR/FL25XL	120	45	6,000	2,025	25°	—	IR-reflecting
45PAR30/HIR/FL35XL	120	45	6,000	1,125	35°	—	IR-reflecting
50PAR30/H/NSP10	120	50	3,000	8,250	10°	—	
50PAR30/H/NFL30	120	50	2,000	1,950	30°	—	

ANSI Lamp Designation	Design Volts	Watts	Design Life (Hrs.)	Initial Candle-power	Beam-Spread 50%	Beam-Spread 10%	Notes
50PAR30/H/FL40	120	50	2,000	1,500	40°	—	
50PAR30/HIR/NSP9	120	50	3,000	13,000	9°	—	IR-reflecting
50PAR30/HIR/NFL25	120	50	3,000	2,900	25°	—	IR-reflecting
50PAR30/HIR/FL35	120	50	3,000	1,500	35°	—	IR-reflecting
50PAR30L/H/NSP9	120	50	2,000	8,800	9°	—	
50PAR30L/H/SP16	120	50	2,000	4,200	16°	—	
50PAR30L/H/NFL30	120	50	2,000	1,900	30°	—	
50PAR30L/H/FL40	120	50	2,000	1,250	40°	—	
50PAR30L/H/WFL60	120	50	2,000	550	60°	—	
60PAR30/H/NSP10	120	60	2,500	10,000	10°	—	
60PAR30/H/NFL30	120	60	2,500	2,800	30°	—	
60PAR30/H/FL40	120	60	2,500	1,850	40°	—	
75PAR30/H/NSP10	120	75	2,000	15,400	10°	—	
75PAR30/H/NFL25	120	75	2,000	3,100	27°	—	
75PAR30/H/FL35	120	75	2,000	2,000	35°	—	
75PAR30L/H/NSP9	120	75	2,000	15,400	9°	—	
75PAR30L/H/SP16	120	75	2,000	6,700	16°	—	
75PAR30L/H/NFL30	120	75	2,000	3,400	30°	—	
75PAR30L/H/FL40	120	75	2,000	2,200	40°	—	
75PAR30L/H/WFL60	120	75	2,500	1,100	50°	—	
25PAR36/VNSP5	6	25	1,000	19,700	—	5.5° × 4.5°	Filament shield
25PAR36/NSP9	12	25	2,000	2,600	10° × 8°	19° × 17°	Filament shield
25PAR36/WFL30	12	25	2,000	360	37° × 26°	49° × 41°	Filament shield
25PAR36/VWFL55	12	25	2,000	160	55°	—	Filament shield
35PAR36/H/VNSP5	12	35	4,000	25,000	5°	—	
35PAR36/H/NSP8	12	35	4,000	20,000	8°	—	
35PAR36/H/WFL30	12	35	4,000	900	25° × 35°	—	
36PAR36/H/VNSP5	12	36	4,000	17,000	5°	—	
36PAR36/H/NSP13	12	36	4,000	3,500	13°	—	
36PAR36/H/WFL32	12	36	4,000	1,000	32°	—	
50PAR36/NSP6	12	50	4,000	25,000	6°	—	Filament shield
50PAR36/NSP10	12	50	2,000	1,100	10°	20° × 17°	Filament shield
50PAR36/WFL35	12	50	2,000	1,300	37° × 27°	48° × 41°	Filament shield
50PAR36/VWFL55	12	50	2,000	1,100	55°	80° × 80°	Filament shield

ANSI Lamp Designation	Design Volts	Watts	Design Life (Hrs.)	Initial Candle-power	Beam-Spread		Notes
					50%	10%	
50PAR36/H/NSP5	12	50	4,000	35,000	5°	—	
50PAR36/H/NSP8	12	50	4,000	30,000	8°	—	
50PAR36/H/WFL30	12	50	4,000	1,300	25° × 35°	—	
45PAR38/H/NSP9	120	45	2,500	10,000	9°	—	
45PAR38/H/SP11	120	45	2,500	8,800	11°	—	
45PAR38/H/FL30	120	45	2,500	1,500	32°	—	
45PAR38/HIR/SP12XL	120	45	6,000	4,000	12°	—	IR-reflecting
45PAR38/HIR/FL40XL	120	45	6,000	1,100	40°	—	IR-reflecting
50PAR38/HIR/SP6	120	50	3,000	20,000	6°	—	IR-reflecting
50PAR38/HIR/SP9	120	50	3,000	14,000	9°	—	IR-reflecting
50PAR38/HIR/S/SP10	120	50	4,000	14,000	10°	—	IR, silverized reflector
50PAR38/HIR/S/FL25	120	50	4,000	3,000	25°	—	IR, silverized reflector
55PAR38/HIR/SP12XL	120	55	6,000	9,000	12°	—	IR-reflecting
55PAR38/HIR/FL40XL	120	55	6,000	2,000	40°	—	IR-reflecting
60PAR38/HIR/SP10	120	60	3,000	20,000	10°	—	IR-reflecting
60PAR38/HIR/SP12	120	60	3,000	12,000	12°	—	IR-reflecting
60PAR38/HIR/S/SP12	120	60	4,000	20,000	12°	—	IR, silverized reflector
60PAR38/HIR/FL30	120	60	3,000	3,600	29°	—	IR-reflecting
60PAR38/HIR/FL40	120	60	3,000	2,000	40°	—	IR-reflecting
60PAR38/HIR/WFL55	120	60	3,000	1,250	53°	—	IR-reflecting
70PAR38/HIR/SP10	120	70	3,000	16,000	10°	—	IR-reflecting
70PAR38/HIR/FL25	120	70	3,000	4,600	25°	—	IR-reflecting
75PAR38/H/NSP8	120	75	2,500	18,400	8°	—	
75PAR38/H/NFL25	120	75	2,500	4,000	26°	—	
80PAR38/HIR/SP10	120	80	3,000	25,000	10°	—	IR-reflecting
80PAR38/HIR/SP12	120	80	3,000	19,000	12°	—	IR-reflecting
80PAR38/HIR/SP25	120	80	3,000	5,500	25°	—	IR-reflecting
90PAR38/H/SP10	120	90	2,000	18,500	12°	—	
90PAR38/H/NFL25	120	90	2,000	4,000	25°	—	
90PAR38/H/3WSP12	120	90	2,500	14,300	12°		Side-prong base
90PAR38/H/3FL30	120	90	2,500	3,500	30°		Side-prong base
90PAR38/CB/H/FL25	120	90	2,500	4,100	25°		Cool-beam

ANSI Lamp Designation	Design Volts	Watts	Design Life (Hrs.)	Initial Candle-power	Beam-Spread 50%	Beam-Spread 10%	Notes
90PAR38/HIR/SP12XL	120	90	6,000	12,000	12°	—	IR-reflecting
90PAR38/HIR/FL40XL	120	90	6,000	2,800	40°	—	IR-reflecting
100PAR38/H/SP10	120	90	2,000	17,000	10°		
100PAR38/H/FL25	120	90	2,000	4,800	25°		
100PAR38/HIR/SP10	120	100	3,000	29,000	10°	—	IR-reflecting
100PAR38/HIR/FL25	120	100	3,000	6,300	25°	—	IR-reflecting
100PAR38/HIR/FL40	120	100	3,000	3,400	40°	—	IR-reflecting
120PAR38/3SP	120	120	2,000	9,200	18°		Side-prong base
120PAR38/3FL	120	120	2,000	3,600	30°		Side-prong base
120PAR38/H/SP10	120	120	3,000	22,500	10°	—	
120PAR38/H/NFL25	120	120	3,000	7,700	25°		
120PAR38/H/FL30	120	120	3,000	4,600	30°	—	
120PAR38/H/WFL55	120	120	3,000	2,000	55°	—	
150PAR38/2FL	120	120	2,000	3,400	24°	60°	Cool-beam
150PAR38/3SP	120	120	2,000	10,500	12°	30°	Side-prong base
150PAR38/3FL	120	120	2,000	3,400	24°	60°	Side-prong base
Q250PAR38/SP10	120	250	4,500	46,500	11°	—	
Q250PAR38/FL30	120	250	4,500	9,000	22°	—	
25PAR46/NSP5	6	25	1,000	55,000	—	5.5° × 4.5°	Filament shield
150PAR46/3MFL	125	150	2,000	8,000	26° × 13°	39° × 25°	Side-prong base
200PAR46/3NSP	120	200	2,000	31,000	12° × 8°	23° × 19°	Side-prong base
200PAR46/3MFL	120	200	2,000	11,500	27° × 13°	40° × 24°	Side-prong base
120PAR56/VNSP	12	120	2,000	60,000	8° × 6°	15° × 10°	
120PAR56/MFL	12	120	2,000	19,000	18° × 9°	29° × 15°	
120PAR56/WFL	12	120	2,000	5,625	35° × 18°	50° × 25°	
200PAR56/MFL	120	200	2,000	15,000	22° × 13°	34° × 22°	
240PAR56/VNSP	12	240	2,000	140,000	90° × 6°	17° × 10°	
240PAR56/MFL	12	240	2,000	46,000	19° × 8°	28° × 15°	
240PAR56/WFL	12	240	2,000	13,000	35° × 18°	50° × 27°	
300PAR56/NSP	120	300	2,000	68,000	10° × 8°	20° × 14°	
300PAR56/MFL	120	300	2,000	24,000	23° × 11°	34° × 19°	
300PAR56/WFL	120	300	2,000	11,000	37° × 18°	57° × 27°	
Q500PAR56/NSP	120	500	4,000	96,000	13° × 8°	32° × 15°	

ANSI Lamp Designation	Design Volts	Watts	Design Life (Hrs.)	Initial Candle-power	Beam-Spread		Notes
					50%	10%	
Q500PAR56/MFL	120	500	4,000	43,000	26° × 10°	42° × 20°	
Q500PAR56/WFL	120	500	4,000	19,000	44° × 20°	66° × 34°	
500PAR64/NSP	120	500	2,000	110,000	12° × 7°	19° × 14°	
500PAR64/MFL	120	500	2,000	45,000	9° × 25°	35° × 19°	
500PAR64/WFL	120	500	2,000	10,500	20° × 55°	55° × 32°	
Q1000PAR64/NSP	120	1,000	4,000	135,000	8° × 20°	31° × 14°	
Q1000PAR64/MFL	120	1,000	4,000	82,000	10° × 30°	45° × 22°	
Q1000PAR64/WFL	120	1,000	4,000	23,000	20° × 60°	72° × 45°	
Reflector (R) lamps							
15R14SC/SP	12	15	2,000	135	14°	—	Single contact base
25R14SC/SP15	12	25	2,000	1,200	16°	32°	Single contact base
25R14SC/FL35	12	25	2,000	200	36°	102°	Single contact base
25R14/WFL60	120	25	1,500	150	60°	120°	
50BR19/25/SP	120	50	2,000	—	25°	—	
30R20/FL40	120	30	2,000	300	38°	—	
50R20/FL40	120	50	2,000	550	38°	—	
75R20/FL120	120	75	2,000	800	—	120°	
100BR25/25	120	100	2,000	—	25°	—	
65BR30/SP20	120	65	2,000	1,625	20°	—	
65BR30/SP20XL	120	65	2,500	1,575	20°	—	
65BR30/FL55	120	65	2,000	525	55°	—	
65BR30/FL55XL	120	65	2,500	510	55°	—	
85BR30/SP20	120	85	2,000	3,100	20°	—	
85BR30/FL55	120	85	2,000	700	55°	—	
65BR40/FL60	120	65	2,000	500	60°	—	
85BR40/SP20	120	85	2,000	3,100	20°	—	
85BR40/FL60	120	85	2,000	700	60°	—	

ANSI Lamp Designation	Design Volts	Watts	Design Life (Hrs.)	Initial Candle-power	Beam-Spread 50%	Beam-Spread 10%	Notes
120BR40/SP20	120	120	2,000	4,600	20°	—	
120BR40/FL60	120	120	2,000	1,000	60°	—	
300R40/SP40	120	300	2,000	14,000	40°	—	
300R40/FL120	120	300	2,000	2,900	120°	—	
Elliptical reflector (ER) lamps							
50ER30/FL30	120	50	2,000	1,300	28°	70°	
75ER30/FL30	120	75	2,000	1,800	28°	70°	
120ER30/FL30	120	120	2,000	2,900	28°	70°	

TABLE 3

FLUORESCENT LAMP DESIGNATIONS AND PROPERTIES

Lamp Description	Designation	Impres-sion	Light Output (%)	Color Temper-ature in Kelvin (K)	Color Render-ing Index (CRI)	Life (Hours)	Initial Lumens	Mean Lumens
Cool white	CW	Cool	100	4100	62	20,000+	3,050	2,650
Cool white deluxe	CWX	Cool	72	4100	89	20,000+	2,200	1,800
Warm white	WW	Warm	102	3000	52	20,000+	3,100	2,700
Warm white deluxe	WWX	Warm	68	2800	77	20,000+	2,200	1,805
Soft white	SW	Warm	68	3000	79	20,000+	2,150	1,800
Natural	N	Neutral	69	3700	90	20,000+	2,100	1,870
Lite white	LW	Cool	102	4200	51	20,000+	3,050	2,650
Daylight	D	Daylight	83	6500	79	20,000+	2,600	2,250
Daylight Deluxe	DX	Daylight	76	6500	84	20,000+	2,300	2,000
RE–730	730	Warm	105	3000	70	20,000+	3,200	2,880
RE–735	735	Neutral	105	3500	73	20,000+	3,200	2,880
RE–741	741	Cool	105	4100	70	20,000+	3,200	2,880
RE–750	750	Daylight	90	5000	76	20,000+	3,200	2,880
RE–830	830	Warm	108	3000	85	20,000+	3,300	2,970
RE–835	835	Neutral	108	3500	85	20,000+	3,300	2,970
RE–841	841	Cool	108	4100	85	20,000+	3,300	2,970
RE–850	850	Daylight	93	5000	85	20,000+	3,280	2,950
RE–930	930	Warm	66	3000	95	20,000+	2,100	1,870
RE–950	950	Daylight	66	5000	98	20,000+	2,100	1,870
Chroma 50	C50	Daylight	72	5000	92	20,000+	2,200	1,915
Chroma 75	C75	Daylight	66	7500	95	20,000+	2,000	1,720
T8/ADV/830	ADV830	Warm	105	3000	86	20,000+	3,300	2,970
T8/ADV/835	ADV835	Neutral	105	3500	86	20,000+	3,300	2,970
T8/ADV/841	ADV841	Cool	105	4100	86	20,000+	3,300	2,970
T8/ADV/850	ADV850	Daylight	105	5000	86	20,000+	3,300	2,970
T12/ADV/830	ADV30	Warm	118	3000	82	20,000+	3,600	3,100
T12/ADV/835	ADV35	Neutral	118	3500	82	20,000+	3,600	3,100
T12/ADV/841	ADV41	Cool	118	4100	82	20,000+	3,600	3,100
T12/ADV/850	ADV50	Daylight	118	5000	82	20,000+	3,600	3,100
Red	R	—	6	—	—	20,000+	195	60
Pink	PK	—	35	—	—	20,000+	1,160	695
Gold	GO	—	60	—	—	20,000+	2,400	1,765
Green	G	—	140	—	—	20,000+	4,400	2,200
Blue	B	—	35	—	—	20,000+	1,200	720

TABLE 4

EFFICACY OF ELECTRIC LIGHT SOURCES

Lamp Type	Wattage Range	Initial Lamp Efficacy (Lumens per watt)	Color Temperature in Kelvin (K)	Color Rendering Index (CRI)	Design Life (Hours)
Incandescent	6–1,500	4–24.5	2700–2800	100	750–4,000
Tungsten-halogen	5–1,500	10–22	2900–3100	100	1,000–6,000
Fluorescent	4–215	10–104.5	2700–7500	53–95	6,000–24,000+
Compact fluorescent	5–80	28–76	2700–4100	81–82	6,000–14,000
Mercury vapor	40–1,000	19–59	3300–5900	15–52	12,000–24,000+
Metal halide	32–1,500	35–100	3000–4400	65–96	3,000–20,000
High-pressure sodium	33–1,000	31–127	1800–2800	22–85	7,500–24,000+
Low-pressure sodium	18–180	58–185	1740–1750	0	14,000–18,000

TABLE 5

COMPARATIVE LUMINANCE OF INCANDESCENT AND FLUORESCENT LAMPS
(APPROXIMATE CANDELAS PER SQUARE INCH)

Lamp Description	Shape	Characteristics	Luminance (cd/sq in)
Incandescent			
150 W	A21	(IF)	150.0
Fluorescent			
Preheat			
8 W	T5	(12")	8.1
15 W	T8	(18")	6.7
15 W	T12	(18")	4.1
20 W	T12	(24")	4.6
Rapid Start			
30 W	T12	(36")	5.3
32 W	T8	(48")	7.4
40 W	T8	(60")	7 4
40 W	T12	(48")	5.4
40 W	T12	(48" ES)	4.7
40 W	T12	(22$\frac{7}{16}$" U-bent)	5.0
High Output			
24"	T12	(35 W)	6.1
48"	T12	(60 W)	7.3
72"	T12	(85 W)	7.3
96"	T12	(110 W)	7.3
96"	T12	(95 W ES)	6.6
Very High Output			
48"	T12	(116 W)	12.0
72"	T12	(162 W)	12.0
96"	T12	(212 W)	12.0
96"	T12	(185 W ES)	11.2
Instant Start			
40 W	T12	(48")	5.3
40 W	T12	(60")	2.3
Slimline			
42"	T8	(23 W)	5.3
64"	T8	(35 W)	5.3

Lamp Description	Shape	Characteristics	Luminance (cd/sq in)
72"	T8	(37.5 W)	5.0
96"	T8	(50 W)	5.0
48"	T12	(38.5 W)	5.0
72"	T12	(56 W)	5.0
96"	T12	(75 W)	5.0
96"	T12	(60W ES)	4.5
Circline			
20 W	T9	(6½" dia.)	5.9
22 W	T9	(8¼" dia.)	5.2
32 W	T9	(12" dia.)	4.8
40 W	T9	(16" dia.)	4.8

TABLE 6

RELATIVE OUTPUT OF COLORED LAMPS

Lamp Color Description	Light Output (%)	Lamp Color Description	Light Output (%)
Incandescent—tinted lamps		**Fluorescent**	
Clear	100	Cool white	100
White	85	Cool white deluxe	72
Ivory	73	Warm white	102
Flame tint	58	Warm white deluxe	72
Rose	35	Natural	69
Red	5	Lite white	104
Orange	35	Daylight	85
Yellow	65	Daylight Deluxe	76
Green	5	RE-730	93
Blue	3	RE-735	93
		RE-741	93
Incandescent—sign lamps		RE-750	90
Clear	100	RE-830	98
White	85	RE-835	98
Ivory	73	RE-841	98
Flame tint	58	RE-850	97
Rose	35	RE-930	66
Red	5	RE-950	66
Orange	35	Chroma 50	72
Yellow	65	Chroma 75	66
Green	5	T8/ADV/830	105
Blue	3	T8/ADV/835	105
		T8/ADV/841	105
Lumiline lamps		T8/ADV/850	105
Clear	100	T12/ADV/830	118
White	85	T12/ADV/835	118
		T12/ADV/841	118
		T12/ADV/850	118
		Blue	39
		Gold	79
		Red	6
		Pink	45
		Green	160
		Deep blue	17

TABLE 7

RELATIVE LAMP WATTS FOR APPROXIMATE EQUAL QUANTITY OF LIGHT

Filament (clear color)	30 W	Clear
	60 W	Pink
	90 W	Blue-white
	200 W	Red
	90 W	Amber
	36 W	Yellow or gold
	300 W	Green
	300 W	Blue
Filament (diffuse color)	30 W	Silica coat
	39 W	Pink tint
	36 W	Gold tint
	60 W	Green tint
	75 W	Blue tint
Fluorescent	10 W	Cool white
	22 W	Pink
	165 W	Red
	13 W	Yellow or gold
	11 W	Yellow-green
	6 W	Green
	22 W	Blue
	65 W	Deep blue

TABLE 8

RELATIVE BRIGHTNESS
FOR EQUAL ATTRACTION

White light	10
Yellow light	12
Red light	3
Green light	4
Blue light	6

TABLE 9

RECOMMENDED WIRE SIZE AND SECONDARY WIRE LENGTH FOR LIGHTING CIRCUITS USING 120 V PRIMARY/12 V SECONDARY TRANSFORMERS

Wire Size (Gauge)	Watts (VA) per Circuit																								
	20	40	60	80	100	120	140	160	180	200	220	240	260	280	300	320	340	360	380	400	420	440	460	480	500
	Maximum Secondary Wire Length in Feet																								
14	75	37	25	19	15	12	11	9	8	7	7	6	6	5	5	5	4	4	4	4	4	3	3	3	3
12	118	59	39	30	24	20	17	15	13	12	11	10	9	8	8	7	7	7	6	6	6	5	5	5	5
10	188	94	63	47	38	31	27	24	21	19	17	16	14	13	13	12	11	10	10	9	9	9	8	8	8
8	299	149	100	75	60	50	43	37	33	30	27	25	23	21	20	19	18	17	16	15	14	14	13	12	12
6	476	238	159	119	95	79	68	60	53	48	43	40	37	34	32	30	28	26	25	24	23	22	21	20	19

This chart is based on SPT-3 wire and a maximum 0.63 voltage drop at the end of the run.

Exceeding the maximum secondary wire lengths noted in the chart above will cause the voltage to drop along the length of the wire. Lamps positioned closer to the transformer will burn at a higher color temperature than those farther from it because the lamps nearest the transformer are receiving greater voltage than those farther away.

When dimming low-voltage loads, use dimmers designed for low-voltage magnetic loads with magnetic transformers and dimmers designed for electronic low-voltage loads with electronic transformers.

Based on the Recommended Wire Size and Voltage Drop chart from Acme Electric Corporation Catalog ATD-01. Used with permission from the Acme Electric Corporation Power Distribution Products Division.

TABLE 10

TRIGONOMETRIC FUNCTIONS: SINES AND COSINES OF ANGLES

$\theta°$	$\sin \theta$	$\cos \theta$	$\theta°$	$\sin \theta$	$\cos \theta$	$\theta°$	$\sin \theta$	$\cos \theta$	$\theta°$	$\sin \theta$	$\cos \theta$
0	0.0000	1.000	22	.375	0.927	45	.707	.707	68	.927	.375
			23	.391	.921	46	.719	.695	69	.934	.358
1	.0175	1.000	24	.407	.914	47	.731	.682	70	.940	.342
2	.0349	0.999	25	.423	.906	48	.743	.669			
3	.0523	.999	26	.438	.899	49	.755	.656	71	.946	.326
4	.0698	.998	27	.454	.891	50	.766	.643	72	.951	.309
5	.0872	.996	28	.470	.833				73	.956	.292
6	.105	.995	29	.485	.875	51	.777	.629	74	.961	.276
7	.122	.993	30	.500	.866	52	.788	.616	75	.966	.259
8	.139	.990				53	.799	.602	76	.970	.242
9	.156	.988	31	.515	.857	54	.809	.588	77	.974	.225
10	.174	.985	32	.530	.848	55	.819	.574	78	.978	.208
			33	.545	.839	56	.829	.559	79	.982	.191
11	.191	.982	34	.559	.829	57	.839	.545	80	.985	.174
12	.208	.978	35	.574	.819	58	.848	.530			
13	.225	.974	36	.588	.809	59	.857	.515	81	.988	.156
14	.242	.970	37	.602	.799	60	.866	.500	82	.990	.139
15	.259	.966	38	.616	.788				83	.993	.122
16	.276	.961	39	.629	.777	61	.875	.485	84	.995	.105
17	.292	.956	40	.643	.766	62	.883	.470	85	.996	.0872
18	.309	.951				63	.891	.454	86	.9976	.0698
19	.326	.946	41	.656	.755	64	.899	.438	87	.9986	.0523
20	.342	.940	42	.669	.743	65	.906	.423	88	.9994	.0349
			43	.682	.731	66	.914	.407	89	.9998	.0175
21	.358	.934	44	.695	.719	67	.921	.391	90	1.0000	0.0000

TABLE 11

LAMP LUMEN DEPRECIATION FACTORS

Lamp Description	Shape	Nominal Wattage	Lamp Lumen Depreciation (LLD) Factors
Incandescent			
Extended service	A, PS	15–70	0.85
General service	A, PS, S	To 40	0.85
		50–1,500	0.89
Projector	PAR 38-64	75–1,000	0.84
Reflector	R40	150–500	0.86
	R52-57	500–1,000	0.81
Rough service	A, PS	50–200	0.79
Showcase	T10	25–40	0.78
Silver-bowl	A, PS	200–500	0.75
Three-way	A, T	30–150	0.85
	PS	100–300	0.72
Tungsten-halogen	T	200–1,500	0.96
Vibration	A19	50	0.72
Fluorescent			
Cool white	T12	40	0.87
Cool white deluxe	T12	40	0.82
Warm white	T12	40	0.87
Warm white deluxe	T12	40	0.82
Natural	T12	40	0.89
Lite white	T12	40	0.87
Daylight	T12	40	0.87
Cool green	T12	40	0.82
RE-700 series	T8	40	0.90
RE-800 series	T8	25–40	0.93
	T12	30–40	0.90
Chroma 50	T12	40	0.87
Chroma 75	T12	40	0.86

Lamp Description	Shape	Nominal Wattage	Lamp Lumen Depreciation (LLD) Factors
Fluorescent, continued			
Compact, twin-tube	T4	5	0.84
Compact, twin-tube	T4	7–13	0.85
Compact, quad-tube	T4	13–26	0.85
Compact, triple-tube	T4	18–70	0.85
Compact, long twin-tube	T5	18–80	0.90
High-intensity discharge			
Standard mercury clear	E28	250	0.88
Mercury warm deluxe white	E28	250	0.81
Mercury deluxe white	E28	250	0.81
Standard clear metal halide	E28	175	0.74*
			0.69**
	BT56	1,000	0.76
Standard coated metal halide	E28	175	0.71*
			0.65**
	BT56	1,000	0.76
Ceramic metal halide	T7	150	0.89
Ceramic metal halide	T8	250	0.80
Ceramic metal halide	T6½	70	0.82
Deluxe high-pressure sodium	B17	70	0.80
White high-pressure sodium	B17	95	0.80
Low-pressure sodium	T16	55	0.87

*Vertical lamp orientation

**Horizontal lamp orientation

TABLE 12

LUMINAIRE MAINTENANCE CATEGORIES

PROCEDURE FOR DETERMINING LUMINAIRE MAINTENANCE CATEGORIES

To assist in determining luminaire dirt depreciation (LDD) factors, luminaires are separated into six maintenance categories (I through VI). To arrive at categories, luminaires are arbitrarily divided into sections—a *top enclosure* and a *bottom enclosure*—by drawing a horizontal line through the light center of the lamp or lamps. The characteristics listed for the enclosures are then selected as best describing the luminaire. Only one characteristic for the top enclosure and one for the bottom enclosure are used in determining the category of a luminaire. Percentage of uplight is based on 100% light output for the luminaire. The maintenance category is determined by the characteristics in both enclosure columns. If a luminaire falls into more than one category, the lower-numbered category is used.

Maintenance Category	Top Enclosure	Bottom Enclosure
I	1. None	1. None
II	1. None	1. None
	2. Transparent with 15% or more uplight through apertures	2. Louvers or baffles
	3. Translucent with 15% or more uplight through apertures	
	4. Opaque with 15% or more uplight through apertures	
III	1. Transparent with less than 15% upward light through apertures	1. None
	2. Translucent with less than 15% upward light through apertures	2. Louvers or baffles
	3. Opaque with less than 15% upward light through apertures	
IV	1. Transparent unapertured	1. None
	2. Translucent unapertured	2. Louvers or baffles
	3. Opaque unapertured	
V	1. Transparent unapertured	1. Transparent unapertured
	2. Translucent unapertured	2. Translucent unapertured
	3. Opaque unapertured	
VI	1. None	1. Transparent unapertured
	2. Transparent unapertured	2. Translucent unapertured
	3. Translucent unapertured	3. Opaque unapertured
	4. Opaque unapertured	

Reprinted from the *IES Lighting Handbook, 9th Ed.* Used with permission from the Illuminating Engineering Society of North America.

TABLE 13

LUMINAIRE DIRT DEPRECIATION (LDD) FACTORS FOR SIX LUMINAIRE CATEGORIES (I THROUGH VI) AND FOR FIVE DEGREES OF DIRTINESS

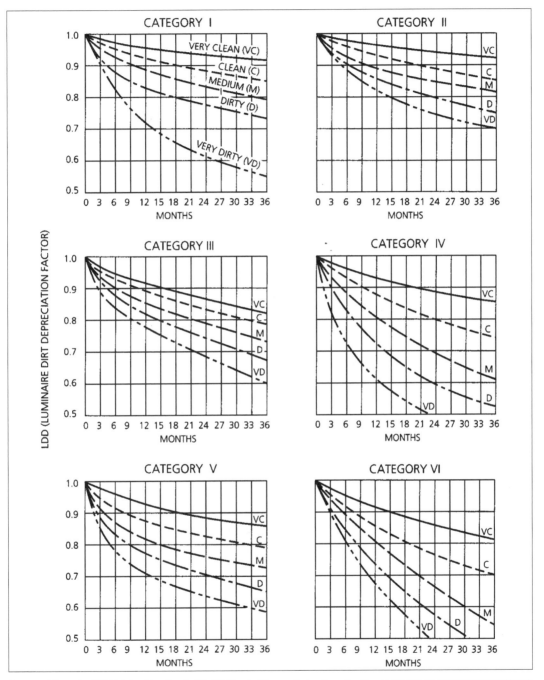

Reprinted from the *IES Lighting Handbook, 9th Ed.* Used with permission from the Illuminating Engineering Society of North America.

TABLE 14

SAMPLE COEFFICIENT OF UTILIZATION TABLE

Coefficients of Utilization—Zonal Cavity Method Effective Floor Cavity Reflectance 0.20																			
RC	80				70				50			30			10			0
RW	70	50	30	10	70	50	30	10	50	30	10	50	30	10	50	30	10	0
0	86	86	86	86	84	84	84	84	80	80	80	77	77	77	74	74	74	72
1	82	80	78	76	80	78	76	75	75	74	72	72	71	70	70	69	68	67
2	77	74	71	68	76	72	70	67	70	68	66	68	66	64	66	64	63	62
3	73	68	64	61	71	67	63	60	65	62	59	63	61	58	61	59	58	56
4	69	63	58	55	67	62	58	55	60	57	54	59	56	53	57	55	53	51
5	64	58	53	49	63	57	52	49	55	52	49	54	51	48	53	50	48	47
6	60	53	48	44	59	52	48	44	51	47	44	50	46	44	49	46	43	42
7	56	48	43	39	55	48	43	39	47	42	39	46	42	39	45	41	39	38
8	52	44	39	35	51	43	38	35	42	38	35	42	38	35	41	37	34	33
9	48	39	34	31	47	39	34	31	38	34	31	38	33	31	37	33	30	29
10	44	36	30	27	43	35	30	27	35	30	27	34	30	27	33	29	27	26

Note: the coefficient of utilization values in this table are based on relative photometry which assumes a ballast factor of 1.0. Any calculations prepared from these data should include an appropriate ballast factor.

TABLE 15

RECOMMENDED ILLUMINANCE VALUES

	General Lighting			Task Lighting		
	Public Spaces	**Simple Orien-tation**	**Occa-sional Visual Task**	**Large Visual Task**	**Small Visual Task**	**Very Small Visual Task**
Activity	*3 fc*	*5 fc*	*10 fc*	*30 fc*	*50 fc*	*100 fc*
GENERAL						
Circulation						
Corridors		•				
Elevators		•				
Lobbies			•			
Stairs		•				
Service						
Toilets and washrooms		•				
Storage						
Active			•			
Inactive		•				
HOSPITALITY FACILITIES						
Bathrooms, for grooming				•		
Bedrooms, for reading				•		
Cleaning			•			
Dining			•			
Kitchen, critical seeing					•	
Laundry				•		
Sewing						•
INDUSTRY						
Assembly						
Simple				•		
Moderately difficult					•	
Difficult						•
Inspection						
Simple				•		
Moderately difficult					•	
Difficult						•
Locker rooms			•			

	General Lighting			Task Lighting		
	Public Spaces	**Simple Orien-tation**	**Occa-sional Visual Task**	**Large Visual Task**	**Small Visual Task**	**Very Small Visual Task**
Activity	*3 fc*	*5 fc*	*10 fc*	*30 fc*	*50 fc*	*100 fc*
OFFICES						
Accounting				•	*	
Conference rooms				•		
Drafting, high contrast					•	
Drafting, low contrast						•
General/private offices				•	**	
Lounges and reception			•			
RESIDENCES						
Bathrooms, for grooming				•		
Bedrooms, for reading				•		
Conversation areas	•					
Dining		•				
Kitchen, critical seeing					•	
Laundry				•		
Sewing					•	
SCHOOLS						
Assembly						
Auditoria			•			
Social activity		•				
Classrooms						
General				•		
Lecture demonstration						•
Science laboratories					•	
STORES						
Circulation			•			
Feature displays						•
Merchandise displays					•	
Sales transactions				•	***	
Wrapping and packaging				•		

*If #4 pencil or harder leads are used for handwritten tasks.

**If tasks involve poor copies, photographs, maps, or 6 point type.

***If handwritten carbon copies.

Based on the IESNA Lighting Design Guide, *IES Lighting Handbook, 9th Ed.* Used with permission from the Illuminating Engineering Society of North America.

TABLE 16

DETERMINATION OF ILLUMINANCE CATEGORIES

Orientation and simple visual tasks. Visual performance is largely unimportant. These tasks are found in public spaces where reading and visual inspection are only occasionally performed. Higher levels are recommended for tasks where visual performance is occasionally important.

A	Public spaces	3 fc
B	Simple orientation for short visits	5 fc
C	Working spaces where simple visual tasks are performed	10 fc

Common visual tasks. Visual performance is important. These tasks are found in commercial, industrial, and residential applications. Recommended illuminance values differ because of the characteristics of the visual task being lighted. Higher values are recommended for visual tasks with critical elements of low contrast or small size.

D	Performance of visual tasks of high contrast and large size	30 fc
E	Performance of visual tasks of high contrast and small size, or visual tasks of low contrast and large size	50 fc
F	Performance of visual tasks of low contract and small size	100 fc

Special visual tasks. Visual performance is of critical importance. These tasks are highly specialized, including those with very small or very low contrast critical elements. The recommended illuminance values are often achieved with supplementary task lighting. The higher recommended values are frequently achieved by moving the light source closer to the task.

G	Performance of the visual task near the threshold	300 to 1,000 fc

Based on the Determination of Illuminance Categories, *IES Lighting Handbook, 9th Ed.* Used with permission from the Illuminating Engineering Society of North America.

References

Anderson, Bruce, with Michael Riordan. *The Solar Home Book*. Andover: Brick House Publishing Co., 1976.

Arnheim, Rudolf. *The Dynamics of Architectural Form*. Berkeley: University of California Press, 1977.

Evans, Benjamin H., AIA. *Daylight in Architecture*. New York: McGraw-Hill Book Company, 1981.

Flynn, John E. "A Study of Subjective Responses to Low Energy and Nonuniform Lighting Systems." *Lighting Design + Application* February 1977: 6–14.

———. "The Psychology of Light." *Electrical Consultant* December 1972–August 1973. Series of 8 articles.

Flynn, John E., and Samuel M. Mills. *Architectural Lighting Graphics*. New York: Reinhold Publishing Corporation, 1962.

Flynn, John E., and Arthur W. Segil. *Architectural Interior Systems*. New York: Van Nostrand Reinhold Co., 1970.

Flynn, John E. and Terry J. Spencer. "The Effects of Light Source Color on User Impression and Satisfaction." *Journal of the Illuminating Engineering Society* April 1977: 167–179.

Flynn, John E., Terry J. Spencer, Osyp Martyniuk, and Clyde Hendrik. "Interim Study of Procedures for Investigating the Effect of Light on Impression and Behavior. *Journal of the Illuminating Engineering Society* October 1993: 87–94.

Gordon, Gary. "The Design Department." *Architectural Lighting* November 1986–May 1987. Series of 6 articles.

———. "Specialty Lighting." *Encyclopedia of Architecture: Design, Engineering, and Construction*. New York: John Wiley & Sons, 1989.

Graham, Frank D. *Audel's Handy Book of Practical Electricity*. New York: Theo. Audel & Co., 1941.

Gregory, Richard L. *Eye and Brain*. 5th ed. Princeton: Princeton University Press, 1997.

Guide to Dimming Low Voltage Lighting. Coopersburg: Lutron Electronics Co., 1989.

Guide to Fluorescent Lamps. Somerset: Philips Lighting Company, 1988.

Guide to High Intensity Discharge Lamps. Somerset: Philips Lighting Company, 1991.

Guide to Incandescent Lamps. Somerset: Philips Lighting Company, 1986.

Hall, Edward T. *The Hidden Dimension.* Garden City: Doubleday, 1966.

High Intensity Discharge Lamps. Cleveland: General Electric Company, 1975.

Hurvich, Leo M., and Dorothea Jameson. *The Perception of Brightness and Darkness.* Boston: Allyn and Bacon, Inc., 1966.

Incandescent Lamps. Cleveland: General Electric Company, 1984.

Kahn, Louis I. *Light is the Theme.* Fort Worth: Kimbell Art Foundation, 1975.

Lambert, Johann Heinrich. *Photometry or On the Measure and Gradations of Light, Colors and Shade.* Trans. David L DiLaura. New York: Illuminating Engineering Society of North America, 2001.

Lamp and Ballast Product Catalog 2002. Danvers, MA: Osram Sylvania, 2002.

Lamp Products Catalog 2001–2002. Cleveland: General Electric Company, 2001.

Lamp Specification and Application Guide 2001/ 2002. Somerset: Philips Lighting Company, 2001.

Light and Color. Cleveland: General Electric Company, 1978.

Marsteller, John. "A Philosophy of Light: Recalling Richard Kelly's Three Functional Elements." *Interior Design* February 1987: 78–80.

MasterColor Metal Halide Lamps. Somerset: Philips Lighting Company, 1999.

Mehrabian, Albert. *Public Spaces and Private Spaces.* New York: Basic Books Inc., 1976.

Moon, Parry. *The Scientific Basis of Illuminating Engineering.* New York: McGraw-Hill Book Company, Inc., 1936.

Moore, Fuller. *Concepts and Practice of Architectural Daylighting.* New York: Van Nostrand Reinhold Company, 1985.

Parker, Bertha Morris. *Electricity.* Evanston: Row, Peterson and Company, 1944.

Rea, Mark S., ed. *Lighting Handbook.* 9th ed. New York: Illuminating Engineering Society of North America, 2000.

Robb, Christina. "Light: An Illumination." *The Boston Globe Magazine* 1 September 1985: 12+.

Smith, Robert L. "Lessons in Luminance." *Lighting Design + Application* August 1992: 10–12.

Tanizaki, Jun'ichiro. *In Praise of Shadows.* New Haven: Leete's Island Books, 1977.

The ABC's of Electronic Ballasts. Rosemont: Advance Transformer Co., 1989.

Thomson, Garry. *The Museum Environment.* London: Butterworths, 1978.

Credits

COLOR PLATES

1	Courtesy of GE Lighting.
2	Courtesy of GE Lighting.
3	Courtesy of GE Lighting.
4	Courtesy of GE Lighting.
5	Gagosian Residence, Francois de Menil Architect. Photo by Paul Warchol.
6	Prudential Insurance Company of America, Grad Associates. Photo by Peter L. Goodman.
7	Prudential Insurance Company of America, Grad Associates. Photo by Peter L. Goodman.
8	Gagosian Residence, Francois de Menil Architect. Photo by Paul Warchol.
9	Courtesy of GE Lighting.
7	Courtesy of GE Lighting.
11	Courtesy of GE Lighting.
12	Courtesy of GE Lighting.
13	Courtesy of GE Lighting.
14	Courtesy of Philips Lighting.
15	Courtesy of Philips Lighting.
16	Courtesy of Philips Lighting.
17	Courtesy of Philips Lighting.
18	Courtesy of GE Lighting.
19	Courtesy of Philips Lighting.
20	Courtesy of Philips Lighting.
21	Courtesy of Philips Lighting.

22   Courtesy of Philips Lighting.
23   Courtesy of Philips Lighting.
24   Courtesy of Philips Lighting.
25   Courtesy of Philips Lighting.
26   Courtesy of GE Lighting.
27   Courtesy of GE Lighting.
28   Courtesy of GE Lighting.
29   Courtesy of GE Lighting.
30   Courtesy of GE Lighting.
31   Courtesy of Philips Lighting.

LUMINAIRE DRAWINGS

Many of the drawings in Chapter 12 are based on luminaires originally manufactured by Edison Price Incorporated. The following illustrations are based on luminaires first designed by Edison Price:

Figure 12.7   for the First Unitarian Church, Rochester, 1963.
Figure 12.8   for the Hartford Fire Insurance Building, 1961.
Figure 12.11   for the CIT Building Headquarters Lobby, 1958.
Figure 12.13   for the Philadelphia Academy of Music, 1957.
Figure 12.15   for the Knoll Chicago Showroom, 1954.
Figure 12.17   the first parabolic, low-brightness, fluorescent downlight was designed for the Upjohn Executive Headquarters Building, 1961.
Figure 12.19   for the Chicago Civic Center, 1965.
Figure 12.21   for the Munson-Williams-Proctor Museum, 1960.
Figure 12.22   for the Museum of Modern Art, 1958.
Figure 12.24   for the Munson-Williams-Proctor Museum, 1960.
Figure 12.25   for the Lyndon Baines Johnson Library, 1971.
Figure 12.26   for the Lyndon Baines Johnson Library, 1971.
Figure 12.28   for 9 West 58 Street, New York City, 1971.
Figure 12.31   for the Seagram Building Lobby,1957.
Figure 12.47   for the Yale Art Gallery Building, 1953.
Figure 12.49   for St. John's College, 1965.

PHOTOGRAPHS

The lighting for all projects was designed by Gary Gordon LLC except figures 13.9, 13.33, 13.34, and 13.35, as noted below.

Figure 2.1   Prudential Insurance Company of America, Grad Associates. Photo by Peter L. Goodman.
Figure 2.2   Armenian Evangelical Church, Lee H. Skolnick Architect. Photo by Stan Reiss.
Figure 2.3   Offices for Gary Gordon LLC, Donna Selene Seftel Architect.
Figure 2.4   One Fifth Avenue Restaurant, Pentagram Architectural Services. Photo by Peter Mauss/Esto.
Figure 2.5   Martinez Valero Shoe Store, Zivkovic Associates. Photo by Ashley Ranson.
Figure 2.6   City Bakery, Turett Collaborative Architects. Photo by Paul Warchol.
Figure 2.7   Australia Broadcasting Corporation, Zivkovic Associates Architects. Photo by Ashley Ranson.

Figure 2.8   Private Residence, Frank and Marcotullio Design Associates. Photo by Michael Gordon.

Figure 2.15   Club Monaco, Deborah Berke Architect. Photo by Catherine Bogert.

Figure 2.16   Marketplace at Newport, Turett Collaborative Architects. Photo by Paul Warchol.

Figure 2.17   One Fifth Avenue Restaurant, Pentagram Architectural Services. Photo by Peter Mauss/ Esto.

Figure 2.18   Tommy Boy Records, Turett Collaborative Architects. Photo by Paul Warchol.

Figure 3.3   Private residence, Sidnam|Petrone Architect. Photo by Peter L. Goodman.

Figure 3.5   Armenian Evangelical Church, Lee H. Skolnick Architect. Photo by Stan Reiss.

Figure 3.7   Lillian Vernon Residence, Hardy Holzman Pfeiffer Associates. Photo by Gideon Louis.

Figure 3.8   Sedona Store, Andaloro Associates. Photo by George Mott.

Figure 3.10   Morton Productions, BumpZoid. Photo by Langdon Clay.

Figure 3.12   Armenian Evangelical Church, Lee H. Skolnick Architect. Photo by Stan Reiss.

Figure 3.14   Yale University School of Art, Deborah Berke Architect. Photo by Catherine Bogert.

Figure 3.16   Offices for Omon Ltd., Zivkovic Associates Architects. Photo by Ashley Ranson.

Figure 3.17   Lillian Vernon Residence, Hardy Holzman Pfeiffer Associates. Photo by Gideon Louis.

Figure 3.18   Gagosian Residence, Francois de Menil Architect. Photo by Paul Warchol.

Figure 3.19   Yale University School of Art, Deborah Berke Architect. Photo by Catherine Bogert

Figure 3.20   City Bakery, Turett Collaborative Architects. Photo by Paul Warchol.

Figure 3.22   Photo by Photosphere.

Figure 3.24   Photo by Photosphere.

Figure 3.25   Photo by Photosphere.

Figure 3.26   Photo by Photosphere.

Figure 3.27   Photo courtesy of GE Lighting.

Figure 3.28   Photo courtesy of GE Lighting.

Figure 12.57   The New Gotham Lobby, Stephen Alton Architects. Photo by Eduard Hueber.

Figure 12.58   Armenian Evangelical Church, Lee H. Skolnick Architect. Photo by Stan Reiss.

Figure 12.59   Neuman and Bogdanoff, Pentagram Architectural Services. Photo by Peter Mauss/Esto.

Figure 12.60   Findler Residence, Bruce Bierman Design. Photo by Andrew Bardwin.

Figure 12.61   The New Gotham Lobby, Stephen Alton Architects. Photo by Eduard Hueber.

Figure 13.1   Offices for Gary Gordon LLC, Donna Selene Seftel Architect.

Figure 13.2   Club Monaco, Deborah Berke Architect. Photo by Catherine Bogert.

Figure 13.3   Prudential Insurance Company of America, Grad Associates. Photo by Peter L. Goodman.

Figure 13.7   Gagosian Residence, Francois de Menil Architect. Photo by Paul Warchol.

Figure 13.8   Residence for Adam R. Rose and Peter R. McQuillan, Stuart Mager Incorporated. Photo by David Mager.

Figure 13.9   Photo courtesy of Halo Lighting.

Figure 13.11   Findler Residence, Bruce Bierman Design. Photo by Andrew Bardwin.

Figure 13.22   Prudential Insurance Company of America, Grad Associates. Photo by Peter L. Goodman.

Figure 13.27   Gagosian Residence, Francois de Menil Architect. Photo by Paul Warchol.

Figure 13.28   Lillian Vernon Residence, Hardy Holzman Pfeiffer Associates. Photo by Gideon Louis.

Figure 13.29   Martinez Valero Shoe Store, Zivkovic Associates. Photo by Ashley Ranson.

Figure 13.30   Club Monaco, Deborah Berke Architect. Photo by Catherine Bogert.

Figure 13.31   Martinez Valero Shoe Store, Zivkovic Associates. Photo by Ashley Ranson.

Figure 13.32   St. Mark's Bookshop, Zivkovic Associates Architects. Photo by Ashley Ranson.

Glossary

"Accent" light: an advertising term misapplied to adjustable, directional luminaires that are properly termed object lights. See *object light*.

Accommodation: the automatic adjustment of the eye for seeing at varied distances, accomplished by changes in focus.

Acuity (*also called* **visual acuity**): the ability of the eye to make out fine detail.

Adaptation: the change in the sensitivity of the visual system based on the amount of light the retina has been exposed to in the recent past. *Dark adaptation* is an increase in visual sensitivity that occurs over time in darkness.

Ambient light: general or background illumination.

Ampere: measurement of the rate of flow of an electric current; it is equivalent to the steady current produced by one volt applied across a resistance of one ohm.

Anodize: to coat a metal (usually aluminum) with a protective film by subjecting it to electrolytic action.

Aperture (of a luminaire): the diameter of the opening of a recessed luminaire.

Apparent color temperature: See *correlated color temperature*.

Axial (filament): a filament situated in the direction of the lamp axis.

Baffle: a single opaque or translucent element to shield glare at normal viewing angles in one direction, along a single axis. For small-aperture luminaires, a baffle around the perimeter provides shielding from all directions. See also *louvers*.

Ballast: an auxiliary device for an electric discharge source that provides the proper starting voltage and regulates the lamp operating current. All fluorescent and HID lamps require a ballast for proper operation.

Ballast factor: the ratio of light output produced by lamps operated by a commercially-available ballast to light output produced by lamps powered by a laboratory-reference ballast.

Beam angle: the angle between the two directions for which the intensity is 50% of the maximum, as measured in a plane through the beam centerline. See also *field angle*.

Beam-spread: the angular cone of light created by the distribution of the lamp or luminaire, in the plane of the beam axis. See also *beam angle* and *field angle*.

Borosilicate: a silicate glass containing oxide of boron that has high heat-resistance.

Brightness: a subjective experience that occurs in the consciousness of a human observer, a result of the intensity of light falling on a given region of the retina at a certain time, the intensity of light that the retina has been subject to in the recent past, and the intensities of light falling on other regions of the retina. See also *luminance*.

Bulb: the outer hard, soft, or quartz glass envelope of an electric lamp, which may contain a vacuum, elemental inert gas, or metal, and a means of light generation. Also, the layman's term for an electric lamp.

Candela (cd): the unit of luminous intensity emitted in a specific direction by a source, equal to one lumen per steradian.

Candlepower: a vernacular term for luminous intensity expressed in candelas.

Candlepower distribution curve: properly called a *luminous intensity distribution curve*, it depicts the amount of luminous intensity (expressed in candelas) generated in each direction by a light source in a plane through the center of the source.

Capacitive: the part of an electric circuit that exhibits the ability to store charge.

Capacitor: an electric circuit element included in some magnetic ballasts that consists of two metallic plates, separated and insulated from each other, used for storing charge temporarily.

Cathode: one of two electron-emitting electrodes hermetically sealed into a fluorescent lamp, consisting of metal cylinders (cold cathode) or coiled tungsten wire (hot cathode), and usually coated with an electron-emissive material.

Clerestory: a window located in the upper portion of a wall that admits natural light into the center of a room.

Coefficient of utilization: the ratio of the number of lumens expected to reach the work plane divided by the number of lumens generated by the bare lamps of a specific luminaire in a specific room.

Color constancy: knowledge of the normal color of objects. We tend to see surface and object colors as the same despite changes to the color of light illuminating the surface or object.

Color rendering index (CRI): the comparison between the color-rendering ability of a given light source and a reference light source, expressed as an R_a factor on a scale of 1 to 100.

Color rendition: how surface and object colors appear under a given light source, in comparison with their color appearance under a reference light source.

Color spectrum: the continuum of color formed when a beam of white light is dispersed (as by a prism) so that its component wavelengths are arranged in order.

Color temperature: the color appearance of the light that emanates from a source, measured in Kelvin (K). Not a measure of the surface temperature of a lamp, it is the absolute temperature of a laboratory blackbody radiator when its visible radiation matches the color of the light source.

Contrast: the relationship between the intensities of an object and its surrounding areas; the degree of difference between light and dark. See also *luminance contrast*.

Correlated color temperature (CCT): the color appearance of the light that emanates from an electric light source with a discontinuous spectrum, measured in Kelvin (K).

Cove: a concave or canted interior corner or molding, especially at the transition from wall to ceiling; sometimes used to shield light sources that distribute light across the ceiling plane.

Current: the flow of electricity in a circuit; the rate of flow of an electric current is measured in *amperes* (amps, A).

Cutoff: measured up from *nadir*, the angle of the first line of sight at which the bare light source is not visible.

Daylighting: the illumination of indoor spaces by natural light.

Dichroic: the property of transmitting certain wavelengths of light while reflecting those not transmitted, usually with little absorption.

Diffraction grating: a glass or polished metal surface that has a large number of very fine parallel grooves or slits, used to change the directions and intensities of a group of wavelengths of reflected or transmitted light.

Diffuse light: a distribution of light that is dispersed in a wide pattern and not incident from any particular direction.

Diffuser: a glass or plastic material that disperses light from a source in all directions, eliminating the directional quality of the beam; in fluorescent downlights, used to redirect light from the glare zone down toward work surfaces.

Dimmer: a device that provides variation in the intensity of a luminaire by controlling the voltage or current available.

Direct glare: excessive light misdirected toward the eye. It refers to glare from the direct view of luminaries or bare lamps. See also *reflected glare*.

Direct/indirect: light emitted in a downward and upward direction, with little or no light emitted at angles near the horizontal.

Direct (light): a distribution of light emitted in a downward direction.

Downlight: a recessed, surface-mounted, or pendant-mounted luminaire which emits light in a downward direction with no upward component of light.

Downlighting: a distribution of light emitted in a downward direction.

Discharge source: a lamp that produces light by the passage of an electric current through a vapor or gas, rather than through a tungsten wire as in incandescent lamps. (These include cold-cathode, fluorescent, high-pressure sodium, low-pressure sodium, mercury vapor, metal halide, and neon lamps.)

Efficacy: the ratio of lumens produced to electricity consumed when referring to a light source, expressed in lumens per watt.

Efficiency: the ratio of lumens emitted by a luminaire to that emitted by the lamp(s) contained within it, expressed as a percentage.

Ellipsoidal: in the shape of an ellipse, which has two focal points. In a reflecting contour, a ray of light originating at one focal point is reflected through the second focus.

Emissive material: in electric lamps, a substance that discharges electrons, usually applied as a coating to the cathode of a discharge source.

Energy-effective: when referring to electric lighting, using the available watts to supply light where it is needed and when it is needed, and limit light from where it is unwanted.

Exitance: the total quantity of light emitted, reflected, or transmitted in all directions from a surface. Properly defined as *density of flux leaving a surface*, it is measured in lumens per square foot (lm/ft^2) or lumens per square meter (lm/m^2).

Fenestration: The arrangement, proportioning, and design of windows and doors in a building for the admission of daylight.

Fiber optics: thin, flexible fibers of glass or plastic that are enclosed by a material of a lower index of refraction, transmitting light throughout their length by internal reflection.

Field angle: the angle between the two directions for which the intensity is 10% of the maximum, as measured in a plane through the beam centerline. See also *beam angle*.

Filament: the fine tungsten wire in an electric lamp, which acts as a conductor and becomes incandescent by the passage of an electric current.

Filter: a transparent material that modifies the color or quantity of light by transmission or reflection.

"Fixture": layman's term for a luminaire. See *luminaire*.

"Floor lamp": layman's term for a torchère. See *torchère*.

Fluoresce: the emission of visible light caused by the absorption of radiation of shorter wavelengths followed by a nearly immediate re-radiation at a longer wavelength.

Fluorescent lamp: a low-pressure, mercury-vapor, electric-discharge lamp having a phosphor coating on its inner surface that transforms the ultraviolet energy generated by the discharge into visible light.

Flux: see *luminous flux*.

Focused light or focal glow: concentrated light of greater intensity on a particular area or object, compared to its background illuminance, intentionally establishing a hierarchy between foreground and background.

Footcandle (fc): the unit measurement of illuminance equal to one lumen per square foot, originally defined with reference to a standardized candle burning at one foot from a given surface.

Footlambert (fL): unit measurement of reflected light from a perfectly diffusing surface that emits or reflects one lumen per square foot; equal to $1/\pi$ candela per square foot; now deprecated.

Fresnel (pronounced fra-nel') lens: a thin, optical lens that consists of a series of concentric lens sections regressed into a planar array; in luminaires, it produces a concentrated beam of light while also reducing the brightness of the source.

General diffuse: a multidirectional lighting distribution produced by luminaires that deliver both upward and downward components of light.

Glare: the sensation produced by an extreme luminance within the normal field of view that is sufficiently greater than the luminance to which the eyes are adapted.

High-bay lighting: interior lighting where mounting height is greater than approximately 25 ft above the floor.

High contrast: a lighting condition characterized by a large proportion of focused light (on an object or the foreground) and a small amount of diffuse light (the background).

High load: an elevated degree of psychological stimulation or arousal, caused by activities or environments that are complex, crowded, asymmetrical, novel, unfamiliar, surprising, or random.

High-pressure sodium: a high-intensity discharge lamp in which light is produced by radiation from the combined vapors of mercury and sodium, with the latter dominating the yellow-amber color.

Hue: spectral color; light of a specific wavelength.

Hydroform: a method of machine-forming metal that consists of a draw ring, flexible die, punch, and a pressurized forming cavity. (In luminaires, it is used to form reflectors from aluminum.)

Illuminance: the density of light received at a point on a surface. Properly defined as *density of flux incident on a surface measured perpendicular to the surface*, it is measured in footcandles (fc).

Incandescence: the emission of light from an object as a result of its being heated.

Incandescent lamp: an electric lamp in which a filament produces light when heated to incandescence by an electric current.

Incident: light rays falling upon or striking a surface.

Included angle: formed between or within two intersecting straight lines.

Indirect: an upward distribution of light which produces illumination on the horizontal workplane via reflection from the ceiling and upper walls.

Inductive: the property of an electric circuit in which an electromagnetic charge is induced in it as the result of a changing magnetic flux.

Infrared: wavelengths in the region of the electromagnetic spectrum immediately above the visible spectrum, from 770 to 10^6 nm.

Intensity: the physical energy of light emitted in a specific direction by a source. Properly called *luminous intensity* and defined as *flux per solid angle in a given direction*, it is measured in candelas (cd).

Interreflection: the multiple reflection of light by the various room surfaces before it reaches the workplane.

Iodide: a salt of hydriodic acid, a compound of iodine; used in metal halide lamps.

Ionize: to convert into ions; a group of atoms that carry a positive or negative electrical charge as a result of having lost or gained one or more electrons.

Isofootcandle plot: a computer-generated diagram on the Cartesian coordinate system showing contour lines of varying illuminance values from a specific luminaire in a specific application; a shaded plan with gray scales representing the range of illuminance values.

Kelvin: the unit of absolute temperature used to designate the color temperature of a light source.

Kilowatt: a unit of power equal to 1,000 watts.

Lamp: a source that converts electricity into light; it is the technical word for what is commonly referred to as a "light bulb."

Lampholder: the component of a luminaire that accepts the lamp base and supplies it with electricity; it is the technical word for what is commonly referred to as a "socket."

Laser: acronym for *l*ight *a*mplification by stimulated emission of *r*adiation; most lasers are oscillators (generators or sources of light) not amplifiers, producing a monochromatic beam of radiation by steady oscillation maintained in a resonator.

LED: acronym for *l*ight-*e*mitting *d*iode; a semiconductor diode that emits light when voltage is applied to it.

Lens: a glass or plastic element used in luminaires to control the direction and distribution of transmitted light by refraction.

Light: a narrow band of electromagnetic energy, ranging from approximately 380 nanometers (nm) to 760 nm, which stimulates receptors in the eye that enable vision.

Lime glass: glass with a high calcium oxide content consisting of silica, alumina, and iron that has greenish hue.

Louver: a series of baffles or shielding elements used to shield glare at normal viewing angles, usually arranged in a geometric pattern to provide shielding from many directions with minimum interference to the desired beam distribution.

Low contrast: a lighting condition characterized by a large proportion of diffuse light and a small amount of focused light.

Low load: a small amount of psychological stimulation or arousal, resulting from activities or environments that are simple, uncrowded, symmetrical, conventional, familiar, unsurprising, or organized.

Low-pressure sodium: a discharge lamp in which light is produced by radiation from sodium vapor, with a monochromatic yellow color.

Lumen (lm): the unit measurement of luminous flux equal to the light emitted in a solid angle by a uniform point source of one candela intensity.

Luminaire: a complete lighting unit consisting of a housing; lamp(s); light controlling elements; brightness controlling element; lampholder(s); auxiliary equipment, such as ballast or transformer, if required; and a connection to the power supply.

Luminance: the objective measurement of intensity of light entering the eye, per unit of projected area. It is the accepted term for light that is reflected from a surface in a given direction (back towards the eyes). Properly defined as *intensity of flux leaving a surface in a given direction*, it is measured in candelas per square foot (cd/ft^2) or candelas per square meter (cd/m^2).

Luminance contrast: the ratio of the luminance of an object or the foreground to the luminance of its immediate background or surround.

Luminous: emitting or reflecting energy in the visible portion of the electromagnetic spectrum.

Luminous flux: light emitted in all directions by a source. Properly defined as *time rate flow of light*, it is measured in lumens (lm).

Matte: a dull finish or surface lacking in luster, gloss, shine, or highlights.

Mercury lamp (properly called a **mercury vapor lamp**): a high-intensity discharge lamp in which light is produced by an electric discharge through mercury vapor.

Metal halide: a high-intensity discharge lamp in which light is produced by an electric discharge through the combined vapors of mercury and metal halides, which are introduced into the arc tube as compound iodides.

milliAmpere: a unit of electric current equal to one thousandth of an ampere.

Monochromatic: having or consisting of only one color or hue, or radiation of a single wavelength or very small range of wavelengths.

Motion sensor: see *occupancy sensor*.

Nadir: straight down (0-degree angle).

Nanometer: a unit of wavelength equal to one billionth (10^{-9}) of a meter.

Object light: an adjustable, directional luminaire that provides an asymmetric distribution of light aimed at one or several objects. Also called "spot lights," they are used to provide focal glow and add contrast to a setting.

Occupancy sensor: a device that provides on-off control of luminaires in response to the presence or absence of occupants in a space, sensed by audio, ultrasonic, passive infrared, or optical means.

Ohm: the standard unit of electrical resistance of a conductor, such that a current of one ampere in its circuit produces a decrease in voltage across it of one volt.

Opaque: blocking the passage of light; neither transparent nor translucent.

Parabolic: having the form of a parabola, a plane curve generated by the intersection of the surface of a cone with a plane parallel to one of its sides.

Pendant (luminaire): a luminaire that is suspended from the ceiling by a support cable, chain, cord, rod, or stem.

Phosphor: a chemical substance that converts invisible ultraviolet radiation into visible light.

Photometer: an instrument for measuring luminous intensity, luminous flux, illuminance, or luminance.

Photometry: the science that measures light.

Photosensor: a light-sensing device used to control luminaires and dimmers in response to detected illuminance values.

Photopic: vision, using the cones of the retina, under relatively high illuminance values.

Prism: a transparent body with three rectangular plane faces, or sides, and two equal and parallel triangular ends or bases, used to refract or disperse a beam of light.

Quad-phosphor: a combination of four narrow spectra, rare-earth phosphors used in fluorescent lamps to produce a wide-range spectrum of visible light. The individual phosphors correspond to the short-, middle-, and long-wavelength regions of the visible spectrum.

Reflected glare: excessive uncontrolled luminance reflected from objects or surfaces in the field of view.

Reflection: the return of light from a surface. *Specular reflection* occurs when the surface alters the direction of a beam of light without changing its form; the angle of reflection is equal to the angle of incidence. *Spread reflection* partially disperses this reflected beam. *Diffuse reflection* occurs when an incident ray of light is reflected in all directions.

Refraction: the deflection of a light ray when it passes obliquely from one medium (such as air) into another (such as water) in which it travels at a different speed.

Relamp: to replace a lamp or lamps.

Restrike: after a high-intensity discharge lamp is extinguished, it must cool sufficiently to reduce the vapor pressure to a point where the arc can be reignited.

Scotopic: vision, using the rods of the retina, under relatively dim light.

Semi-specular: an irregular surface that partially disperses or spreads the reflected beam, with the greatest intensity of light reflected at an angle near the angle of incidence.

Shielding angle: the zone within which shielding (baffles or louvers) conceals the light source and controls glare.

Sight line: the line extending from an observer's eye to the point at which a bare light source first becomes visible.

Skylight: 1. the diffused and reflected light of the sky; it is light from the sun redirected by the atmosphere. 2. an opening in the roof of a building, glazed with a transparent or translucent material, that is designed to admit natural light.

Slimline: a linear fluorescent lamp with a single-pin base that is capable of being operated at more than one current and wattage.

Soffit: the exposed underside of any overhead component of a building, such as an arch, balcony, beam, cornice, lintel, or vault.

Spacing criterion (SC) or **spacing-to-mounting-height ratio (S/MH)**: an estimated maximum ratio of luminaire spacing to luminaire mounting height above the workplane, necessary to achieve uniform, horizontal illuminance.

Spectral: of, relating to, or made by the color spectrum or electromagnetic spectrum.

Specular: having the reflecting properties of a mirror; a smooth reflecting surface. The angle of reflection is equal to the angle of incidence.

Splice: the electrical connection of luminaire wires to the building branch circuit wires.

Stroboscopic: when rapidly moving objects are observed under discharge sources, blurred "ghost" images are sometimes observed that cause the objects to appear slowed, stopped, or moving in reverse.

Torchère: a portable luminaire suitable for standing on the floor, which directs most, or all, of its light upward.

Toroidal: doughnut-shaped.

Total internal reflection: occurs when light passes into a transparent medium, such as glass or plastic, at an appropriate angle so that it travels inside the medium repeatedly reflecting from side to side.

Transformer: a device with two or more coupled windings, used to convert the supply of electric power at one voltage in a primary circuit to a lower voltage in a secondary circuit.

Translucent: having the property of transmitting diffused light but obscuring vision, so that objects beyond cannot be seen clearly.

Transmission: the passage of light through space or a medium; it is altered by the reflections at each surface of the medium, and by the absorption and reflection within the medium.

Transparent: having the property of transmitting light without altering its distribution, so that objects beyond are seen clearly.

Triphosphor: a combination of three narrow spectra, rare-earth phosphors used in fluorescent lamps to produce a wide-range spectrum of visible light. The individual phosphors correspond to the peak spectral sensitivities of human vision: blue-violet, pure green, and orange-red.

"Troffer": layman's term for a recessed, rectilinear fluorescent downlight; perhaps derived from "trough" and "coffer."

Trough: a long, narrow opening, usually in the ceiling plane; sometimes called a *slot*.

Tungsten-halogen: an incandescent lamp with a selected gas of the halogen family sealed into it to stop evaporated tungsten from depositing on the bulb wall.

Ultraviolet (UV): radiant energy having a wavelength shorter than wavelengths of visible light and longer than those of x-rays; within the range of 10 nanometers (nm) to 380 nm.

Uplight: a luminaire that emits light in an upward direction toward the ceiling, with no downward component of light.

Uplighting: a distribution of light emitted in an upward direction.

Valance: a longitudinal shielding panel mounted over a window with draperies to conceal light sources that provide both uplight and downlight.

Veiling reflection: a reflection of incident light that partially or completely obscures the details on a surface by reducing its contrast. See also *reflected glare*.

Visual comfort: the degree of visual satisfaction produced by the luminous environment, resulting from the reduction of glare and distracting luminance in the field of view.

Visible spectrum: wavelengths of electromagnetic energy, ranging from approximately 380 nanometers (nm) to 760 nm.

Volt: the standard unit of measurement for electrical potential; when applied across a resistance of one ohm, it will result in a current flow of one ampere.

Wall-washer: a luminaire with an asymmetric distribution used for illuminating vertical surfaces from ceiling to floor without noticeable variation in intensity.

Watt: the unit of electrical power; it is equal to the power produced by a current of one ampere across a potential difference of one volt.

Wattage: the amount of power expressed in watts.

Wavelength: the distance between one peak or crest of a wave of light, heat, or other energy, and the next corresponding peak or crest.

Workplane: the plane on which visual tasks are usually done; a horizontal plane 2 ft 6 in. above the floor, unless otherwise indicated.

Index